Introduction to Software Development

Learning to Program

Black & White Edition

Marwan Shaban

Icons by Google under Apache 2 license.

This product has no ISBN. It is a special black and white edition.

Library of Congress Control Number: 2021909532

About the cover: An astrolabe (ăs'trŭlāb) is an instrument probably used originally for measuring the altitudes of heavenly bodies and for determining their positions and movements. Although its origin is ancient and obscure, its invention is frequently ascribed either to Hipparchus or to Apollonius of Perga. For many centuries it was used by both astronomers and navigators (The Columbia Encyclopedia).

Cover design by Yasmeen Shaban.

Contents

List of Figures

List of Tables

List of Techniques

List of Tips

List of Examples

Preface

This book focuses on helping the reader develop an intuitive understanding of how to write good code. While learning Java, the reader will acquire principles and techniques that are presented in the context of realistic examples, with minimal jargon and constant reinforcement so that they're internalized and become habits. The techniques presented apply to any computer language, and have stood the test of time—techniques such as taking the extra time to simplify your code, starting your testing as soon as you can, and avoiding repeated code. Using a tutorial style and a steady progression from basic to advanced, the book allows the reader to follow along and try each example for him- or herself. The reader learns by doing.

Care was taken at each point to include only enough detail for the reader to progress to the next topic, avoiding discussion that would distract many readers from the main mission: learning how to write good code. As the focus is on learning to write code, software development processes and tools, such as source control and unit testing, aren't presented—indeed, it is my opinion that a good coder can easily learn those ancillary topics, while the reverse is not true.

The book is suitable for use in a two- or three-semester course on introductory programming.

My reviewers have saved me from many embarrassing oversights. I wish to thank professors Dick Grant, Lisa Macon, Ian O'Toole, Bill Gaught, Craig Tidwell, Adam Rocke, Mahendra Gossai, John Delgado, Ron Villmow, Holger Findling and Steven Zimmerman for their valuable feedback on early drafts of this book. I owe special thanks to professors Grant, Macon and O'Toole for their numerous insights and in-depth feedback. Any remaining shortcomings are mine alone. Error reports can be sent to ProfessorShaban@gmail.com.

I'm fortunate to have a family who are kind and supportive, and each inspirational in his or her own way—my wife Wyeleen, daughter Yasmeen, son Ramsey, parents Fuad and Mary, brothers Sami and Omar, and sister Rana. With gratitude, I dedicate this book to them.

Marwan Shaban
Orlando, May 2021

Introduction

Writing code is the essence of software development. This book is your introduction to the art of writing good code. After learning the materials in this book, you'll be able to move on to learn other kinds of programming or specialize in a particular language.

Some readers benefit more from in-depth discussion, while others need more of a tutorial style. I've tried to maintain a tutorial theme while covering essential information and avoiding programming topics that are best kept in reference texts. This allows the focus to remain on the main mission: developing solid coding skills.

How to use this book

You are encouraged to read the book's chapters sequentially; I have tried to introduce the reader to concepts when it makes sense to do so, and maintain a steady progression roughly in order of difficulty. Consequently, it didn't make sense to organize the book strictly in terms of language features, although each chapter has a focus and a theme.

Learning how to program is like learning to ride a bike. You can't learn it by reading a book. It takes constant practice for the ideas to take hold, and persistence is key. Learning the *syntax* is fast. Learning *how to program* takes time, and you can't expect it to be a fast process. As you study each chapter, you should follow along by typing in each example and making sure you get the expected output. Do each example over and over until you can write it without looking at the book. Your goal is to internalize the concepts and *get to the point where you are writing code easily without referring to examples*. You're not done until you reach that level of skill, and it's impossible to say how long this will take you, as each person is different—it takes as long as it takes. Remember, you don't learn programming by reading a book—you learn by doing!

Tip 1. Learning how to program is like learning to ride a bike. You must practice!

Syntax: The grammatical rules of a language.

Do each example over and over until you can write it without looking at the book. Your goal is to write code easily without referring to examples.

Tip 2. Copy/paste is the enemy of learning.

When addressing the danger of copy/paste, I'm referring to copying other people's code. Copying your own code is not only okay—you'll do it very often.

The book also tries to get you used to problem solving on your own. When studying or working on your homework, it's okay to search online now and then, but if you're a beginning programmer, you should avoid it to the extent possible. Conduct an Internet search only after you are stuck, and if you do use code that you find online, don't just copy and paste it into your program without understanding it. Copy/paste is the enemy of learning, because it makes it easy to skip ahead without going through the full learning process. It's important that you type the code yourself, to help you understand the details and help build that muscle memory. If you do copy code that you find online, be sure to understand how it works, and look up any language features that you don't recognize. Once you are past the learning stage and have completed this text, this advice no longer applies, and it's quite common for programmers to go online to look up techniques or languages features.

What you'll learn

The focus of this book is on learning the fundamentals. Thus, it doesn't teach how to build a graphical user interface. Rather, you will construct programs that interact with the user on the command line. This allows the focus to remain on learning core programming logic and programming basics. These core concepts apply to every kind of programming: desktop, database, cloud, web, enterprise, mobile, and more. What you learn here is a prerequisite to all those skills.

Since the book seeks to focus on teaching the basics and minimize distractions, you should consider each concept in the book to be essential. What's not in the book is as important as what's in it—if a language feature or programming technique is not covered, you can assume that it's not needed as part of the essential skill set. If you go through the book and master all its concepts, I believe you'll be done with the hard part, and all other software development skills will be relatively easy for you to master.

Unless you're already a programmer, resist the urge to skip sections. Don't rush it. If you learn the right way and get there in time, you'll have a solid foundation forever.

Getting Started | 1

1.1 Computer Languages and Compilers

Your computer executes machine language. Programming in such a low-level language is difficult for humans, so very early in the computer age, high-level languages were developed. The high-level language is translated into machine language by a compiler. When we create programs in high-level languages, there are many details of the program's execution that we don't need to worry about. The compiler takes care of those details for us. This is an example of abstraction, an important topic we'll discuss in later chapters.

In this book, the high-level language we use is Java. There are many high-level languages we could choose as a first language, but Java is a good choice due to its relative simplicity and also its prevalence, which makes it among the most in-demand language skills.

The Java compiler translates the Java source code into a machine language program. We make a distinction between compile-time, which is when the program is compiled, and run-time, which is when the program is executed. A program that is compiled once can be run many times, during which the program may interact with the user.

In this chapter, we'll download the tools needed to compile and run Java programs, and illustrate compiling and running a simple Java program. The main development tool that we'll interact with is Eclipse, which runs the Java compiler, and offers features that make Java development easier.

High-Level Language: A computer language that humans can read.

Machine Language: A computer's native language.

Compiler: A program that translates a high-level language into machine language.

Eclipse: An Integrated Development Environment (IDE) used to develop Java programs.

1.2 Hello World Program

The first program to write is customarily a simple program that outputs a simple message,

Example 1.1. Hello, World! program.

```
1  // main method
2  public static void main(String[] args) {
3    System.out.println("Hello, World!");
4  }
```

Above is the canonical Hello World program. You enter the program into Eclipse in preparation for compiling and running it. Here are a few things to note about the above code,

- A line that begins with two slashes (//) constitutes a comment. Comments don't cause the program to do anything - they're just there as clarifications for whoever reads the code.
- The main sequence of commands that make up the program is contained within { and } characters, which we call *curly braces* or *curly brackets*. In the above program, there's only one statement between the braces, which is the print statement.
- The word "main" is the name of the block of code enclosed within the curly braces. In Java, this is a special block of code, which will be executed when the program is started.
- The words "public", "static" and "void" will be explained in later chapters. They're keywords that denote properties of the main method.

JDK: The Java Development Kit that includes the Java compiler. It's used by Eclipse to compile Java programs.

Don't worry about the details at this point. Just know for now that the program will print the message "Hello, World!" when it runs. After installing JDK and Eclipse, we'll enter the above program and run it.

1.3 Installing the JDK

The first thing you need to download and install is the JDK (Java Development Kit). Installing the JDK also installs the Java compiler, which is invoked by Eclipse when it compiles your program. At the time of this writing, the JDK can be downloaded from this web page:

Web links that you see in this book may have changed by the time you read this. If that is the case, you should be able to easily search for the proper web page.

https://www.oracle.com/java/technologies/javase-downloads.html. Note that this is the Java SE edition. On this web page, you'll see a link to download the JDK (Figure 1.1).

Your operating system

The screen shots here show macOS. If you're on Windows, you

will choose the "Windows x64 Installer", and go through a typical Windows installation experience instead of using the standard macOS DMG file. Through the rest of the book, screen shots showing Eclipse on macOS should be very close to what a Windows user would see, as Eclipse looks the same on both operating systems.

Java editions

There are multiple editions of Java, including SE (Standard Edition), EE (Enterprise Edition) and ME (Micro Edition). In this book, we'll use the Standard Edition.

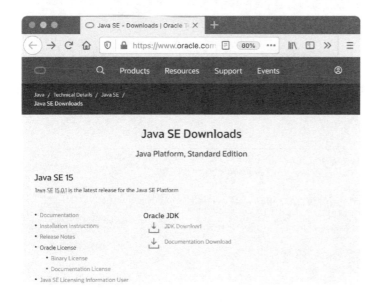

Screen shots that you see in this book may be different than what you see by the time you try this. If that is the case, do your best to use the new layouts to accomplish the same steps that you see here.

Figure 1.1: The JDK download page.

Clicking on the "JDK Download" link will take you to a second web page containing download links for each supported operating system (Figure 1.2).

Version numbers

By default, you should choose the latest version of software that you install. Here, we're installing JDK 15, which is the latest version at the time of this writing. Some programmers prefer to install the latest LTS (long term support) version of the JDK,

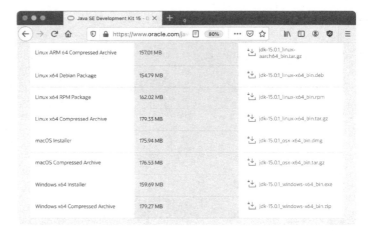

Figure 1.2: The JDK download page with download links for each operating system.

instead of the latest JDK version.

After downloading the appropriate installer for your operating system, you will start the installation process and go through a series of simple screens to complete the installation. Figure 1.3 shows the initial screen of the installer. Make sure the installer has completed before moving on to the next step.

Figure 1.3: The JDK installer's initial screen.

1.4 Installing Eclipse

As we did with the JDK, we'll download and install Eclipse. Go to `https://www.eclipse.org/downloads/` and click the download link (see Figure 1.4). At the second download page, click Download again to start the download. Wait for the download to complete, and start the installation. The installer will show a number of different installation types. For our purposes, we need to choose the "Eclipse IDE for Java Developers" (see Figure 1.5).

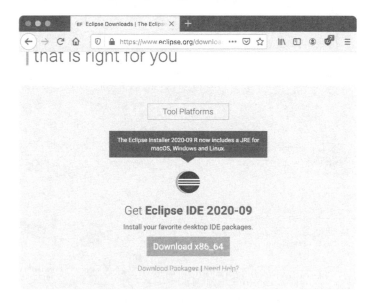

Figure 1.4: The Eclipse download page.

Next you will encounter the configuration screen which should show the path to the JDK that you just installed (Figure 1.6). Hit the Install button to start the installation. Wait for the installation process to finish, and then start Eclipse.

Upon launching Eclipse, you'll see the Eclipse workspace directory screen (Figure 1.7). Here you can override the location of the main Eclipse workspace, but we'll leave it with the default path and turn on the "Use this as the default and don't ask again" checkbox, then click Launch. The Eclipse main window is shown in Figure 1.8.

You'll learn what an Eclipse workspace is on page 40

At the moment, Eclipse is showing the Welcome view. Click on the "x" next to the tab's title to close the Welcome view. Also, close each of the Donate, Outline, Problems, Javadoc and Declaration views. You now have a minimal Eclipse window as shown in Figure 1.9.

View: A window within Eclipse.

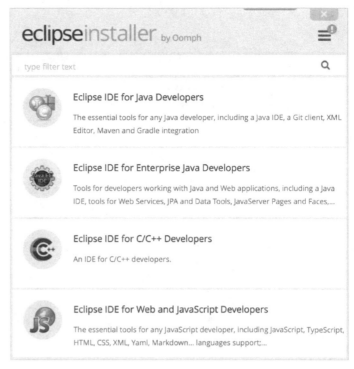

Figure 1.5: The Eclipse install options.

Figure 1.6: The Eclipse configuration screen.

Figure 1.7: The Eclipse workspace directory screen.

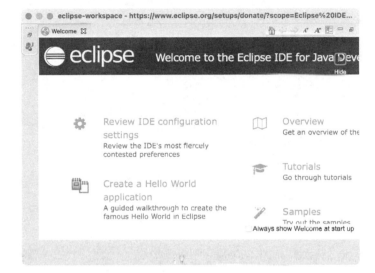

Figure 1.8: The Eclipse main window when started for the first time.

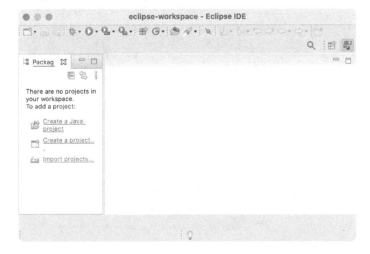

Figure 1.9: The Eclipse main window.

1.5 Creating a Program

Now that we've installed the JDK and Eclipse, we can create our first program. In Eclipse, open the File menu, and choose the New → New Java Project option to create the boilerplate project. Enter HelloWorld as the project name, and hit the Finish button (Figure 1.10). At the next screen, asking whether to create a module-info.java file, hit the Don't Create button (Figure 1.11).

Boilerplate: Standardized text used as a placeholder.

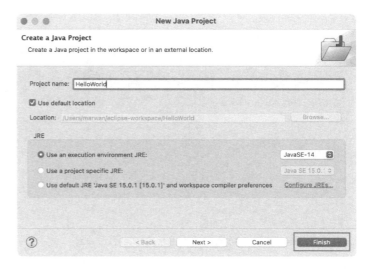

Figure 1.10: New Java Project window.

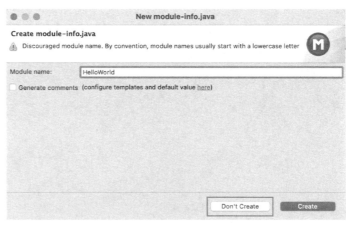

Figure 1.11: The module-info.java window.

You've just created the project called HelloWorld. Next, we'll create the main Java class. Back at the File menu, choose the New → Class option. Again, enter HelloWorld as the class name, turn on the "public static void main(String[] args)" checkbox, and hit the Finish button (Figure 1.12). At this point we've got a basic program with a class containing the `main` method (Figure 1.13).

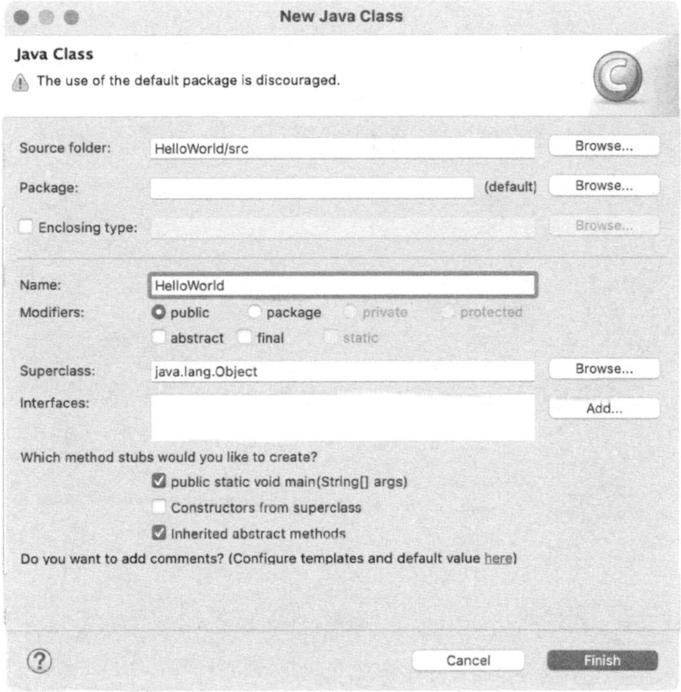

Figure 1.12: New Java Class window.

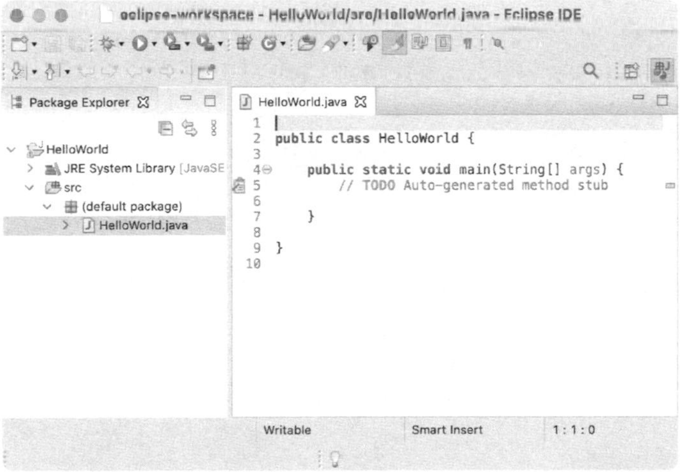

Figure 1.13: Boilerplate project with `main` method.

1.6 Running Programs

We've gone through the process of creating a new program. Next, we'll modify it to match our Hello World program as shown at the top of section 1.2 (Hello, World). We only need to add the comment at the top, remove the placeholder comment within `main`, and add the print statement. See Figure 1.14.

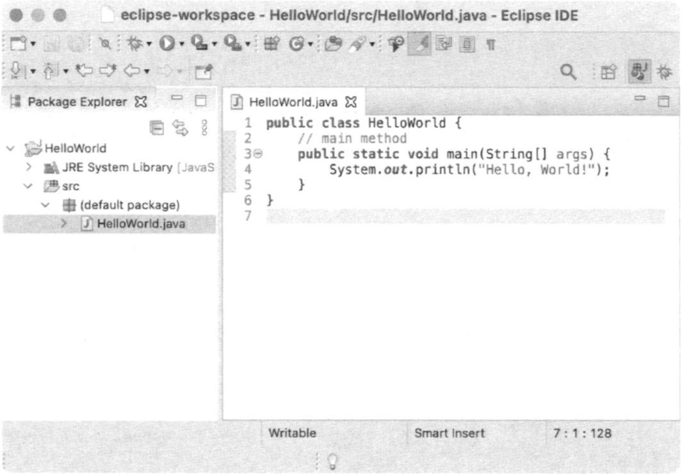

Figure 1.14: Eclipse with Hello World program.

Our program is now ready to test. The toolbar has a run button that looks like a white triangle within a green circle. Hit the run button on the toolbar, and you should see the program's output correctly displayed in the Console view. See Figure 1.15.

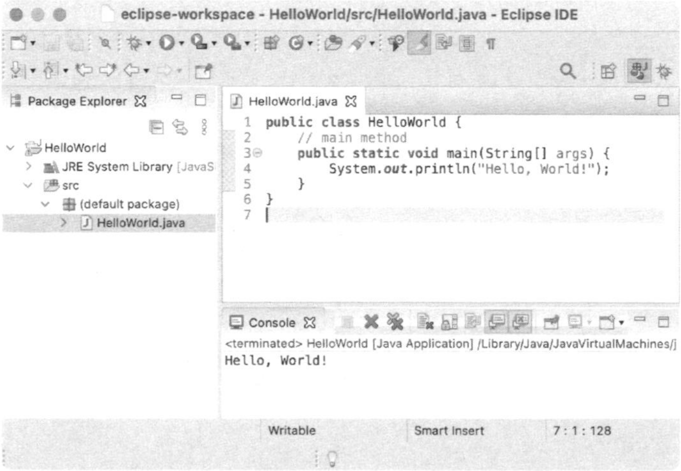

Figure 1.15: Hello World program's output correctly displayed in the Console view.

We'll have much more to say in chapter 3 about the various features available to you in Eclipse. Right now, it's time to move on to the next chapter and the basics of input and output in Java.

Exercises

1.1 Change the message that the program outputs, to print out your name. Run it and observe the output in the Console view.

1.2 Duplicate the print command (the entire line that prints Hello World) six times. Print out a different day of the week in each of the seven lines.

1.3 Create a new project by following the same process. You'll have to give the new project a different name. Test to make sure the second project also works.

Chapter Summary

- Install the JDK (Java Development Kit).
- Install Eclipse (the integrated development environment, or IDE).
- Use the New Java Project command in Eclipse to create a new program.
- Use the Run command in Eclipse to run a Java program. The output appears in Eclipse's Console view.
- The traditional "Hello, world" program is shown below with some of its notable components labeled:

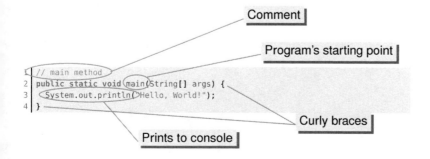

Exercise Solutions

1.1
```
1  // main method
2  public static void main(String[] args) {
3    System.out.println("Your Name");
4  }
```

```
Your Name
```

1.2
```
1   // main method
2   public static void main(String[] args) {
3     System.out.println("Sunday");
4     System.out.println("Monday");
5     System.out.println("Tuesday");
6     System.out.println("Wednesday");
7     System.out.println("Thursday");
8     System.out.println("Friday");
9     System.out.println("Saturday");
10  }
```

```
Sunday
Monday
Tuesday
Wednesday
Thursday
Friday
Saturday
```

1.3
```
1  public static void main(String[] args) {
2    System.out.println("Second Project");
3  }
```

Input, Processing and Output | 2

2.1 Variables

When your program runs, it stores its data in memory. It keeps track of the location within memory of each piece of data that is being processed. These memory locations can have names, and they can be referenced from the program's code. We call these variables. Example 2.1 shows an example of a variable,

```
1  public static void main(String[] args) {
2      int price;
3      price = 10;
4      System.out.println("The price is " + price);
5  }
```

In the above example, we have a variable called price, and its value is set to the number 10. A variable has a *type*. Our price has type `int`, which means it can store integers. Running this program produces the following output,

Example 2.1. Simple variable.

Variable: A location within memory that holds a data value.

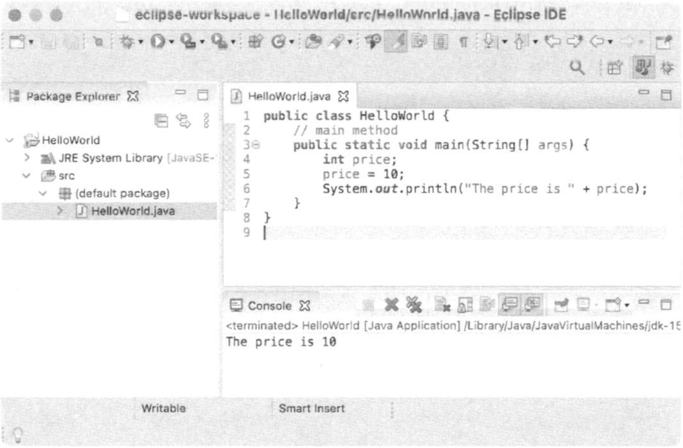

Figure 2.1: Using the variable price.

Henceforth, we'll save some space by illustrating program output inline, like this,

Using the variable `price`.

```
The price is 10
```

Assignment: Changing the value contained within a variable.

Your program can change the value contained within a variable. One way to do this is to use the assignment operator. Technically, a variable is merely the name that we use to refer to the location within memory that contains the data. A variable name in Java can be any sequence of letters, numbers, the dollar sign symbol and underscore. It must begin with a letter. In addition, variable names are case sensitive, which means that uppercase and lowercase letters are different—so `price` and `Price` are different.

In your Java program, a variable is declared by stating its type, then its name. The semicolon is required at the end of the declaration. For example, the following program (example 2.2) displays remaining inventory after a sale,

Example 2.2. Computing remaining inventory after a sale.

```
1  int quantityOnHand;
2  quantityOnHand = 100;
3  int quantitySold;
4  quantitySold = 25;
5  int quantityRemaining;
6  quantityRemaining = quantityOnHand - quantitySold;
7  System.out.println("Quantity remaining = " + quantityRemaining);
```

I've omitted the main method's signature and braces, for brevity. The above code produces the expected remaining quantity,

```
Quantity remaining = 75
```

Initialization: assigning an initial value to a variable.

A variable's declaration may include an initial assignment after the variable name and before the semicolon. So the above program can be rewritten as in example 2.3,

Example 2.3. Simplified version.

```
1  int quantityOnHand = 100;
2  int quantitySold = 25;
3  int quantityRemaining = quantityOnHand - quantitySold;
4  System.out.println("Quantity remaining = " + quantityRemaining);
```

This form is preferred to the one above since it's shorter and, I would argue, clearer. This brings us to a very important principle, one that you should always remember and apply:

Technique 1. Simplify your code whenever you can

Always take the time to simplify your code before moving on. Code should be as brief as possible, without sacrificing clarity.

Your code is organized in blocks, delimited by the curly braces that we referred to earlier. For example, the `main` method defines a block of code that is run when the program is invoked, and when that block is finished executing, the program stops. Variables are declared within blocks, and their lifetimes end when the corresponding blocks finish executing. We say that the variable's *scope* is within the block in which it is defined.

Code block: Lines of code delimited by curly braces.

To **delimit** something is to surround it or mark its boundaries.

Variable scope: Variable use is limited to the blocks in which they're defined.

As you've noticed, variable names by convention begin with a lowercase letter, and each word after the first starts with an uppercase letter. This is called *camel case*.

Statements in Java

Most statements in Java have to end in a semicolon, as you've seen in example 2.3. A statement is not a line of code. Statements can span multiple lines, and one line can contain multiple statements. A statement corresponds to one valid Java instruction, such as the variable declaration on line 1 of example 2.3, or the assignment on line 3 of example 2.3.

2.2 Data Types

Each unit of data that your program processes has a particular type. Java makes sure that each variable only holds the type of data that it was declared as. For example, a variable declared as an integer only holds whole numbers in the proper range. Table 2.1 shows some of the basic data types in Java, with an example, and the range of possible values for each type.

Type	Example	Minimum value	Maximum value
int	1000	-2,147,483,648	2,147,483,647
float	3.14	$-3.4x10^{38}$	$3.4x10^{38}$
boolean	true	n/a	n/a
String	"Mary"	n/a	n/a

Table 2.1: Basic data types in Java.

Integer variables can have values in the range of $-2,147,483,648$ to $2,147,483,647$. Therefore, they can have $4,294,967,296$ different values, which is 2^{32}—because integers are represented with 32 bits, or 4 bytes.

Floating point variables are declared with the **float** keyword, and they hold decimal numbers in the range of approximately $-3.4x10^{38}$ to $3.4x10^{38}$.

Boolean variables only have a true or false value. They can be used in situations where data values determine different execution paths.

String variables contain text data, which can be of any length. Strings can be manipulated with Java code, for example to extract substrings, or concatenate (merge) different strings. Here is example code illustrating each of the above data types,

Example 2.4. Usage of int, boolean, float and String.

```java
int quantitySold = 25;
boolean soldOut = false;
float taxRate = 0.06f;
String customerName = "John Doe";
System.out.println("Quantity sold: " + quantitySold);
System.out.println("Sold out: " + soldOut);
System.out.println("Tax rate: " + taxRate);
System.out.println("Customer name: " + customerName);
```

```
Quantity sold: 25
Sold out: false
Tax rate: 0.06
Customer name: John Doe
```

Hardcoded value: A constant value of a particular type in the program's source code.

Here we've declared four variables, each of a different type. Each of the four has been assigned a value of the appropriate type, then output to the console. Note that we've assigned specific values that are *hardcoded*, that is, specific values entered into the program's source code, as opposed to data that was entered by the user while the program is running. These are called *literal values* or *literal constants*.

Using string literals.

Note that the string literal is delimited by double quotes, and that these double quotes aren't part of the string data itself. Also note that the floating point literal is followed by lowercase "f". This is to distinguish it from a double-precision floating point literal which doesn't require the "f" suffix. We'll discuss the double precision floating point type in section 6.5.

Type Conversion

Some data types can be converted to one another. For example, an integer value can be assigned to a floating point variable, since the range of values for a floating point variable includes the possible integer values,

```
1   int intVariable = 123;
2   float floatVariable = intVariable;
3   System.out.println("floatVariable: " + floatVariable);
```

Example 2.5. Assigning an `int`'s value to a `float`.

```
floatVariable: 123.0
```

On the other hand, assigning a floating point value to an integer variable results in a compile error, but we can convert the floating point value to an integer value using an operation known as *type casting*, or just *casting*,

Casting: Converting a value from one type to another.

```
1   float floatVariable = 3.14f;
2   int intVariable = (int) floatVariable;
3   System.out.println("intVariable: " + intVariable);
```

Example 2.6. Type casting.

```
intVariable: 3
```

The cast operator is `(int)`. It converts the floating point value to an integer value. This is done by rounding down, not by rounding to the nearest integer.

Often you will need to extract numbers from strings. You can do this using Integer.parseInt() and Float.parseFloat(). For example,

```
1   String yearString = "2021";
2   int year = Integer.parseInt(yearString);
3
4   String taxRateString = "7.5";
5   float taxRate = Float.parseFloat(taxRateString);
6
7   System.out.println("The year is " + year + ", and the tax rate is " + taxRate
        + "%");
```

Example 2.7. Converting strings into numbers.

```
The year is 2021, and the tax rate is 7.5%
```

In example 2.7, the program creates two strings containing numbers, then converts them to numeric data types using `parseInt` and `parseFloat`.

2.3 Output

Method: A named block of code that can be executed from your Java code.

Calling a method: The act of using the method's name to execute its code.

Method argument: Data that you pass to a method.

Parameter: The name that we give to an argument within the method.

In Java, a *method* is a named block of code that you can execute just by invoking its name followed by a pair of parentheses. The `println` method is an example, and we've already seen how to execute `println` to print data to the Console view in Eclipse. We say that the section of code defined by the method is *executed*, *invoked*, or *called* when you use its name followed by parentheses. For example, `System.out.println("Hello, world!")` prints the string "Hello, world!". In the preceding example, the *literal string* contained within the pair of parentheses is called an *argument* that is passed to the method. A method can accept parameters and use their values within the method's block of code, or *body*. You can write your own methods; in fact, you've already written one: your `main()` method is called by the system when you tell Eclipse to run your program.

The `print()` method does the same thing as `println()`, except that it doesn't advance the output to the next line after printing. Both `print()` and `println()` can accept a parameter of various types, such as string, integer and float.

You can use `println()` without any parameters to move the output to the next line. If nothing has already been printed to the current line of output, this has the effect of printing an empty line. Together, `print()` and `println()` can be used to print almost anything you need to the Console view in Eclipse. Here's an example of using these two method together,

Example 2.8. Using `print` and `println`.

The `import` statement brings in a specific system identifier so that we can refer to it within a program.

```
1  import static java.lang.System.out;
2
3  public class HelloWorld {
4    public static void main(String[] args) {
5      out.println("THE TEMPEST");
6      out.println("");
7
8      String playCharacter = "Master";
9      out.print(playCharacter);
10     out.println();
11     out.print(1);
12     out.println(" Boatswain!");
13     out.println();
14
```

```
15      playCharacter = "Boatswain";
16      out.print(playCharacter);
17      out.println();
18      out.print(2);
19      out.println(" Here, master: what cheer?");
20      out.println();
21
22      playCharacter = "Master";
23      out.print(playCharacter);
24      out.println();
25      out.print(3);
26      out.println(" Good, speak to the mariners: fall to't, yarely,");
27      out.print(4);
28      out.println(" or we run ourselves aground: bestir, bestir.");
29      out.println();
30    }
31 }
```

```
THE TEMPEST

Master
1 Boatswain!

Boatswain
2 Here, master: what cheer?

Master
3 Good, speak to the mariners: fall to't, yarely,
4 or we run ourselves aground: bestir, bestir.
```

Note that we've added an `import` statement at the top, which allows us to use the syntax `out.println` instead of `System.out.println`. I like the short form better since it's less typing and less visual clutter.

As illustrated in the example above, `print` is used when we want to output bits of data that should all be on the same output line, whereas `println` is used when we want to output data, and then start a new line. The play script's line numbers 1, 2, 3 and 4 are printed, each followed by the script line. There is an empty line between the first character's lines and the second character's lines, which was produced using `out.println()`, that is, `println` with empty parentheses indicating no arguments are passed into the method.

Note also that the default font used by Eclipse in the Console view is fixed-width, meaning each character takes up the same width. This allows you to play with ASCII art, which is one way we had fun with graphics before the advent of graphical user interfaces,

Using print and println.

*A **character** is a single letter, digit or symbol, not to be confused with the play characters in the last example.*

Example 2.9. Fixed-width font in the Console view.

```
1   out.println("       oo0000");
2   out.println("       oo            ");
3   out.println("    _I__n_n__||_||  _____");
4   out.println("  >(_____|_7_|-|_____|");
5   out.println("   /o ()() ()() o    oo   oo");
```

More ASCII art can be found at the ASCII Art Archive, https://www.asciiart.eu.

```
        oo0000
       oo
    _I__n_n__||_||  _____
  >(_____|_7_|-|_____|
   /o ()() ()() o    oo   oo
```

Using `printf`.

Java helps you format output in various ways when printing out different data types. To do this, you can use the `printf` method. It differs from `print` and `println` in that it takes multiple parameters separated by commas. The first parameter is a string containing *format specifiers*, and the rest of the parameters are the data items to be printed. For example, `out.printf("%5.3f", interestRate)` prints out the value of a floating point variable called `interestRate`. It will use at least five characters to print the number, and will print three digits after the decimal point. If `interestRate` has more than three digits after the decimal point, `printf` will round up or down appropriately,

Example 2.10. Rounding with `printf`.

```
1   float interestRate = 3.1259f;
2   out.printf("%5.3f", interestRate);
```

```
3.126
```

Each parameter after the first needs its own format specifier within the format string. A format specifier begins with a percent sign (%) followed by optional modifiers then a character denoting the format type. Table 2.2 shows three of the most important format types that `printf` offers.

To left justify the output, add a hyphen before the number of characters, such as `%-5d`. To advance to a new line, add a %n within the format string. Example 2.11 shows another example of `printf`,

Example 2.11. Another `printf` example.

```
1   String customer = "John Doe";
2   float price = 48.99f;
3   float taxRate = 0.073f;
4   float total = price * (1 + taxRate);
5   out.printf("%s's total is $%.2f", customer, total);
```

```
John Doe's total is $52.57
```

Format	Type	Example	
s	String	%10s	Prints a string using at least ten characters.
d	int	%d	Prints an integer.
		%5d	Prints an integer, using at least five characters.
f	float	%5.3f	Prints a floating point number using at least five characters, and prints three digits after the decimal point.
		%.3f	Prints a floating point number with three digits after the decimal point.

2.4 Input

Your Java program can get input from the user, and store that input in data variables. For this, we'll use the **Scanner** class,

```java
import java.util.Scanner;
...
  Scanner input = new Scanner(System.in);

  out.print("What's your name? ");
  String name = input.nextLine();
  out.print("Hello, " + name + "!");

  input.close();
```

Example 2.12. Using Scanner to read input from the keyboard.

```
What's your name? Billy
Hello, Billy!
```

In the above example, we've created an object of type **Scanner**, and we've named it **input**. Note the new **import** statement that we've added to the top of our program. An import statement such as this allows us to abbreviate `java.util.Scanner` to `Scanner` when used in the rest of our program.

A method can **return** a value to the code that invoked it, which can be assigned to a variable or used in a computation.

To get input from the keyboard, we call the `nextLine` method of the `Scanner` object. This method returns a string which we then store in the `String` variable called `name`. The screen shot above shows the program's prompt followed by the user's input. The `nextLine` method suspends the program's execution and waits for the user's input. It doesn't return to the caller until the user has hit the enter key.

A `Scanner` object can be used to get keyboard input repeatedly, but in example 2.12 we've only used it to retrieve one string, the user's name. After our program has finished getting its input from the keyboard, the `Scanner` object is closed using the `input.close()` statement. If you don't close a `Scanner` object, your program will still work, but will contain a *resource leak*, and having too many resource leaks during runtime will affect your program's performance or cause it to stop working.

You can use the `Scanner` object to read integer and floating point input using its `nextInt` and `nextFloat` methods. The following (2.13) is an example program that reads string, integer and floating point data from the user (we've omitted the `Scanner` object's declaration as well as the call to its `close` method, for brevity),

Example 2.13. Getting input of different data types.

```
1   out.print("Enter product: ");
2   String product = input.nextLine();
3   out.print("Enter quantity: ");
4   int quantity = input.nextInt();
5   input.nextLine();
6   out.print("Enter price per unit: ");
7   float pricePerUnit = input.nextFloat();
8   input.nextLine();
9
10  out.printf("%d units of %s will cost $%.2f", quantity, product, pricePerUnit
        * quantity);
```

```
Enter product: 16 oz. Pepsi
Enter quantity: 3
Enter price per unit: 1.21
3 units of 16 oz. Pepsi will cost $3.63
```

Reading multiple types with `Scanner`

When reading both strings and numbers with an object of type `Scanner`, you should call `nextLine` after you read a number from the keyboard, as shown on line 8 of the above example. This is because `nextInt` and `nextFloat` only read the *number* from the keyboard. The following call to `nextLine` will instruct the `Scanner` object to *consume* the newline character generated by the enter key. Without the call to `nextLine` following `nextInt`, subsequent reading of string data with `nextLine` won't read the intended input properly.

2.5 Processing Numeric Data

Now that we know how to get input and generate output, it's time for our program to do something useful. A typical pattern is gathering input, processing the input and outputting a result. To process the input, our Java program will use data manipulation statements.

Numeric data is processed with mathematical expressions that combine numeric variables with mathematical operators. For example, `int birthYear = thisYear - age` will subtract your current age from this year to compute the year you were born,

```
1  import java.util.Calendar;
2  ...
3    out.print("Enter your age: ");
4    int age = input.nextInt();
5    input.nextLine();
6
7    int thisYear = Calendar.getInstance().get(Calendar.YEAR);
8    int birthYear = thisYear - age;
9
10   out.println("You were born in " + birthYear);
```

Example 2.14. Simple computation.

This simplistic formula doesn't take into account the month and day, so it may display an answer that is off by one year.

```
Enter your age: 31
You were born in 1989
```

`thisYear - age` is an example of an expression, and it computes the user's year of birth. An expression has inputs and produces an output. In this instance, the inputs are `thisYear` and `age`, both of which are of type `int`. The result of this expression is also of type `int` because the minus operator takes two integers and produces an integer. We say that the minus operator takes two *arguments*. Always keep in mind that an expression has a specific type, which is the type of data that it produces.

Expression: A formula that can include constants, variables and operators, which produces a result of a certain type.

We've already seen type conversion using casting. If we use the minus operator to subtract a floating point number from an integer, the minus operator automatically converts the integer to a floating point

Table 2.3: Common mathematical operators.

Operator	Example	
+	`birthYear + age`	Adds the user's age to his year of birth to get the current year.
-	`thisYear - age`	Subtracts the user's age from the current year to compute the user's year of birth.
*	`quantity * pricePerUnit`	Computes total price, given the price per unit and the number of units.
/	`miles / gallons`	Computes a vehicle's fuel efficiency (miles per gallon).
	`hours / 24`	Computes days from hours. This integer division returns the number of whole days without the remaining fraction, for example if hours is 36, the result is one day.
%	`hours % 24`	The *remainder* operator gives the remainder after performing integer division. For example, if hours is 36, the remainder is 12.

number, then performs the subtraction and produces a floating point result. Table 2.3 shows a list of some of the important operators.

Of course, expressions can be more complex than the example we just saw. Here's an example of converting temperature units,

```
1   out.print("Enter degrees Celsius: ");
2   int celsius = input.nextInt();
3   input.nextLine();
4
5   int fahrenheit = celsius * 9 / 5 + 32;
6
7   out.printf("%d Celsius is %d Fahrenheit", celsius, fahrenheit);
```

Example 2.15. Temperature conversion.

```
Enter degrees Celsius: 100
100 Celsius is 212 Fahrenheit
```

The formula to convert Celsius degrees to Fahrenheit is:

$$Fahrenheit = 9/5\ Celsius + 32$$

which corresponds to our Java expression `celsius * 9 / 5 + 32`. The multiplication will be performed first, then the division and then the addition. In our test run above, `celsius` has the value 100. Since `celsius` is of type `int`, the multiplication will result in the integer value 900. The division is performed next, and will be integer division since both operands are integers (the two division operands being 900 and 5). The result of this integer division is the integer value 180. Then 180 is added to 32, resulting in 212.

Suppose our Java expression was `9 / 5 * celsius + 32`. Though that is equivalent mathematically to the previous expression, in practice the result will be different. The division operation occurs first, and since both operands are integers, the result of 1.8 will be rounded down to the integer value 1, which when multiplied by `celsius` is 100. Next 32 is added with a final result of 132. You should be aware of this pitfall with integer division. To force floating point division, one of the operands should be a floating point number. Two easy ways to fix this are,

Integer division: The division operator rounds down and produces an integer if both operands are integers.

- Use a floating point constant for one of the division arguments, and cast the final result to an integer: `int fahrenheit = (int) (9f / 5 * celsius + 32)`. This causes it to be a floating point division, producing a floating point result.
- Cast one of the division arguments to a floating point number, which again forces a floating point division: `int fahrenheit = (int) ((float) 9 / 5 * celsius + 32)`.

Our next example (2.16) involves adding the price of two items, multiplying the total by 1.05 to add 5% tax, and printing the total,

Example 2.16. Incorrect expression due to operator precedence.

```
1  float price1 = 19.95f;
2  float price2 = 2.80f;
3  float totalWithTax = price1 + price2 * 1.05f;
4  out.println("Total with tax is $" + totalWithTax);
```

```
Total with tax is $22.890001
```

The result is $22.89, which is incorrect. This is because we meant to add the tax to both prices. The tax was only added to `price2` due to *operator precedence*. The multiplication operator has higher precedence than the addition operator, so the multiplication is performed first, then the addition. To fix this, we must enclose the addition in parentheses,

Example 2.17. Corrected expression.

```
1  float price1 = 19.95f;
2  float price2 = 2.80f;
3  float totalWithTax = (price1 + price2) * 1.05f;
4  out.println("Total with tax is $" + totalWithTax);
```

```
Total with tax is $23.887499
```

This time, the addition was performed first, then the 5% sales tax was added to both prices. Operator precedence is another thing to keep in mind when working with numeric expressions. Table 2.4 shows operator precedence for the basic mathematical operators.

Table 2.4: Operator precedence in Java (abbreviated).

Precedence	Operator
1	cast operator
2	- (unary negation)
3	+, -
4	*, /, %

We'll add one more enhancement to example 2.17 by rounding the output to two decimal places using `printf`,

Example 2.18. After rounding to two decimal places.

```
1  float price1 = 19.95f;
2  float price2 = 2.80f;
3  float totalWithTax = (price1 + price2) * 1.05f;
4  out.printf("Total with tax is $%.2f", totalWithTax);
```

```
Total with tax is $23.89
```

Exercises

2.1 Write a program that converts miles to kilometers. Have the user enter the value in miles, multiply it by 1.61 and output the result.

2.2 Write a program that asks the user for a vehicle's fuel tank capacity in gallons and its fuel efficiency in miles per gallon. It should then output the vehicle's range, that is, the number of miles it can travel on a full tank.

2.3 Write a program that asks the user for three items' prices and a tax rate. Output the total price including tax.

2.4 Write a program that asks the user for his or her year of birth, and output how old he or she is.

2.5 Write a program that asks the user for a sphere's radius in inches, and output its volume in cubic inches using the formula $v = 4/3\pi r^3$.

2.6 Modify example 2.15 to use the expression `9 / 5 * celsius + 32`, then demonstrate both methods of forcing floating point division as discussed on page 27. Run your program and make sure it produces the correct result.

2.6 Processing String Data

Using the addition operator with two strings concatenates them, creating a new string with the combined contents of the two operands. We've done this earlier in this chapter,

```
1  out.print("What's your name? ");
2  String name = input.nextLine();
3  out.print("Hello, " + name + "!");
```

Example 2.19. String concatenation with the + operator.

```
What's your name? Billy
Hello, Billy!
```

Line 3 concatenates three strings, two literals and a `String` variable. After the three strings are concatenated, the resulting string is passed

String concatenation: Merging two strings to make a new combined string.

in to the `print` method as a parameter. Here's another example of string concatenation,

```
1   out.print("Enter your first name: ");
2   String firstName = input.nextLine();
3   out.print("Enter your last name: ");
4   String lastName = input.nextLine();
5   String fullName = firstName + " " + lastName;
6   out.printf("Hello, %s", fullName);
```

```
Enter your first name: Isaac
Enter your last name: Newton
Hello, Isaac Newton
```

We can extract first and last names from a string containing a full name. To do that, we look for the space character, then extract the first and last names separately,

Example 2.20. Extracting words from a string.

```
1   out.print("Enter your full name: ");
2   String name = input.nextLine();
3   int spaceIndex = name.indexOf(' ');
4   String firstName = name.substring(0, spaceIndex);
5   String lastName = name.substring(spaceIndex + 1);
6   out.printf("First name: %s, last name: %s", firstName, lastName);
```

```
Enter your full name: Isaac Newton
First name: Isaac, last name: Newton
```

`indexOf` and `substring` methods of the `String` class.

The `indexOf` method of the `String` class returns the index (position) of a certain character within the string. After we've retrieved the position of the space within the string containing first and last name, we extract the first and last name separately using the `substring` method of the `String` class. When passing one parameter into `substring()`, it returns the contents of the string starting at the specified index. When passing two parameters, it returns the contents of the string starting at the first index and ending at the second index. Note that the first character in a string has the index zero, thus we say that string indexing is zero-based.

String indexing is zero-based.

`char` data type.

One primitive data type in Java that we haven't seen yet is the `char` type. A variable of type `char` can hold a single character. `char` literals are enclosed in single quotes, and this is what we've passed into the `indexOf` method of the `String` class.

Exercises

2.7 Write a program that asks the user for his or her first, middle and last names, and outputs the full name.

2.8 Write a program that asks the user for three sentences separated by commas, then prints each sentence separately. Hint: you can do this by using indexOf to find the index of the first comma, then use substring to get a string containing the second and third sentences, then again use indexOf and substring to separate the second and third sentences.

2.9 Fix the two syntax errors in the following program, and test it with the retail price $15.50, which should produce a sale price of $16.27,

```
1  import static java.lang.System.out;
2  import java.util.Scanner;
3
4  public class Test {
5    public static void main(String[] args) {
6
7      Scanner input = new Scanner(System.in);
8
9      out.print("Enter retail price: ");
10     float retailPrice = input.nextFloat();
11     input.nextline();
12
13     float taxRate = 0.05;
14     float salePrice = retailPrice * (1 + taxRate);
15
16     out.printf("The price with tax is %.2f", salePrice);
17
18     input.close();
19   }
20 }
```

2.7 Processing Dates

Occasionally your programs will need to process dates and times. Java provides the LocalDate and LocalTime classes to help with this. Let's suppose you want to display the current date and time. This can be done as in the following example (2.21),

Example 2.21. Printing current date and time.

```
1  import java.time.LocalDate;
2  import java.time.LocalTime;
3  ...
4
5     LocalDate date = LocalDate.now();
6     out.println("The date is " + date);
7
8     LocalTime time = LocalTime.now();
9     out.println("The time is " + time);
```

```
The date is 2021-02-16
The time is 20:19:58.868667
```

The **LocalDate** and **LocalTime** classes provide methods that retrieve the date and time's components (year, month, day, hour, minute, etc.), in case you need individual components or want to print it out in a different way than the output in the previous example. In the next example (2.22), you can see how to retrieve these individual components and use them to print the current date and time,

Example 2.22. Getting date and time components.

```
1    LocalDate date = LocalDate.now();
2    out.printf("The date is %d-%02d-%02d\n", date.getYear(), date.getMonthValue()
       , date.getDayOfMonth());
3
4    LocalTime time = LocalTime.now();
5    out.printf("The time is %02d:%02d:%02d\n", time.getHour(), time.getMinute(),
       time.getSecond());
```

```
The date is 2021-02-16
The time is 20:39:06
```

To initialize a **LocalDate** object with a specific day, you can use the **LocalDate.of()** method, passing it three integer parameters for the year, month and day. You can also use a string to initialize a **LocalDate** variable using the **LocalDate.parse()** method, which takes a string and optionally a date format. The following example (2.23) illustrates all three of these techniques of creating a date object,

Example 2.23. Initializing a LocalDate object.

```
1   import java.time.format.DateTimeFormatter;
2   ...
3     LocalDate date = LocalDate.of(2021, 7, 21);
4     out.printf("The date is %d-%02d-%02d\n", date.getYear(), date.getMonthValue()
        , date.getDayOfMonth());
5
6     LocalDate date2 = LocalDate.parse("2004-03-02");
7     out.println("The date is " + date2);
8
9     DateTimeFormatter formatter = DateTimeFormatter.ofPattern("MM/dd/yyyy");
10    LocalDate date3 = LocalDate.parse("04/03/2005", formatter);
```

```
11 | out.println("The date is " + date3);
```

```
The date is 2021-07-21
The date is 2004-03-02
The date is 2005-04-03
```

`LocalDate` has many other useful features. Other common operations include,

- Adding a certain number of days to a `LocalDate` object can be done with the `plusDays()` method.
- Getting the number of days between two `LocalDate` objects can be done with the syntax `java.time.temporal.ChronoUnit.DAYS.between(date1, date2)`, which returns a long integer.

Chapter Summary

- Variables hold your programs' data. Your programs can read from and write to variables.
- Variables have specific data types.
- Data types have a range of allowed values.
- Output is displayed on the Console view in Eclipse. The `println` method allows you to write output, and the `printf` method allows greater flexibility in formatting output.
- The `Scanner` class allows your programs to get input from the user.
- Numeric data, string data and dates can be manipulated by your programs.
- A sample program is shown below, with labels for notable input, processing and output components:

```
1  import static java.lang.System.out;                          Import System.out
2  import java.util.Calendar;
3  import java.util.Scanner;                                     Import Scanner class
4
5  public class Test {
6    public static void main(String[] args) {                   Creates Scanner object
7
8      Scanner input = new Scanner(System.in);
9
10     out.print("Enter your age: ");                            Read a number
11     int age = input.nextInt();
12     input.nextLine();
13
14     out.print("Enter your full name: ");                      Read a string
15     String name = input.nextLine();
16
17     int thisYear = Calendar.getInstance().get(Calendar.YEAR);
18     int birthYear = thisYear - age;                           Numeric computation
19
20     int spaceIndex = name.indexOf(' ');                       String manipulation
21     String firstName = name.substring(0, spaceIndex);
22     String lastName = name.substring(spaceIndex + 1);
23
24     out.printf("First name: %s, last name: %s\n", firstName, lastName);
25     out.println("You were born in " + birthYear);
26                                                               Formatted output with printf
27     input.close();
28   }
29 }
```

Output with println

Closing Scanner object

Exercise Solutions

2.1
```
1  out.print("Enter distance in miles: ");
2  float miles = input.nextFloat();
3  input.nextLine();
4
5  float kilometers = miles * 1.60934f;
6
7  out.printf("%.2f miles = %.2f kilometers", miles, kilometers);
```

```
Enter distance in miles: 3
3.00 miles = 4.83 kilometers
```

2.2
```
1  out.print("Enter fuel tank capacity in gallons: ");
2  float gallons = input.nextFloat();
3  input.nextLine();
4
```

```
 5    out.print("Enter miles per gallon: ");
 6    float mpg = input.nextFloat();
 7    input.nextLine();
 8
 9    float range = mpg * gallons;
10
11    out.printf("Your vehicle's range is %.2f miles", range);
```

```
Enter fuel tank capacity in gallons: 13.3
Enter miles per gallon: 37
Your vehicle's range is 492.10 miles
```

2.3
```
 1    out.print("Enter prices for three items: ");
 2    float price1 = input.nextFloat();
 3    float price2 = input.nextFloat();
 4    float price3 = input.nextFloat();
 5    input.nextLine();
 6
 7    out.print("Enter tax rate: ");
 8    float taxRate = input.nextFloat();
 9    input.nextLine();
10
11    float price = (price1 + price2 + price3) * (1 + taxRate);
12
13    out.printf("Total price = $%.2f", price);
```

```
Enter prices for three items: 1.99 12 5.99
Enter tax rate: 0.06
Total price = $21.18
```

2.4
```
 1    out.print("What year were you born? ");
 2    int birthYear = input.nextInt();
 3    input.nextLine();
 4
 5    int thisYear = java.time.LocalDate.now().getYear();
 6
 7    out.println("You are " + (thisYear - birthYear) + " years old");
```

```
What year were you born? 2002
You are 19 years old
```

2.5
```
 1    out.print("Enter sphere's radius in inches: ");
 2    float radius = input.nextFloat();
 3    input.nextLine();
 4
 5    float volume = radius * radius * radius * 3.14159f * 4 / 3;
 6
 7    out.printf("The sphere's volume is %.2f cubic inches", volume);
```

```
Enter sphere's radius in inches: 3
The sphere's volume is 113.10 cubic inches
```

2.6
```
 1    out.print("Enter degrees Celsius: ");
 2    int celsius = input.nextInt();
 3    input.nextLine();
 4
```

```
5   int fahrenheit = (int) (9f / 5 * celsius + 32);
6   out.printf("%d Celsius is %d Fahrenheit \n", celsius, fahrenheit);
7
8   fahrenheit = (int) ((float) 9 / 5 * celsius + 32);
9   out.printf("%d Celsius is %d Fahrenheit \n", celsius, fahrenheit);
```

```
Enter degrees Celsius: 100
100 Celsius is 212 Fahrenheit
100 Celsius is 212 Fahrenheit
```

2.7
```
1   out.print("Enter your first name: ");
2   String firstName = input.nextLine();
3   out.print("Enter your middle name: ");
4   String middleName = input.nextLine();
5   out.print("Enter your last name: ");
6   String lastName = input.nextLine();
7   String fullName = firstName + " " + middleName + " " + lastName;
8   out.printf("Hello, %s", fullName);
```

```
Enter your first name: Galileo
Enter your middle name: di Vincenzo
Enter your last name: Galilei
Hello, Galileo di Vincenzo Galilei
```

2.8
```
1   out.print("Enter a three-sentence poem: ");
2   String poem = input.nextLine();
3   int index = poem.indexOf(',');
4   String sentence1 = poem.substring(0, index);
5   poem = poem.substring(index+1);
6   index = poem.indexOf(',');
7   String sentence2 = poem.substring(0, index);
8   String sentence3 = poem.substring(index+1);
9   out.printf("%s\n%s\n%s", sentence1, sentence2, sentence3);
```

```
Enter a three-sentence poem: Everyone young or old, needs someone to listen, as their stories are told
Everyone young or old
needs someone to listen
as their stories are told
```

2.9
```
1   out.print("Enter retail price: ");
2   float retailPrice = input.nextFloat();
3   input.nextLine();
4
5   float taxRate = 0.05f;
6   float salePrice = retailPrice * (1 + taxRate);
7
8   out.printf("The price with tax is %.2f", salePrice);
```

```
Enter retail price: 15.50
The price with tax is 16.27
```

Working with the IDE (Integrated Development Environment)

3

3.1 Managing Programs

This isn't a book about Eclipse, so we won't go into too much detail here. We'll cover just what you need to learn about the IDE in order to move on to the next chapter.

The IDE (Integrated Development Environment) in our case is Eclipse, and its main window is shown in Figure 3.1.

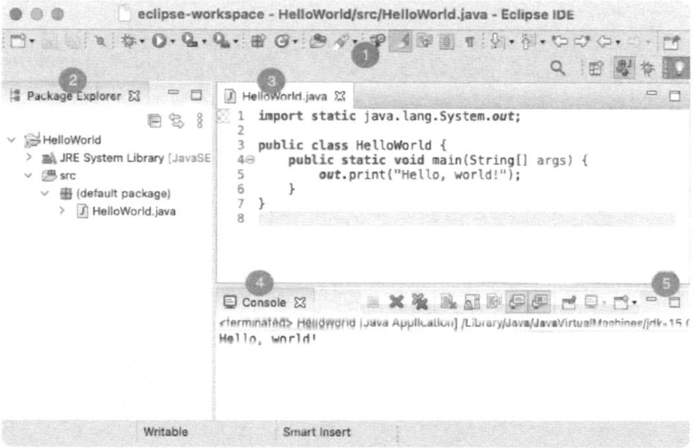

Figure 3.1: The Eclipse main window.

The toolbars (labeled 1 in the figure) each have a handle which looks like four vertical dots. You can grab toolbars by the handle and move them around the window. The Package Explorer view (2) shows a tree hierarchy of each of your projects. We only have one project so far, HelloWorld, and you can see its tree which contains HelloWorld.java under the "src" folder. The HelloWorld.java file (3) contains our main program's source code. The Console view (4) shows the program's output. Views such as Console and Package Explorer have their own minimize/maximize buttons on the top right (5). You can grab a view by its tab, where you see the view's name, and drag it around the window to dock it somewhere else. Views can be docked separately, and can also be docked together as tabs. You should practice moving some of the views around the window to get the hang of it.

If you accidentally minimize one of these views, you can get it back by clicking on its icon in the toolbar that it minimized to, or by choosing "Window → Show View" from the main menu, followed by the view that you want, e.g., "Window → Show View → Console".

You saw in section 1.5 how to create a new program. Follow the same process to create a second project, and name it "GeometryWiz". Add a class to your new project called "CircleArea", and enter the following code into the new file CircleArea.java,

Example 3.1. CircleArea class.

```java
 1  import static java.lang.System.out;
 2  import java.util.Scanner;
 3
 4  public class CircleArea {
 5
 6    public static void main(String[] args) {
 7      Scanner input = new Scanner(System.in);
 8
 9      out.print("Please enter circle's radius in feet: ");
10      float radius = input.nextFloat();
11      input.nextLine();
12      float area = radius * radius * 3.14f;
13      out.print("The circle with radius " + radius + " feet has an area of " +
          area + " square feet.");
14
15      input.close();
16    }
17  }
```

You can get a more accurate answer by using (float) Math.PI instead of 3.14f. We'll see Math.PI later on, in section 9.6.

At this point, your main window will look like Figure 3.2.

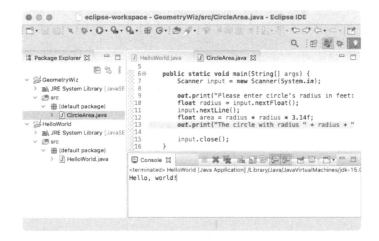

Figure 3.2: Eclipse window with two projects.

The Package Explorer window now has both of your projects, HelloWorld and GeometryWiz, each with its tree of assets. Hitting the

Run button in the toolbar will run your new class, CircleArea, *if you have its code in focus*. Click within the CircleArea.java window, then hit the Run button in the toolbar, to run it:

```
Please enter circle's radius in feet: 10
The circle with radius 10.0 feet has an area of 314.0 square feet.
```

Alternatively, you can right-click in the code window and choose "Run As → Java Application" from the context menu, or right-click on CircleArea.java in the Package Explorer view, then choose "Run As → Java Application". You can have multiple programs in your Eclipse workspace, and you need to make sure you're running the right one to avoid the confusion that can result if the wrong program runs in the Console view.

Above, I've used the terms *project* and *program* somewhat loosely. You run a program by invoking the `main` method belonging to one of your classes. A project can have many classes, and more than one of them can have a `main` method. If you aren't able to run the `main` method that you intend, you should go into the "Run Configurations" dialog box (colloquially, a *dialog box* is also called a *dialog*, a term we'll use occasionally), which you open using "Run → Run Configurations" from the main menu. The Run Configurations dialog is shown in Figure 3.3.

Run configuration: A definition telling Eclipse how to run your program. This definition is created automatically when you run your program for the first time.

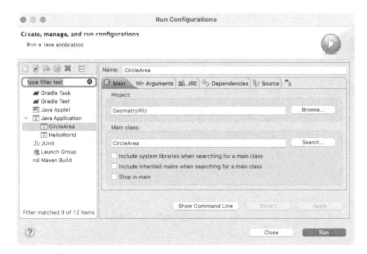

Figure 3.3: The Run Configurations dialog in Eclipse.

On the left-hand side of the Run Configurations dialog box, under Java Application, you will see the Java Application run configurations defined in your workspace (we'll deal with what a *workspace* is later in this chapter). If you're having trouble running your program, you can manually create a run configuration here, or delete a run configuration and re-create it. You can see in Figure 3.3 that the CircleArea run configuration invokes the `main` method in the CircleArea class of the GeometryWiz project.

If you have two programs running at the same time, the Console view shows both of them. To see how this works, run the CircleArea program and leave it waiting for user input. Then run the HelloWorld program. You'll see the Hello World output in the Console view, and the ⊟▾ icon in its toolbar will become enabled. Clicking the triangle to its right brings up a menu of running programs, which you can use to switch between the different programs that are running simultaneously. See Figure 3.4.

Figure 3.4: Multiple programs running in the Console view.

Two more toolbar buttons on the Console view that you should be aware of are the Stop and Close buttons (Figure 3.5). If a program is still running, the Stop button will be enabled (the one that looks like a red square). You can use it to force a program to stop, if for example you inadvertently created an infinite loop in your code. The Close button, which looks like a black "x", is next to the Stop button. It lets you close a program's output, which is handy if you have too many sessions open and you don't want confusion about which session is the most recent.

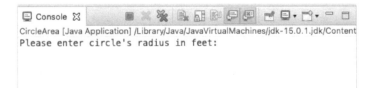

Figure 3.5: The Console view's toolbar.

Java Project: A collection of related Java classes in Eclipse.

Eclipse workspace: A collection of related Java projects along with Eclipse configuration settings.

A Java Project in Eclipse is a set of related Java classes, all under one tree within the Package Explorer view. An Eclipse workspace is the set of projects you currently have in Package Explorer, plus Eclipse's configuration settings. You can have multiple workspaces, for example, one for the assignments in your Java course, and another for the assignments in your Advanced Java course. You can switch workspaces at any time, using the "File → Switch Workspace" menu option. Choosing "Other" leads to the New Workspace dialog as shown in Figure 3.6. There, you can enter a directory to use as the root of a new workspace.

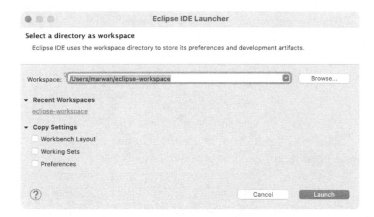

Figure 3.6: The New Workspace dialog in Eclipse.

The tree structure within the Package Explorer view is close but doesn't exactly mirror the tree of files and directories in your workspace. Rather, it's more of a logical organization of the files and other artifacts that make up a Java project. Occasionally you'll want to locate a Java file on disk. You can do that in Package Explorer by right-clicking on the Java file and choosing the "Show In → System Explorer" option. This opens a Windows Explorer window (or Finder window on MacOS) with the Java file selected.

Exercises

3.1   Refer to the bibliography and navigate to the Eclipse online help URL. Click around to familiarize yourself with the Eclipse help content.

3.2   Use the "Window → Show View" command on the main toolbar to open three or four views of your choosing, and peruse the views that appear.

3.2 Compile Errors

As you write code, Eclipse points out syntax errors. You'll see error symbols in the left margin, as well as red underlines where Eclipse thinks the error is. Hovering the mouse over either of those will show a tool tip with error information. I've illustrated this in Figure 3.7 by removing the semicolon at the end of the `print` statement.

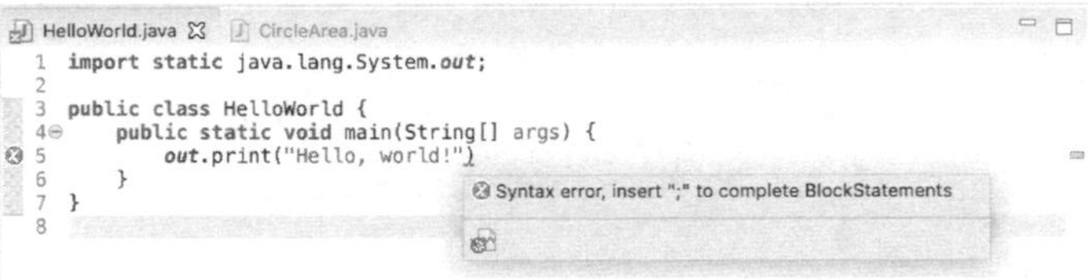

```
HelloWorld.java 83    CircleArea.java
 1  import static java.lang.System.out;
 2
 3  public class HelloWorld {
 4⊖     public static void main(String[] args) {
 5          out.print("Hello, world!")
 6      }
 7  }                                   Syntax error, insert ";" to complete BlockStatements
 8
```

Figure 3.7: Compile-time error.

Eclipse will remove the error message after you restore the semicolon and save the file. Recall from chapter 1 that a compiler translates a high-level language such as Java into machine language. Eclipse compiles your source code as you are typing, and shows you compile errors in real-time. These are called compile-time errors since they're detected as Eclipse compiles your code. A Java program can't be run until all compile errors are fixed.

Often, multiple errors show up in your code. You should fix them one by one. Since coding mistakes sometimes result in more than one error message, sometimes it helps to fix the first error, which clears up other error messages in subsequent lines. Figure 3.8 shows an example of a single syntax error causing multiple error messages,

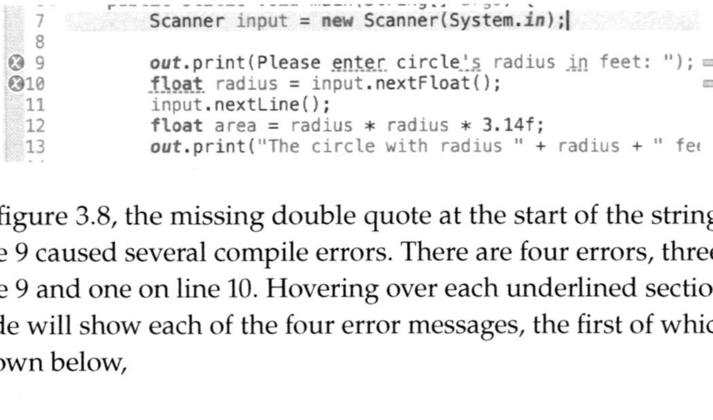

```
 7          Scanner input = new Scanner(System.in);
 8
 9          out.print(Please enter circle's radius in feet: ");
10          float radius = input.nextFloat();
11          input.nextLine();
12          float area = radius * radius * 3.14f;
13          out.print("The circle with radius " + radius + " fee
```

Figure 3.8: Multiple compile errors.

In figure 3.8, the missing double quote at the start of the string on line 9 caused several compile errors. There are four errors, three on line 9 and one on line 10. Hovering over each underlined section of code will show each of the four error messages, the first of which is shown below,

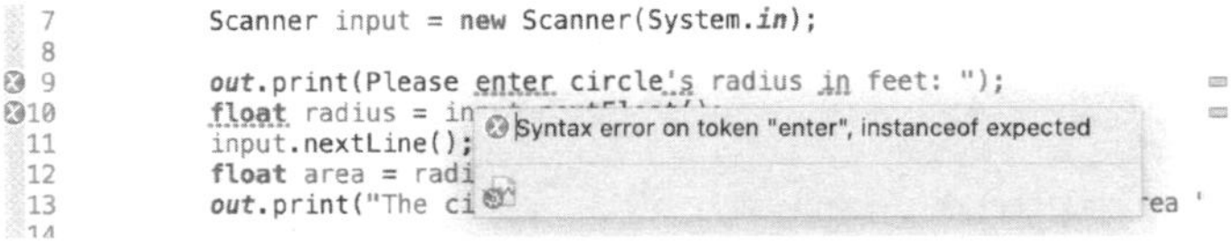

```
 7          Scanner input = new Scanner(System.in);
 8
 9          out.print(Please enter circle's radius in feet: ");
10          float radius = in                                   ⊟
11          input.nextLine();     Syntax error on token "enter", instanceof expected
12          float area = radi
13          out.print("The ci                                          ea '
14
```

None of the four error messages actually says what the real problem is, but the first error message, "Syntax error on token "enter", instanceof expected", gives a hint that something is wrong near the word 'enter', and examining that area reveals the real problem. Adding double quotes after the opening parenthesis fixes the error. Compile errors aren't a bad thing—they're a normal part of software development. The compiler is helping you correct problems in your program.

Exercises

3.3   Enter the code in example 3.1. Remove the opening bracket that follows `public class CircleArea` on line 4 and read the compile error. Now restore the opening bracket and remove the corresponding closing bracket. Read the ensuing compile error.

3.4   Enter the following program, find the compile errors and fix them, then run it to make sure it works.

```
1    out.print("Enter your first name: ");
2    String firstName = input.nextLine;
3    out.print("Enter your last name: ");
4    String lastName = input.nextLine;
5    String fullName = firstName + " " + lastName;
6    out.printf("Hello, %s", fullName);
```

3.5   Enter the following program, find the compile errors and fix them, then run it to make sure it works.

```
1    float price1 = 19.95;
2    float price2 = 2.80;
3    float totalWithTax - price1 + price2 * 1.05;
4    out.println("Total with tax is " + totalWithTax);
```

3.3 Runtime Errors

Another kind of error you will encounter is the runtime error. These occur at runtime due to a variety of problems that can occur while your program is running. They can't be predicted by the compiler at compile-time. An example is when an integer is divided by another, and the denominator has the value zero at the time. The result is an error message at runtime, followed by the Java system terminating your program. Example 3.2 shows this,

Example 3.2. Runtime divide-by-zero error.

```java
import static java.lang.System.out;
import java.util.Scanner;

public class HelloWorld {
  public static void main(String[] args) {
    Scanner input = new Scanner(System.in);

    out.print("Please enter the rectangle's area: ");
    int area = input.nextInt();
    input.nextLine();
    out.print("Please enter the rectangle's height: ");
    int height = input.nextInt();
    input.nextLine();
    int width = area / height;
    out.print("The rectangle's width is: " + width);

    input.close();
  }
}
```

```
Please enter the rectangle's area: 10
Please enter the rectangle's height: 0
Exception in thread "main" java.lang.ArithmeticException: / by zero
        at HelloWorld.main(HelloWorld.java:14)
```

As you see in the above screen shot, the Java system produced an error message and the program terminated before reaching the `print` statement on line 15. Java refers to runtime errors as *exceptions*. The error message provides a lot of information about the error that occurred. From the error message in the screen shot above, we can get the following information,

Exception: An exceptional situation causing the Java program to terminate.

- The exception that occurred is of type "java.lang.ArithmeticException", and the specific error is "/ by zero".
- The error occurred in the thread called "main". Threads are simultaneous execution paths within your program, but in this simple program there is only one thread, the main thread.
- The error occurred in "HelloWorld.main", that is, the `main` method of the `HelloWorld` class.
- The error occurred in the file HelloWorld.java at line 14. Clicking the link in the error message will open that file, if it isn't already open, and highlight that line.

That's plenty to go on, and it doesn't take much detective work to get to the bottom of the issue. In chapter 4, you'll learn how to test for specific values and modify execution if a certain condition is met. In this case, the way to fix the problem is to test for the denominator being zero, and if it is, tell the user that zero is an invalid input value,

```
1   out.print("Please enter the rectangle's area: ");
2   int area = input.nextInt();
3   input.nextLine();
4   out.print("Please enter the rectangle's height: ");
5   int height = input.nextInt();
6   input.nextLine();
7   if (height == 0) {
8     out.print("The height can't be zero.");
9   }
10  else {
11    int width = area / height;
12    out.print("The rectangle's width is: " + width);
13  }
```

Example 3.3. Runtime divide-by-zero error averted.

```
Please enter the rectangle's area: 10
Please enter the rectangle's height: 0
The height can't be zero.
```

We'll leave the `if` statement's specifics for chapter 4. For now, we'll just say that the error condition was detected and the exception averted. We'll also discuss exceptions in more detail in chapter 12. In general, runtime errors are more difficult to correct than compile errors, but still are part of normal everyday life as a software developer. You'll get used to dealing with them with ease and they won't be a problem. Quite the opposite, these exceptions provide a lot of information that helps you to correct mistakes in your code.

3.4 Logic Errors

The last type of error we'll discuss is the logic error. Often, these are harder to detect and correct than compile or runtime errors, because they don't generate an error message. The program's logic is incorrect and the output will be wrong, at least for certain input values, but it's up to you to catch and correct them. We've already seen a good example of this in chapter 2, which we'll repeat here as example 3.4,

```
1   out.print("Enter degrees Celsius: ");
2   int celsius = input.nextInt();
3   input.nextLine();
4
5   int fahrenheit = 9 / 5 * celsius + 32;
6
7   out.printf("%d Celsius is %d Fahrenheit", celsius, fahrenheit);
```

Example 3.4. Example of a logic error.

```
Enter degrees Celsius: 100
100 Celsius is 132 Fahrenheit
```

This example implements the formula $Fahrenheit = 9/5\,Celsius + 32$. One hundred degrees Celsius is 212 degrees Fahrenheit. But when we run our program and enter 100 as the Celsius temperature, the output is 132 degrees Fahrenheit. The problem as discussed in section 2.5 is that line 5 first divides 9 by 5, an integer division resulting in the value 1. To fix it, we change line 5 to use floating point division by using a floating point 9 (9f), then cast the final answer to an integer, as in example 3.5, which produces the right answer,

Example 3.5. Logic error corrected.

```
1  out.print("Enter degrees Celsius: ");
2  int celsius = input.nextInt();
3  input.nextLine();
4
5  int fahrenheit = (int) (9f / 5 * celsius + 32);
6
7  out.printf("%d Celsius is %d Fahrenheit", celsius, fahrenheit);
```

```
Enter degrees Celsius: 100
100 Celsius is 212 Fahrenheit
```

The programmer may not catch the erroneous computation without adequate testing. As the above example illustrates, you should carefully test your code before moving on to another task. Many professional software developers make a point to step through their code in the debugger at least once whenever they write new sections of code. We'll discuss the debugger later in the book.

Exercises

3.6   The following program has two syntax errors and one logic error. Fix them and test the program to make sure it works,

```
1  import static java.lang.System.out;
2  import java.util.Scannerr;
3
4  public class Test {
5    public static void main(String[] args) {
6
7      Scanner input = new Scanner(System.in);
8
9      out.print("Enter your full name: ");
10     String name = input.nextLine();
```

```
11    int spaceIndex = name.indexOf(' ');
12    String firstName = name.substring(0, spaceIndex));
13    String lastName = name.substring(spaceIndex + 1);
14    out.printf("First name: %s, last name: %s", lastName, firstName);
15
16    input.close();
17  }
18 }
```

Chapter Summary

- The Eclipse IDE calls your program a project. An Eclipse workspace can contain multiple projects.
- You can have multiple Eclipse workspaces, and switch between them using the "File → Switch Workspace" command.
- In Eclipse, a run configuration defines how your program is run.
- The Console view in Eclipse shows your program's output, and multiple programs can be run at once.
- Three common types of errors are:
  - Compile errors: Syntax errors in your Java code. Your program can't run while it has compile errors.
  - Runtime errors: Exceptions are thrown by your code in certain exceptional circumstances, such as attempting to divide by zero.
  - Logic errors: Mistakes in the code can cause the program to show incorrect output.

Exercise Solutions

3.4
```
1    out.print("Enter your first name: ");
2    String firstName = input.nextLine();
3    out.print("Enter your last name: ");
4    String lastName = input.nextLine();
5    String fullName = firstName + " " + lastName;
6    out.printf("Hello, %s", fullName);
```

```
Enter your first name: Rene
Enter your last name: Descartes
Hello, Rene Descartes
```

3.5
```
1    float price1 = 19.95;
2    float price2 = 2.80;
```

```
3   float totalWithTax = price1 + price2 * 1.05;
4   out.println("Total with tax is " + totalWithTax);
```

```
Total with tax is 22.890001
```

3.6
```
1  import static java.lang.System.out;
2  import java.util.Scanner;
3
4  public class Test {
5    public static void main(String[] args) {
6
7      Scanner input = new Scanner(System.in);
8
9      out.print("Enter your full name: ");
10     String name = input.nextLine();
11     int spaceIndex = name.indexOf(' ');
12     String firstName = name.substring(0, spaceIndex);
13     String lastName = name.substring(spaceIndex + 1);
14     out.printf("First name: %s, last name: %s", firstName, lastName)
         ;
15
16     input.close();
17   }
18 }
```

```
Enter your full name: Leonhard Euler
First name: Leonhard, last name: Euler
```

Conditionals | 4

4.1 Boolean Expressions

Conditional execution is when your program executes different code depending on some condition. A condition is evaluated using a boolean expression—an expression that evaluates to true or false. You saw the `boolean` data type in chapter 2. Variables of type `boolean` can only have a true or false value, and are initially false.

Several types of operators result in a boolean value. For example, we test whether two numbers are the same using the equals operator (==), which gives a boolean value that we can then use in an `if` statement. Another operator is `!=` which returns true if its two arguments are not equal. Table 4.1 shows more operators that return a boolean value.

Boolean Expression: An *expression* that has the value true or false.

Table 4.1: Common operators.

Operator	Example	
==	a == b	True if two numbers are equal.
!=	a != b	True if two numbers are not equal.
>	a > b	True if the first argument is larger than the second.
<	a < b	True if the first argument is smaller than the second.
>=	a >= b	True if the first argument is larger than or equal to the second.
<=	a <= b	True if the first argument is smaller than or equal to the second.
&&	(a > b) && (c > d)	and operator—True if a is bigger than b, *and* c is bigger than d.
||	(a > b) || (c > d)	or operator—True if a is bigger than b, *or* c is bigger than d.
!	!(a == b)	not operator—True if its argument is false.

All but the last operator in table 4.1 are *binary*. They each take two `arguments`, one on the left and one on the right. The last one is a *unary* operator, which takes a single argument. Using these operators, you can construct boolean expressions to test various conditions within your programs.

Exercises

4.1   Complete the following table,

Expression	Value
a	120
b	-12
c	0
d	31
a == b	*false*
a != b	
a > b	
a < b	
a >= b	
a <= b	
(a > b) && (c > d)	
(a > b) || (c > d)	
!(a == b)	

4.2 The `if` Statement

Here's an example of a basic `if` statement,

Example 4.1. == operator with a simple `if` statement.

```
1  boolean isEqual = false;
2  int number1 = 99 / 3;
3  int number2 = 22 + 11;
4  isEqual = number1 == number2;
5  if (isEqual) {
6    out.println("The numbers are equal");
7  }
```

```
The numbers are equal
```

Above, we declared a variable named `isEqual` of type `boolean`, and initialized its value to false. Then we declared two integer variables with values 99/3 and 22 + 11. The boolean variable is set to the result of the equality test `number1 == number2`. Since the two variables' values at runtime are equal, the boolean variable `isEqual` is assigned the value 'true'.

The `if` statement is on line 5 of example 4.1. An `if` statement must contain a boolean expression within parentheses, followed by a code block to execute if the expression evaluates to 'true'. In this case, the boolean expression consists of the single boolean variable `isEqual`, and its value is 'true', so the code within the block is executed. A code block is a set of statements enclosed by curly braces (above, this block starts on line 5 and ends on line 7).

Recall from Technique 1 on page 17 that we should always try to simplify our code. We can do this by noticing that `number1` and `number2` are only used in one place, on line 4, so we can combine lines 2-4 as shown in Example 4.2,

```
1    boolean isEqual = false;
2    isEqual = (99 / 3) == (22 + 11);
3    if (isEqual) {
4      out.println("The numbers are equal");
5    }
```

Example 4.2. Simplified version of example 4.1.

If you run the revised example, you'll see the same output. We've simplified our code while maintaining its clarity. But we can still simplify further, as shown in Example 4.3, since `isEqual` is only used in one place, on line 3, so we can get rid of the `isEqual` variable as well,

```
1    if ((99 / 3) == (22 + 11)) {
2      out.println("The numbers are equal");
3    }
```

Example 4.3. Simplified version of example 4.2.

Again, running the code produces the same output. Simplifying your code should be a natural and automatic practice as you write your programs.

An `if` statement has an optional `else` clause which is executed if its condition is false. To illustrate this, we modify our previous example to output 'not equal' in the case that the two numbers aren't equal. In addition, we'll change the program so that it prompts the user to enter the two numbers,

Example 4.4. Use of the `else` clause.

```
1  import static java.lang.System.out;
2  import java.util.Scanner;
3
4  public class HelloWorld {
5    public static void main(String[] args) {
6
7      Scanner input = new Scanner(System.in);
8
9      out.print("Enter first number: ");
10     int num1 = input.nextInt();
11     input.nextLine();
12     out.print("Enter second number: ");
13     int num2 = input.nextInt();
14     input.nextLine();
15
16     if (num1 == num2) {
17       out.println("The numbers are equal");
18     }
19     else {
20       out.println("The numbers are not equal");
21     }
22
23     input.close();
24   }
25 }
```

```
Enter first number: 17
Enter second number: 21
The numbers are not equal
```

Though we've gotten used to omitting the top few and bottom few lines of our programs in code examples, I've included them in example 4.4 to illustrate our next technique. Notice the deliberate use of blank lines between each group of related lines of code. The import statements at the top are grouped together. The declaration of the `Scanner` variable is by itself. The six lines that get the user's input are grouped together. And, the lines that make up the `if` block are grouped together. This logical grouping of lines is so that you can *quickly and easily* look at your code and visually see each section. Each section of your code is a distinct part that serves its own function within the overall *algorithm* that your code embodies. It's very important that your code be easy to traverse in this way. You will be making lots of changes as you develop and refine your programs, and having these visual groupings is essential both for the ease and speed with which you modify your program.

Technique 2. Group related code together

Organize the code within your program into logical groupings, separated by blank lines.

Another thing that you'll notice in example 4.4, as well as the other examples you've seen, is the consistent style of indenting lines of code. The lines within each block of code, delimited by curly braces, are indented one level deeper than the enclosing block. The outer block is the `class` declaration on line 4, and its curly braces are on lines 4 and 25. The next block is the `main` method declaration, starting on line 5 and ending on line 24. Notice that the entire `main` method is indented within the `class` block. Likewise, the contents of the `main` method are indented, and so are the contents of the `if` statement and its `else` clause. Eclipse by default indents blocks by four spaces, while code listings here display blocks indented only two spaces to save space. You should get used to maintaining consistent indentation at all times. Without correct indentation, you're more likely to introduce syntax or logical errors into your program.

Technique 3. Maintain proper indentation in your programs

Maintain proper indentation in your programs to keep the logical flow of the program clear, and help prevent syntax or logical errors.

Tip 3. Don't try to *memorize* techniques. Instead, *internalize* them by thinking about why we use each technique.

Eclipse can help fix your indentation via the "Source → Format" command.

Eclipse can help fix your indentation via the "Source › Format" command, but this feature usually doesn't work if you have compile errors in your code, because the compiler can't interpret the code properly in the presence of syntax errors. So we can't always rely on Eclipse to fix our indentation—we must do the work to keep our code tidy.

The two techniques you've just seen, as well as Technique 1 on page 17 are all meant to help you *quickly and easily* navigate and modify your programs. This is important, especially as your programs get longer and more sophisticated.

Java (and many other languages) allows you to omit the opening and closing braces in `if` and `else` blocks, if there is only one statement within the code block. Thus, example 4.4 can be revised as follows,

Example 4.5. Omitting opening/-
closing braces when there's only one
statement within the if or else code
block.

```
1   out.print("Enter first number: ");
2   int num1 = input.nextInt();
3   input.nextLine();
4   out.print("Enter second number: ");
5   int num2 = input.nextInt();
6   input.nextLine();
7
8   if (num1 == num2)
9     out.println("The numbers are equal");
10  else
11    out.println("The numbers are not equal");
```

```
Enter first number: 15
Enter second number: 15
The numbers are equal
```

I prefer the final version to the one before it, since it has fewer lines, but clarity hasn't suffered. Note that the indentation as well as code block separation were maintained.

Compare strings using the equals()
method instead of ==.

When comparing strings, the == operator shouldn't be used. Instead, the **equals** method of the String object should be used. For example, **str1.equals(str2)** returns true or false depending on whether the two strings are equal. The reason you can't use == is that it returns true when the two strings are *the same* string object, whereas **equals** returns true when the two string objects contain identical strings.

You can nest if statements to create a decision tree. Here's an example program that asks a series of questions to diagnose a medical condition,

Example 4.6. Nesting if statements.

```
1   out.print("Do you have a sore throat? ");
2   String answer = input.nextLine();
3   if (answer.equals("Yes")) {
4     out.print("Do you have a fever? ");
5     answer = input.nextLine();
6     if (answer.equals("Yes"))
7       out.print("Possibly the flu.");
8     else
9       out.print("Possibly strep throat.");
10  }
11  else {
12    out.print("are you in pain? ");
13    answer = input.nextLine();
14    if (answer.equals("Yes"))
15      out.print("Try Advil.");
16    else
17      out.print("You appear to be fine.");
18  }
```

```
Do you have a sore throat? No
are you in pain? Yes
Try Advil.
```

In this example of `if` statement nesting, the outer `if` statement, representing the question "do you have a sore throat" has two possible execution paths, one for a "yes" answer, and another for any other response. Each of the two execution paths has another `if` statement. Obviously, you could nest further `if` statements to create a more complex decision tree. Execution at runtime flows down through the decision tree based on the user's answers to each question. Note that we only declare the "answer" variable once, on line 2.

The next example (4.7) asks the user for the name of a country, and outputs its capital,

```
1    out.print("Enter country name: ");
2    String country = input.nextLine();
3
4    if (country.equals("United States"))
5      out.print("The capital is Washington, DC");
6    if (country.equals("Brazil"))
7      out.print("The capital is Brasilia");
8    if (country.equals("Canada"))
9      out.print("The capital is Ottawa");
10   if (country.equals("France"))
11     out.print("The capital is Paris");
12   if (country.equals("India"))
13     out.print("The capital is New Delhi");
```

Example 4.7. Printing the capital of a country.

```
Enter country name: France
The capital is Paris
```

Note the string comparison using the `equals` method. Also note that no output is generated if the user's input doesn't match the country name in any of the `if` statements. What if we want to output a default message, such as "not found", if the user entered an unrecognized country name? For this, we'll use `else`, as in the example 4.8,

```
1    out.print("Enter country name: ");
2    String country = input.nextLine();
3
4    if (country.equals("United States"))
5      out.print("The capital is Washington, DC");
6    else {
7      if (country.equals("Brazil"))
8        out.print("The capital is Brasilia");
9      else {
```

Example 4.8. Multiple nested `if` statements.

```
10        if (country.equals("Canada"))
11          out.print("The capital is Ottawa");
12        else {
13          if (country.equals("France"))
14            out.print("The capital is Paris");
15          else {
16            if (country.equals("India"))
17              out.print("The capital is New Delhi");
18            else
19              out.print("I don't know the capital of " + country);
20          }
21        }
22      }
23    }
```

```
Enter country name: New Zealand
I don't know the capital of New Zealand
```

Look carefully at the way each `if` statement is nested within the previous `if`'s `else` clause. If the user's input doesn't match any of the `if` statements, it keeps falling through the else clauses until it reaches the innermost else clause, where the "not found" message is printed. In Java (as well as similar languages), else clauses can be chained in a simpler way, as shown in example 4.9,

Example 4.9. Chaining if statements.

```
1   out.print("Enter country name: ");
2   String country = input.nextLine();
3
4   if (country.equals("United States"))
5     out.print("The capital is Washington, DC");
6   else if (country.equals("Brazil"))
7     out.print("The capital is Brasilia");
8   else if (country.equals("Canada"))
9     out.print("The capital is Ottawa");
10  else if (country.equals("France"))
11    out.print("The capital is Paris");
12  else if (country.equals("India"))
13    out.print("The capital is New Delhi");
14  else
15    out.print("I don't know the capital of " + country);
```

This syntax is equivalent to that in the prior example, but lacks the extra curly braces on each `else` clause. We're able to do this because each `else` clause only has one statement, which is the next `if` statement. Note that Java, and similar languages, consider `if` as a single statement, including its `else` clause. This syntax is preferable because it's more compact and easier to read—readability isn't sacrificed, nor is runtime efficiency since it generates the same machine code as the longer syntax.

In the above form of chaining `if` statements, each `else` clause is considered to belong to the `if` statement immediately preceding it. This is a language rule meant to clear up the ambiguity that results from omitting the curly braces. Without this rule, it would be unclear whether an else statement belongs to the first or second `if` in the following example:

```
1   if (condition1)
2   if (condition2)
3   {action 2}
4   else
5   {action 3}
```

Visualize the ambiguity in the above using each of the below indentation scenarios:

```
1   if (condition1)
2      if (condition2)
3         {action 1}
4   else
5      {action 2}
```

```
1   if (condition1)
2      if (condition2)
3         {action 1}
4      else
5         {action 2}
```

In the absence of curly braces, `else` belongs to the `if` immediately above it.

The language rule means the second scenario matches the correct runtime behavior. Note that using curly braces would remove the ambiguity, but would increase the number of lines. Also note that in Java, the compiler ignores indentation completely—indentation is there to make it easier for us humans to work with our code.

In some languages such as Python, indentation does affect the program's behavior.

The next example (4.10) shows a program that generates 10 random numbers between 1 and 100, and prints their average. After computing the average, if it's below 40, it prints "too low". If it's above 60, it prints "too high". Otherwise, it prints "normal". The `Math.random` method returns a random floating point number between 0 and 0.99999.... Multiplying it by 100 converts it to a random number between 0 and 99.99999..., then adding 1 makes a random number between 1 and 100.9999.... Finally, casting to an integer retains the integer portion, a random number between 1 and 100.

`Math.random()` generates random numbers.

```
1   int num1 = (int) (Math.random() * 100 + 1);
2   int num2 = (int) (Math.random() * 100 + 1);
3   int num3 = (int) (Math.random() * 100 + 1);
4   int num4 = (int) (Math.random() * 100 + 1);
5   int num5 = (int) (Math.random() * 100 + 1);
6   int num6 = (int) (Math.random() * 100 + 1);
7   int num7 = (int) (Math.random() * 100 + 1);
8   int num8 = (int) (Math.random() * 100 + 1);
```

Example 4.10. `if` statement example—averaging random numbers.

```
9    int num9 = (int) (Math.random() * 100 + 1);
10   int num10 = (int) (Math.random() * 100 + 1);
11   int average = (num1 + num2 + num3 + num4 + num5 + num6 + num7 + num8 + num9 +
        num10) / 10;
12   out.println("The average is: " + average);
13   if (average < 40)
14     out.println("Too low");
15   else if (average > 60)
16     out.println("Too high");
17   else
18     out.println("Normal");
```

```
The average is: 61
Too high
```

Obviously, when you run this, you'll get different results since the program generates different random numbers each time it's run. Our last `if` statement example in this section will ask the user for the name of a country, and output the continent it's in,

Example 4.11. if statement example—output the continent.

```
1    out.print("Enter country name: ");
2    String country = input.nextLine();
3
4    if (country.equals("United States") || country.equals("Canada") || country.
        equals("Mexico"))
5      out.print(country + " is in North America");
6    else if (country.equals("Brazil") || country.equals("Chile") || country.
        equals("Argentina"))
7      out.print(country + " is in South America");
8    else if (country.equals("France") || country.equals("Belgium") || country.
        equals("Spain"))
9      out.print(country + " is in Europe");
10   else if (country.equals("Egypt") || country.equals("South Africa") || country.
        equals("Kenya"))
11     out.print(country + " is in Africa");
12   else if (country.equals("China") || country.equals("India") || country.equals
        ("Cambodia"))
13     out.print(country + " is in Asia");
14   else
15     out.print("I don't know where " + country + " is.");
```

```
Enter country name: Belgium
Belgium is in Europe
```

Note the use of the *or* operator, ||, to test whether the input matches any of a continent's countries.

Exercises

4.2 Write a program that asks the user for his car's mpg (miles per gallon). If it's below 20, the program should output 'not enough'. If it's between 20 and 30, it should output 'ok'. If it's above 30, it should output 'good'.

4.3 Write a program that asks the user for three numbers, and outputs the biggest one.

4.4 Write a program that greets the user with 'Good morning', 'Good afternoon' or 'Good evening', depending on the current hour of day. The current hour of day can be retrieved in Java using this syntax: `java.time.LocalTime.now().getHour()`.

4.5 Write a program that asks the user for a numeric grade between 0 and 100, and outputs the corresponding letter grade.

4.3 The `switch` Statement

The second most often used conditional statement in Java is `switch`. Its general format is,

```
1   switch (expression) {
2       case (literal value 1):
3           (actions 1)
4           break;
5       case (literal value 2):
6           (actions 2)
7           break;
8       case (literal value 3):
9           (actions 3)
10          break;
11      default:
12          (actions 4)
13          break;
14  }
```

`switch` can be used when you want to compare an expression to several possible literal values. If `expression` matches `literal value 1`, then the actions under the corresponding `case` are executed. A `break` statement marks the end of the statements executed in each case block. The last `default` block is executed if none of the other `case` clauses match. Here is example 4.11, rewritten using a `switch` statement,

Example 4.12. `switch` statement example—output the continent.

```
1   out.print("Enter country name: ");
2   String country = input.nextLine();
3
4   switch (country) {
5     case "United States":
6     case "Canada":
7     case "Mexico":
8       out.print(country + " is in North America");
9       break;
10    case "Brazil":
11    case "Chile":
12    case "Argentina":
13      out.print(country + " is in South America");
14      break;
15    case "France":
16    case "Belgium":
17    case "Spain":
18      out.print(country + " is in Europe");
19      break;
20    case "Egypt":
21    case "South Africa":
22    case "Kenya":
23      out.print(country + " is in Africa");
24      break;
25    case "China":
26    case "India":
27    case "Cambodia":
28      out.print(country + " is in Asia");
29      break;
30    default:
31      out.print("I don't know where " + country + " is.");
32      break;
33  }
```

```
Enter country name: Chile
Chile is in South America
```

Note how the expression in the above example is the variable `country`, which is of type `String`. It's compared with the constant values representing country names in each `case` clause. Also note how multiple `case` clauses can be merged so that the same actions are executed if the value matches any of the constants in the `case` clauses. The `default` clause doesn't need a `break` statement, but it's frequently included. For an example like this one, using `if` and `switch` will both work, as you've seen, but I consider `switch` to be more natural, more readable and more maintainable. `switch` does have its limitations, for example, you can only compare the main expression to constant values, and you can only compare for an exact match, so something like example 4.10 that compares a value with a range can't be accomplished using `switch`.

What if the user entered "mexico" as the country name, instead of "Mexico"? If you try that with the above example, you'll see that the program doesn't recognize the country. That's because the `equals` method is *case sensitive*. To allow the program to recognize uppercase as well as lowercase input by the user, we can convert the user's input to lowercase, and compare it with the countries' names in lowercase,

Use `toLowerCase()` and `toUpperCase()` to convert a string to all lowercase or all uppercase.

```
1    out.print("Enter country name: ");
2    String country = input.nextLine();
3
4    switch (country.toLowerCase()) {
5      case "united states":
6      case "canada":
7      case "mexico":
8        out.print(country + " is in North America");
9        break;
10     case "brazil":
11     case "chile":
12     case "argentina":
13       out.print(country + " is in South America");
14       break;
15     case "france":
16     case "belgium":
17     case "spain":
18       out.print(country + " is in Europe");
19       break;
20     case "egypt":
21     case "south africa":
22     case "kenya":
23       out.print(country + " is in Africa");
24       break;
25     case "china":
26     case "india":
27     case "cambodia":
28       out.print(country + " is in Asia");
29       break;
30     default:
31       out.print("I don't know the capital of " + country);
32       break;
33   }
```

Example 4.13. Recognizing lowercase and uppercase input.

```
Enter country name: kenya
kenya is in Africa
```

Exercises

4.6   Write a program that asks the user for the name of a month, and uses a `switch` statement to output the number of days in that month.

4.7 Write a program that asks the user for a letter grade, and uses a `switch` statement to output the corresponding numeric grade range.

4.8 Fix the logic error in the following program, and test it to make sure it works,

```
1  out.print("Enter your car's miles-per-gallon: ");
2  int mpg = input.nextInt();
3  input.nextLine();
4
5  if (mpg < 25)
6    out.println("Too low");
7  if (mpg > 37)
8    out.println("Good");
9  else
10   out.println("Acceptable");
```

4.4 Conditional Expressions

Java has a way to conditionally assign one of two values to a variable based on a condition. A common pattern is using an `if` statement to assign one value or another to a variable based on a condition, such as this,

```
1  if (useSSL)
2    url = "https://" + webAddress;
3  else
4    url = "http://" + webAddress;
```

Java lets us abbreviate the above like this,

```
1  url = useSSL ? "https://" + webAddress : "http://" + webAddress;
```

This is called the question-mark-colon operator (`?:` operator). It's a ternary operator, meaning it takes three operands. The first is the condition, which must be a boolean expression, such as a boolean variable. The second operand is the result if the boolean expression is true, and the third is the result if the boolean expression is false. The question mark is positioned between the first and second operands, and the colon is positioned between the second and third operands. You'll encounter this operator occasionally, so you should be comfortable with its usage. Though it's strange at first, you'll eventually get comfortable using it, and there are times when it's natural to use it. Take for example the following line of code,

```
1  shiftsPerEmployee = numberOfEmployees == 0 ? 0 : numberOfShifts /
     numberOfEmployees;
```

This expression first checks that the number of employees isn't zero, and if so assigns a default value of zero thus avoiding a divide-by-zero exception. If the number of employees isn't zero, it divides the number of shifts by the number of employees to get the shifts per employee. The ternary operator is also useful when combined with certain features that you'll learn about in later chapters, such as testing whether a reference is null, giving a default value if it is, and following the reference if it isn't (more on that later).

You can use ?: to avoid runtime errors.

4.5 Shortcut Evaluation

We haven't yet discussed operator precedence with respect to boolean operators. Recall that in chapter 2 we listed the precedence of common arithmetic operators in table 2.4. We will now add the operators that test boolean conditions to that list:

Precedence	Operator
1	cast operator
2	- (unary negation), ! (logical 'not')
3	+, -
4	*, /, %
5	<, <=, >, >=
6	==, !=
7	&&
8	||
9	?:

Table 4.2: Operator precedence in Java.

With table 4.2 in mind, table 4.3 displays some sample expressions with the corresponding *implied* order of evaluation,

Expression	Implied evaluation order
x > 0 && y < 0	(x > 0) && (y < 0)
x > 10 || x > 0 && y < 0	(x > 10) || ((x > 0) && (y < 0))
x + y * 3 > 10 || x < 0	(x + (y * 3) > 10) || (x < 0)

Table 4.3: Operator precedence examples.

&& and \|\| are *shortcut* operators, meaning they evaluate the left-hand side only, if the right-hand side's value doesn't affect the expression's outcome. To see how this works, consider the following code,

```
1  if (age > 15 && passedDrivingTest) {
2      out.println("You can drive.");
3  }
```

The code checks two conditions, that the age is over 15 years old, and that the driving test has been passed. The code is equivalent to the following,

```
1   if (age > 15) {
2     if (passedDrivingTest) {
3       out.println("You can drive.");
4     }
5   }
```

You can see that the first condition is checked, and if it's true, the second condition is then checked, and if the second condition is also true, the message "you can drive" is printed. But, if the user's age is not over 15 years old, *the second condition isn't checked*. This is known as shortcut evaluation. The right-hand side of the && operator is only evaluated if it needs to be. This has practical implications if evaluating the right-hand side of the expression can have side effects. Consider the following code,

```
1   if (numberOfEmployees == 0 || numberOfShifts / numberOfEmployees > 2) {
2     out.println("Not enough employees are available.");
3   }
```

You can use shortcut evaluation to avoid runtime errors.

This code outputs a warning if there aren't enough employees to cover the shifts. Assuming the maximum number of shifts per employee is two, the code first checks that the number of employees is nonzero. If the number of employees is not zero, it divides the number of shifts by the number of employees, and if the result is more than two shifts per employee, the message "not enough employees" is printed. If the number of employees is zero, the right-hand side of the *or* operator isn't evaluated, thus avoiding a divide-by-zero exception.

4.6 Planning Your Projects

Pseudocode: An English description of the steps that make up a program's algorithm.

As you start each program, or each part of your program, you should plan ahead and break it down into simpler tasks, before you start writing code. To do this, you should write *pseudocode*, that is, an English description of what your program will do. It should have enough detail so that it's clear how to implement each part. It sounds like an obvious strategy, but it takes practice and discipline to get used to it. The pseudocode doesn't need to be elaborate—if you program is simple, the pseudocode will be quite short, which is fine. For example, consider the following exercise,

*Write a program that accepts a date in the format "mm/dd/yyyy",
and outputs the date in a long format such as "July 3, 2021".*

To solve this exercise, we need to devise an algorithm that solves each
requirement. We'll have to get input from the user in the required
format, extract the month, day and year from the user's input, then
output the month's name followed by the day and year. We could
write the pseudocode as follows,

- Ask the user for the date string in the format "mm/dd/yyyy".
- Extract the month, day and year as integers from the date
  string that the user entered.
- Output the date in the required format, with the month name
  first, then day and year.

The above is perfectly good pseudocode for our program, but we
should add more detail for how to accomplish the parts that aren't
obvious. Specifically, how to extract the three integers from the
string, and how to output the month's name given the month's
number. After some thought, we can conclude that extracting three
numbers from a date string in the format "mm/dd/yyyy" can be
done using the two string methods `indexOf` and `substring`, as well
as the `Integer.parseInt` method that we saw in chapter 2. And,
printing the month's name given the month's number can be done
with a `switch` statement. Our revised pseudocode might look like
the following,

- Ask the user for the date string in the format "mm/dd/yyyy".
- Extract the month, day and year as integers from the date
  string that the user entered.
  - Extract three numbers, as strings, from the date string
    using indexOf() and substring().
  - Convert each of the three string numbers into integers
    using Integer.parseInt().
- Output the date in the required format, with the month name
  first, then day and year. The month's name can be output using
  a switch statement.

Example 4.14. Example pseudocode

We wrote down enough detail to convince ourselves that we know
how to accomplish the task, although we haven't written down *all*
the details, and haven't written any code yet. You should get used to
breaking down bigger tasks into smaller ones, and thinking through
how a problem will be solved before writing code. How much detail

to include in your pseudocode is subjective, and depends on your skill level. A rule of thumb is to omit details that are obvious to you.

Technique 4. Plan your projects

Break down projects into smaller tasks, and write down pseudocode before starting to implement your project. Include enough detail to convince yourself that each step can be accomplished. Think of it as the algorithm that your program will implement. It takes practice and discipline to plan your implementation before starting to write code, but you can't be a good developer without this skill. You will keep getting better the more you practice.

Exercises

4.9   Implement the pseudocode given in example 4.14: Write a program that accepts a date in the format "mm/dd/yyyy", and outputs the date in a long format such as "July 3, 2021".

4.10   Write pseudocode for example 4.6 on page 54.

Chapter Summary

- Boolean variables can have two values, true and false.
- Boolean expressions evaluate to true or false.
- The `if` statement evaluates a boolean expression and executes one of two blocks of code based on the result.
- The `switch` statement executes one of many blocks of code based on the result of an expression.
- The question-mark-colon operator (`?:`) produces one of two possible values, depending on the value of a boolean expression.

```
 1   out.print("Enter country name: ");
 2   String country = input.nextLine();
 3
 4   if (country.equals("United States") || country.equals("Canada") || country.
       equals("Mexico"))
 5     out.print(country + " is in North America");
 6   else if (country.equals("Brazil") || country.equals("Chile") || country.
       equals("Argentina"))
 7     out.print(country + " is in South America");
 8   else
 9     out.print("I don't know where " + country + " is.");
10
11   switch (country.toLowerCase()) {
12     case "united states":
13     case "canada":
14     case "mexico":
15       out.print(country + " is in North America");
16       break;
17     case "brazil":
18     case "chile":
19     case "argentina":
20       out.print(country + " is in South America");
21       break;
22     default:
23       out.print("I don't know the capital of " + country);
24       break;
25   }
```

if **statement**

Boolean Expression

else **keyword**

switch **statement**

Switch Expression

case **clause**

default **clause**

Exercise Solutions

4.1

Expression	Value
a	120
b	-12
c	0
d	31
a == b	*false*
a != b	*true*
a > b	*true*
a < b	*false*
a >= b	*true*
a <= b	*false*
(a > b) && (c > d)	*false*
(a > b) || (c > d)	*true*
!(a == b)	*true*

4.2
```
1   out.print("Enter miles per gallon: ");
2   float mpg = input.nextFloat();
```

```
3    if (mpg < 20)
4      out.println("Too low");
5    if (mpg >= 20 && mpg <= 30)
6      out.println("OK");
7    if (mpg > 30)
8      out.println("Good");
```

```
Enter miles per gallon: 37
Good
```

4.3
```
1    out.print("Enter three numbers: ");
2    float num1 = input.nextFloat();
3    float num2 = input.nextFloat();
4    float num3 = input.nextFloat();
5    out.print("The biggest is ");
6    if (num1 > num2) {
7      if (num1 > num3)
8        out.println(num1);
9      else
10       out.println(num3);
11   }
12   else {
13     if (num2 > num3)
14       out.println(num2);
15     else
16       out.println(num3);
17   }
```

```
Enter three numbers: 4 10 -2
The biggest is 10
```

4.4
```
1    int hour = java.time.LocalTime.now().getHour();
2    if (hour < 12)
3      out.print("Good morning");
4    else if (hour < 18)
5      out.print("Good afternoon");
6    else
7      out.print("Good evening");
```

```
Good evening
```

4.5
```
1    out.print("Enter grade (0-100): ");
2    int grade = input.nextInt();
3    if (grade < 60)
4      out.println("F");
5    else if (grade < 70)
6      out.println("D");
7    else if (grade < 80)
8      out.println("C");
9    else if (grade < 90)
10     out.println("B");
11   else
12     out.println("A");
```

```
Enter grade (0-100): 77
C
```

4.6

```
1   out.print("Enter a month: ");
2   String month = input.nextLine();
3   switch (month) {
4   case "February":
5     out.println(month + " has 28 days");
6     break;
7   case "January":
8   case "March":
9   case "May":
10  case "July":
11  case "August":
12  case "October":
13  case "December":
14    out.println(month + " has 31 days");
15    break;
16  default:
17    out.println(month + " has 30 days");
18    break;
19  }
```

```
Enter a month: June
June has 30 days
```

4.7

```
1   out.print("Enter a letter grade: ");
2   String month = input.nextLine();
3   switch (month) {
4   case "A":
5     out.println("90-100");
6     break;
7   case "B":
8     out.println("80-89");
9     break;
10  case "C":
11    out.println("70-79");
12    break;
13  case "D":
14    out.println("60-69");
15    break;
16  case "F":
17    out.println("0-59");
18    break;
19  default:
20    out.println("Unknown letter grade");
21    break;
22  }
```

```
Enter a letter grade: B
80-89
```

4.8

```
1   out.print("Enter your car's miles-per-gallon: ");
2   int mpg = input.nextInt();
3   input.nextLine();
4
5   if (mpg < 25)
```

```
6       out.println("Too low");
7     else if (mpg > 37)
8       out.println("Good");
9     else
10      out.println("Acceptable");
```

```
Enter your car's miles-per-gallon: 21
Too low
```

4.9

```
1     out.print("Enter date in the format 'mm/dd/yyyy': ");
2     String date = input.nextLine();
3
4     int index = date.indexOf('/');
5     int month = Integer.parseInt(date.substring(0, index));
6     date = date.substring(index+1);
7
8     index = date.indexOf('/');
9     int day = Integer.parseInt(date.substring(0, index));
10    int year = Integer.parseInt(date.substring(index+1));
11
12    String monthString = "";
13    switch (month) {
14    case 1: monthString = "January"; break;
15    case 2: monthString = "February"; break;
16    case 3: monthString = "March"; break;
17    case 4: monthString = "April"; break;
18    case 5: monthString = "May"; break;
19    case 6: monthString = "June"; break;
20    case 7: monthString = "July"; break;
21    case 8: monthString = "August"; break;
22    case 9: monthString = "September"; break;
23    case 10: monthString = "October"; break;
24    case 11: monthString = "November"; break;
25    case 12: monthString = "December"; break;
26    }
27    out.printf("%s %d, %d", monthString, day, year);
```

```
Enter date in the format 'mm/dd/yyyy': 04/21/2021
April 21, 2021
```

4.10

- Ask whether the user has a sore throat.
- If the user does have a sore throat, follow these steps:
  - Ask whether the user has a fever.
  - If the user reports having a fever, output 'Possibly the flu'.
  - If the user reports not having a fever, output 'Possibly strep throat'.
- If the user doesn't have a sore throat, follow these steps:
  - Ask whether the user is in pain.
  - If the user reports being in pain, output 'Try Advil'.

- If the user reports not being in pain, output 'You appear to be fine'.

5.1 The `while` Loop

Often we need to repeat an action until a certain condition is met. Let's look back at example 4.6, which we've modified and reproduced here as example 5.1,

```
1   out.print("Do you have a sore throat? ");
2   String answer = input.nextLine().toLowerCase();
3   if (answer.equals("yes")) {
4     out.print("Do you have a fever? ");
5     answer = input.nextLine().toLowerCase();
6     if (answer.equals("yes"))
7       out.print("Possibly the flu.");
8     else
9       out.print("Possibly strep throat.");
10  }
11  else {
12    out.print("are you in pain? ");
13    answer = input.nextLine().toLowerCase();
14    if (answer.equals("yes"))
15      out.print("Try Advil.");
16    else
17      out.print("You appear to be fine.");
18  }
```

Example 5.1. Medical decision tree.

```
Do you have a sore throat? No
are you in pain? Yes
Try Advil.
```

We've modified the example from its original form by converting the user's input on lines 2, 5 and 13 to lowercase, and comparing it to a lowercase "yes". This lets our program recognize "YES" or "yes" in addition to "Yes". Suppose we want to further enhance the program so that the only acceptable inputs by the user are "yes" and "no." We would have to repeat the question until the user enters one of the acceptable answers. For this, we'll use a `while` loop,

Example 5.2. Basic while loop.

```
1   out.print("Do you have a sore throat (yes/no)? ");
2   String answer = input.nextLine().toLowerCase();
3   while (!answer.equals("yes") && !answer.equals("no")) {
4     out.print("Do you have a sore throat (yes/no)? ");
5     answer = input.nextLine().toLowerCase();
6   }
```

```
Do you have a sore throat (yes/no)? A little bit
Do you have a sore throat (yes/no)? maybe
Do you have a sore throat (yes/no)? no
are you in pain? yes
Try Advil.
```

The while statement.

The `while` statement accepts a boolean condition, just like the `if` statement does, and it has a body delimited by curly braces, just like `if`. The difference is that it executes the body repeatedly while the condition evaluates to "true", that is, until the condition evaluates to "false". In the above example, the condition checks that the answer is *not* "yes" and *not* "no". While the answer is neither yes nor no, the question is repeated and the user enters another response. Note that the variable `answer` is declared once on line 2, and used again on line 5, i.e., it's declared in one place and written to in multiple places.

There's another form of the `while` loop that checks the condition at the *bottom* of the code block, so that the code block is executed at least once. We have to add the `do` keyword before the code block, and we have to add a semicolon after the `while` condition. I'll illustrate this in example 5.3,

Example 5.3. do..while loop.

```
1   String answer;
2   do {
3     out.print("Do you have a sore throat (yes/no)? ");
4     answer = input.nextLine().toLowerCase();
5   } while (!answer.equals("yes") && !answer.equals("no"));
```

```
Do you have a sore throat (yes/no)? A little bit
Do you have a sore throat (yes/no)? maybe
Do you have a sore throat (yes/no)? no
are you in pain? yes
Try Advil.
```

This form of the `while` statement is more natural in this case, since we need to ask the question at least one time. The code block is executed, then the condition is checked, and the program repeats the question if necessary. The implementation in example 5.3 is preferable to that in example 5.1 because the two lines that print the prompt and get user input occur only once in example 5.3, but are repeated in example 5.1. Repeated code is bad for two reasons,

1. If you later need to modify the repeated code, for example by modifying the prompt in the above code, you would have to change it in two places instead of one place, and you run the risk of not making the same change, or forgetting to change one of them.
2. Repeated code usually results in a program that isn't as simple as it can be, which goes against technique 1 on page 17.

This brings us to our next technique:

> **Technique 5. Avoid repeating code**
>
> Avoid repeating code, to keep your program simple and maintainable.

You can think of this technique as a corollary to technique 1 (Simplify your code whenever you can), and is sometimes referred to as the DRY (Don't Repeat Yourself) principle.

Suppose we want to repeat an action a certain number of times. Here's an example of a loop that repeats exactly ten times,

```
1  int i = 1;
2  while (i <= 10) {
3    out.print(i + " ");
4    i = i + 1;
5  }
```

Example 5.4. Looping ten times using a `while` loop.

```
1 2 3 4 5 6 7 8 9 10
```

We've used a variable as a counter, starting with the value 1. Each time the loop's body executes, the current value is printed, followed by a space, and the counter's value is incremented by 1. Once the count reaches 11 at the end of the tenth iteration, the `while` loop's condition becomes false and the loop terminates.

It's customary to use i, j and k as loop counters. This custom dates back to the C language, which Java is derived from, and from there probably dates back to the field of mathematics where i, j and k are common variables in summations, such as $\sum_{i=1}^{10} i$.

Exercises

5.1 Write a program that accepts an integer from the user, and prints each digit on a line by itself. Use a `while` loop, repeatedly printing the number *mod* 10, then dividing it by 10, until the number reaches zero.

5.2 Write the program in example 5.1, and use the code in example 5.3 for each of the three diagnostic questions that the user is asked.

5.2 The `for` Loop

A more natural way to count to ten is using the `for` loop. The general structure of a `for` loop is as follows,

```
1   for ((start action); (loop condition); (end action)) {
2       (statements)
3   }
```

where the "start action" is a statement that is executed once before the loop begins, the "loop condition" is the condition to keep looping, and the "end action" is code that gets executed *after each iteration*. Here's the previous example of counting to ten, rewritten as a `for` loop,

Example 5.5. Looping ten times using a `for` loop.

```
1   for (int i = 1; i <= 10; i = i + 1) {
2       out.print(i + " ");
3   }
```

```
1 2 3 4 5 6 7 8 9 10
```

The code in examples 5.4 and 5.5 is equivalent. Each of them initializes the loop counter to 1, keeps looping while the loop counter is less than or equal to 10, increments the loop counter after each iteration, and prints the loop counter each time through the loop.

The `while` and `for` loops are like the `if` statement in that the curly braces can be omitted if code block only contains one statement. So, example 5.5 can be rewritten as follows,

```
1   for (int i = 1; i <= 10; i = i + 1)
2     out.print(i + " ");
```

Java has additional assignment operators that we haven't covered yet. If you're incrementing a variable, there's a shorter syntax. Instead of x = x + 10, we can use x += 10. And, if we're incrementing by one, we can use x++. So, the following three statements are equivalent,

```
1   x = x + 1;
2   x += 1;
3   x ++;
```

So the above loop can now be rewritten as,

```
1   for (int i = 1; i <= 10; i++)
2     out.print(i + " ");
```

Finally, it's customary in Java, and many other languages, to start the for-loop counter at zero. So the usual syntax is,

```
1   for (int i = 0; i < 10; i++)
2     out.print((i + 1) + " ");
```

```
1 2 3 4 5 6 7 8 9 10
```

The reason loop counters customarily start at zero is largely due to the fact that array indexes start at zero—we'll get to that in the next chapter.

Some of this may look strange at first, especially starting the loop counter at zero, but it's the most common pattern and you'll get used to it quickly.

Exercises

5.3   Write a for loop that prints the even numbers from 2 to 20.

5.4   Write a for loop that prints the square root of the integers from 1 to 10. To get the square root of an integer i, use the syntax Math.sqrt(i).

5.3 Loops and Math

Let's look at a few more examples of the for loop. The following program (example 5.6) uses the Math.pow method to calculate the first twenty powers of 2. Math.pow() takes two arguments, the

Math.pow() raises a number to a power.

base and the exponent, and returns the result as a floating point number,

Example 5.6. Using a loop to print the powers of 2.

```
1  for (int i = 0; i <= 20; i++)
2      out.print((int) Math.pow(2, i) + " ");
```

```
1 2 4 8 16 32 64 128 256 512 1024 2048 4096 8192 16384 32768 65536 13
```

The output starts with 1 since the loop counter is 0 the first time through the loop, and 2^0 is 1. Next we print the first ten negative powers of 2,

Example 5.7. Using a loop to print the negative powers of 2.

```
1  for (int i = 0; i >= -10; i--)
2      out.print(Math.pow(2, i) + " ");
```

```
1.0 0.5 0.25 0.125 0.0625 0.03125 0.015625 0.0078125 0.00390625 0.0019
```

This prints the values of 2^0, 2^{-1}, 2^{-2}, and so on, so the loop counter starts at zero and is decremented by one each time through the loop, stopping at -10.

The next example (5.8) prints the value of π rounded to one digit, two digits, and so on,

Example 5.8. Using a loop to print the value of π rounded to one digit, two digits, and so on.

```
1  for (int i = 1; i <= 10; i++)
2      out.print(Math.round(Math.PI * Math.pow(10, i)) / Math.pow(10, i) + " ");
```

```
3.1 3.14 3.142 3.1416 3.14159 3.141593 3.1415927 3.14159265 3.1415926
```

The formula to round a floating point number x to i digits is:

$$Math.round(x * Math.pow(10, i))/Math.pow(10, i)$$

`Math.round()` rounds a floating point number to the nearest integer.

The number x is multiplied by 10 to the power i, rounded, then the result is divided by 10 to the power i. This is illustrated in table 5.1 by showing the intermediate values of the calculation where x is π and i is 3,

We saw in example 4.10 how to generate a random number between 1 and 100. With loops under our belt, we can write a program to print 100 random numbers,

Expression	Value
i	3
10^i	1000
π	3.141593
$\pi * 10^i$	3141.593
$Math.Round(\pi * 10^i)$	3142
$Math.Round(\pi * 10^i) / 10^i$	3.142

Table 5.1: The steps to compute the rounded π value.

```
1  for (int i = 1; i <= 100; i++) {
2    out.print((int) (Math.random() * 100 + 1) + " ");
3    if (i % 20 == 0)
4      out.println();
5  }
```

Example 5.9. Printing 100 random numbers.

```
23 70 99 88 77 3 41 21 88 78 77 84 82 36 89 51 1 79 44 78
26 52 87 60 7 62 12 82 83 57 57 5 96 9 68 53 32 45 58 8
57 22 5 42 73 48 7 40 19 12 59 93 41 84 88 40 49 37 2 46
79 18 54 39 82 28 91 46 77 96 13 72 100 59 100 49 8 88 35 19
8 25 71 79 3 57 34 6 58 46 53 75 44 53 19 55 6 21 26 28
```

We've added code to advance the output to the next line after every 20 random numbers. To do this, the `if` statement tests whether the loop counter is evenly divisible by 20, and if so, `println` is called. We'll enhance our program by computing the overall average of the 100 numbers, and print out the average before the program terminates,

```
1  int sum = 0;
2  for (int i = 1; i <= 100; i++) {
3    int number = (int) (Math.random() * 100 + 1);
4    sum += number;
5    out.print(number + " ");
6    if (i % 20 == 0)
7      out.println();
8  }
9  out.println("The average is: " + sum / 100);
```

Example 5.10. Printing 100 random numbers with their average.

```
46 12 77 52 34 88 18 59 92 47 66 83 23 69 69 5 71 95 13 17
18 38 31 81 91 82 52 21 76 36 4 90 10 89 80 91 38 76 63 89
73 83 5 25 47 16 86 8 37 97 93 88 50 98 62 100 3 65 4 23
77 3 46 25 6 22 62 54 94 20 59 71 46 43 13 70 73 42 38 76
40 79 38 97 45 19 99 5 43 6 39 87 13 58 55 96 62 1 29 91
The average is: 51
```

We've added code to add the random numbers by declaring a new variable, `sum`, initializing it to zero and adding each random number to it within the loop. Then after the loop terminates, we divide the sum by the number of random numbers to get the average.

Let's continue the example of producing an average of several numbers, but this time the user will be asked to enter each of the numbers. The user can enter a zero to exit the program,

Example 5.11. Printing the average of user-entered numbers.

```
1   int sum = 0;
2   int count = 0;
3   int number = 0;
4   do {
5     out.print("Enter a number (0 to exit): ");
6     number = input.nextInt();
7     input.nextLine();
8     if (number != 0) {
9       sum += number;
10      count ++;
11    }
12  } while (number != 0);
13  out.println("The average is: " + sum / count);
```

```
Enter a number (0 to exit): 55
Enter a number (0 to exit): 70
Enter a number (0 to exit): 59
Enter a number (0 to exit): 0
The average is: 61
```

This time, we use a `do...while` loop instead of a `for` loop, since we don't know beforehand how many numbers will be averaged. The user enters each number, entering 0 to exit from the loop. The sum is computed as before, and we've also keep a count of the numbers to be averaged. After the loop terminates, we divide the sum by the count to get the average.

Exercises

5.5   Use a while loop to print random numbers between 1 and 10 until the total of the random numbers exceeds 100.

5.6   Modify example 5.10 to accept a number from the user, and generate that many random numbers, printing the average after the loop terminates.

5.7   Fix the logic error in the following program, and test it to make sure it works,

```
1    int sum = 0;
2    for (int i = 1; i <= 10; i++) {
3      out.print((int) (Math.random() * 100 + 1) + " ");
4      sum += (int) (Math.random() * 100 + 1);
5    }
6    out.printf("\nThe sum of the above random numbers is %d", sum);
```

5.4 The break Statement

Using the `break` statement within a `while` or `for` loop causes it to terminate immediately. We can rewrite the previous example as follows,

```
1    int sum = 0;
2    int count = 0;
3    do {
4      out.print("Enter a number (0 to exit): ");
5      int number = input.nextInt();
6      input.nextLine();
7      if (number == 0)
8        break;
9      sum += number;
10     count ++;
11   } while (true);
12   out.println("The average is: " + sum / count);
```

Example 5.12. Using the `break` statement.

```
Enter a number (0 to exit): 55
Enter a number (0 to exit): 70
Enter a number (0 to exit): 59
Enter a number (0 to exit): 0
The average is: 61
```

When the user enters the value 0, the break statement is executed to exit the loop. Note that the loop condition on line 11 has been changed to `true`, since exiting the loop is done via `break` instead of relying on a loop condition.

When using `break` to terminate a `for` loop, you may not need the loop's condition anymore. Unlike `while` where we changed the loop condition to 'true', a `for` loop's condition can be absent which has the same effect. Note that the second semicolon is still required in this situation,

```
1    for (int i = 1; ; i++) {
2      out.print(i + " ");
3      if (i == 10)
4        break;
5    }
```

Exercises

5.8   Rewrite example 5.2 to use a break statement when the user enters 'yes' or 'no' to terminate the loop.

5.9   Rewrite example 5.10 to use a break statement when the count reaches 100. The `for` loop's condition should be empty, so the `for` statement should look like this: *for (int i = 1; ; i++)*.

5.5 The `continue` Statement

`continue` is another statement that is used to alter the normal flow of control in a loop. It's used to skip the rest of the *current* iteration of the loop, but doesn't cause the program to exit from the loop. It just skips the current iteration and causes the loop to begin the next iteration by evaluating the loop condition again. When used in a `for` loop, the `continue` statement causes the loop counter to be incremented before the loop condition is evaluated again. Example 5.13 loops through the numbers from 1 to 40, and prints those which aren't divisible by any number from 2 to 6,

Example 5.13. Using the `continue` statement.

```
1   for (int i = 1; i <= 40; i++) {
2       if (i % 2 == 0 || i % 3 == 0 || i % 4 == 0 || i % 5 == 0 || i % 6 == 0)
3           continue;
4       out.println("The number " + i + " isn't divisible by 2, 3, 4, 5 or 6");
5   }
```

```
The number 1 isn't divisible by 2, 3, 4, 5 or 6
The number 7 isn't divisible by 2, 3, 4, 5 or 6
The number 11 isn't divisible by 2, 3, 4, 5 or 6
The number 13 isn't divisible by 2, 3, 4, 5 or 6
The number 17 isn't divisible by 2, 3, 4, 5 or 6
The number 19 isn't divisible by 2, 3, 4, 5 or 6
The number 23 isn't divisible by 2, 3, 4, 5 or 6
The number 29 isn't divisible by 2, 3, 4, 5 or 6
The number 31 isn't divisible by 2, 3, 4, 5 or 6
The number 37 isn't divisible by 2, 3, 4, 5 or 6
```

As the loop checks each number from 1 to 40, the "continue" statement is executed if the number is divisible by 2, 3, 4, 5 or 6. This causes the rest of the iteration (which is just the `println` statement in this case) to be skipped, and the loop counter is incremented then the loop condition is checked in preparation for the next iteration.

The continue statement is not used frequently, and you can usually get by without it with ease, but it's important to know and you'll find yourself using it occasionally.

5.6 Nested Loops

Loops are often nested, which allows the programmer to tackle many real-world situations. For example, suppose your program tracks airline flights. You might want to loop through a list of flights, and for each flight, loop through the list of passengers. This is done using a nested loop (that is, a loop within a loop), illustrated by the following pseudocode,

- Initialize total revenue *r* to zero.
- For each flight *f*, perform the following actions:
    - For each passenger *p* on flight *f*, perform the following actions:
        * Add passenger *p*'s ticket price to the total revenue *r*.
- Output the total revenue *r*.

Example 5.14. Pseudocode for a nested loop.

Once we cover arrays and collections, we'll be able to implement the code illustrated by the pseudocode in example 5.14. Here's another simple example of a nested loop, constructing a multiplication table for numbers from 1 to 10,

```
1  for (int i = 1; i <= 10; i++) {
2    for (int j = 1; j <= 10; j++)
3      out.print(i * j + " ");
4    out.println();
5  }
```

Example 5.15. Printing a multiplication table.

```
1 2 3 4 5 6 7 8 9 10
2 4 6 8 10 12 14 16 18 20
3 6 9 12 15 18 21 24 27 30
4 8 12 16 20 24 28 32 36 40
5 10 15 20 25 30 35 40 45 50
6 12 18 24 30 36 42 48 54 60
7 14 21 28 35 42 49 56 63 70
8 16 24 32 40 48 56 64 72 80
9 18 27 36 45 54 63 72 81 90
10 20 30 40 50 60 70 80 90 100
```

The multiplication table's rows are printed one at a time. The outer loop prints each row, with the loop counter i representing the row

number, and the inner loop prints the columns, with the loop counter
j representing the column number. Each iteration through the inner
loop prints one number, the product of row and column numbers,
followed by a space. After the inner loop terminates, `println` is
called to advance to the next line.

We'll make a couple of improvements to this example. We'll print the
row and column headers, and we'll use printf to pad each number
so that it takes up four spaces—that way the columns will line up,

Example 5.16. Improved multiplication table.

```
1    out.print("        ");
2    for (int j = 1; j <= 10; j++)
3      out.printf("%4d", j);
4    out.println();
5    out.println();
6    for (int i = 1; i <= 10; i++) {
7      out.printf("%4d   ", i);
8      for (int j = 1; j <= 10; j++)
9        out.printf("%4d", i * j);
10     out.println();
11   }
```

	1	2	3	4	5	6	7	8	9	10
1	1	2	3	4	5	6	7	8	9	10
2	2	4	6	8	10	12	14	16	18	20
3	3	6	9	12	15	18	21	24	27	30
4	4	8	12	16	20	24	28	32	36	40
5	5	10	15	20	25	30	35	40	45	50
6	6	12	18	24	30	36	42	48	54	60
7	7	14	21	28	35	42	49	56	63	70
8	8	16	24	32	40	48	56	64	72	80
9	9	18	27	36	45	54	63	72	81	90
10	10	20	30	40	50	60	70	80	90	100

Lines 1-3 print the header containing column numbers, followed by
a blank line (lines 4 and 5). Line 7 prints the row header followed by
blank spaces. Each number is now printed with `printf` with "%4d"
as format specifier, which causes the number to be printed within
four characters. The fixed-width font, which is the default for the
Console view, helps to make each column line up correctly.

Here's another example of loop nesting which prints an asterisk
if the row index is less than the column index. This produces a
triangle,

```
1   for (int i = 0; i <= 8; i++) {
2       for (int j = 0; j <= 8; j++)
3           if (j < i)
4               out.print("*");
5       out.println();
6   }
```

Example 5.17. Printing a triangle.

We could print just the diagonal line by printing an asterisk where j == i, and a space character otherwise,

```
1   for (int i = 0; i <= 8; i++) {
2       for (int j = 0; j <= 8; j++)
3           if (j == i)
4               out.print("*");
5           else
6               out.print(" ");
7       out.println();
8   }
```

The other diagonal can be printed by changing our condition from j == i to 8 - j == i (where 8 is one less than the number of columns),

```
1   for (int i = 0; i <= 8; i++) {
2       for (int j = 0; j <= 8; j++)
3           if (8-j == i)
4               out.print("*");
5           else
6               out.print(" ");
7       out.println();
8   }
```

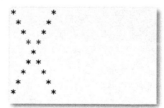

And, we can test for *either* j == i or 8 - j == i to print both diagonals,

```
1   for (int i = 0; i <= 8; i++) {
2       for (int j = 0; j <= 8; j++)
3           if (j == i || 8-j == i)
4               out.print("*");
5           else
6               out.print(" ");
7       out.println();
8   }
```

There's one more thing I want to do—this code can be simplified by combining lines 3-6 using the question-mark-colon operator,

```
1  for (int i = 0; i <= 8; i++) {
2    for (int j = 0; j <= 8; j++)
3      out.print((j == i || 8-j == i) ? "*" : " ");
4    out.println();
5  }
```

Example 5.18. Printing both diagonals.

Here, we've simplified our program without sacrificing clarity or runtime performance, applying technique 1 from page 17.

Exercises

5.10 Use the multiplication table code in example 5.16 to create a 5x5 table of powers. Use `Math.pow()` as in example 5.6 to generate i to the power j for each table cell. You'll have to cast the result of `Math.pow()` to an integer, and you'll have to increase the number of spaces used by each number to 5.

5.11 Use nested loops to print a two-dimensional grid representing a monthly calendar. Assume the first day of the month falls on a Sunday.

5.12 Modify example 5.18 to print an hourglass shape, as shown in this picture:

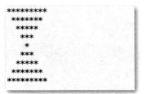

5.7 Printing Log Messages

A common technique for debugging programs is to generate logging output at different points of the program's execution. These are simple `println` statements inserted at key points within the code, to help the programmer find a particular bug. Let's use examples 5.1 and 5.3 to illustrate this. I've reproduced the code here as example 5.19 with an intentional mistake causing incorrect output,

```
1   String answer;
2   do {
3     out.print("Do you have a sore throat (yes/no)? ");
4     answer = input.nextLine().toLowerCase();
5   } while (!answer.equals("yes") || !answer.equals("no"));
6
7   if (answer.equals("yes")) {
8
9     do {
10      out.print("Do you have a fever? ");
11      answer = input.nextLine().toLowerCase();
12    } while (!answer.equals("yes") || !answer.equals("no"));
13
14    if (answer.equals("yes"))
15      out.print("Possibly the flu.");
16    else
17      out.print("Possibly strep throat.");
18  }
19  else {
20
21    do {
22      out.print("are you in pain? ");
23      answer = input.nextLine().toLowerCase();
24    } while (!answer.equals("yes") || !answer.equals("no"));
25
26    if (answer.equals("yes"))
27      out.print("Try Advil.");
28    else
29      out.print("You appear to be fine.");
30  }
```

Example 5.19. Program containing a bug.

```
Do you have a sore throat (yes/no)? No
Do you have a sore throat (yes/no)?
```

The problem is that the program won't let the user past the first question, even though the user's answer is valid. We add a diagnostic output message within the loop to check that our loop condition has the expected value, and then run the program again,

```
1   do {
2     out.print("Do you have a sore throat (yes/no)? ");
3     answer = input.nextLine().toLowerCase();
4
5     out.println("!answer.equals(\"yes\") || !answer.equals(\"no\") = " +
6       (!answer.equals("yes") || !answer.equals("no")));
7
8   } while (!answer.equals("yes") || !answer.equals("no"));
```

```
Console ⊠           ■ ✖ ✖  ▣ ▣ ▣ ▣ ▣   ▣ ▣ ▾ ▣ ▾ ▭
HelloWorld [Java Application] /Library/Java/JavaVirtualMachines/jdk-15.0.1.jdk/Contents/Home
Do you have a sore throat (yes/no)? No
!answer.equals("yes") || !answer.equals("no") = true
Do you have a sore throat (yes/no)? Yes
!answer.equals("yes") || !answer.equals("no") = true
Do you have a sore throat (yes/no)?
```

Infinite Loop: A loop that iterates forever, forcing the user to terminate the program.

As we test this program, we see the value of the loop condition printed out after each answer is entered. Once we've confirmed that the loop condition is true even when the input is valid, we know that's the cause of the infinite loop. Further inspection of the loop condition reveals that the *or* condition should be *and*. We can then correct the program and test it,

```
1    String answer;
2    do {
3       out.print("Do you have a sore throat (yes/no)? ");
4       answer = input.nextLine().toLowerCase();
5    } while (!answer.equals("yes") && !answer.equals("no"));
6
7    if (answer.equals("yes")) {
8
9       do {
10         out.print("Do you have a fever? ");
11         answer = input.nextLine().toLowerCase();
12      } while (!answer.equals("yes") && !answer.equals("no"));
13
14      if (answer.equals("yes"))
15         out.print("Possibly the flu.");
16      else
17         out.print("Possibly strep throat.");
18   }
19   else {
20
21      do {
22         out.print("are you in pain? ");
23         answer = input.nextLine().toLowerCase();
24      } while (!answer.equals("yes") && !answer.equals("no"));
25
26      if (answer.equals("yes"))
27         out.print("Try Advil.");
28      else
29         out.print("You appear to be fine.");
30   }
```

```
Do you have a sore throat (yes/no)? No
are you in pain? Yes
Try Advil.
```

Using log files.

A Production system runs on dedicated servers that are separate from development servers.

Log messages are commonly written to log files, which are particularly useful in production systems where the developer is typically unable to use the debugger (we discuss the debugger in the next section).

Technique 6. Use diagnostic output messages for debugging

Use diagnostic output messages to trace program execution and print values of expressions at runtime. This can help narrow down the cause of bugs in your code.

5.8 Using the Debugger

Another technique you should be familiar with is using the debugger to follow program execution and examine the values of variables as the program is running. To illustrate this, we return to the version of the program containing a bug in example 5.19.

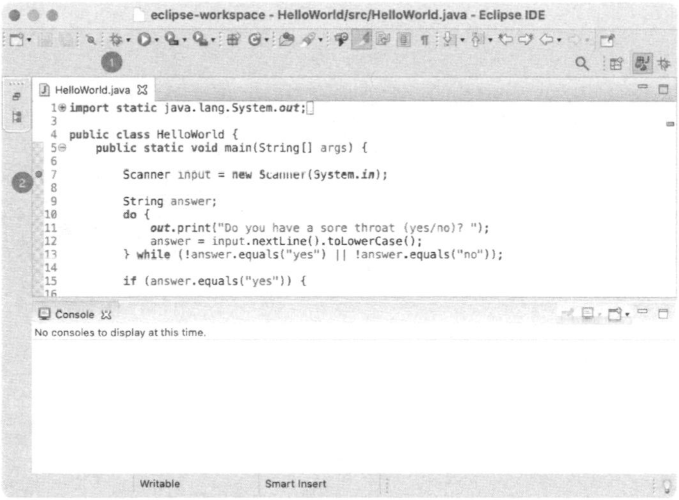

Figure 5.1: Eclipse with a breakpoint.

The blue left margin in the editor view within Eclipse can be double-clicked to add a breakpoint at a line of code. This breakpoint appears as a blue dot, highlighted as "2" in figure 5.1. A debugging session is similar to running the program, but it puts Eclipse in debug mode, and is initiated using the debug button on the toolbar, highlighted as "1" in figure 5.1. Once debugging is started, the program runs normally until it reaches a breakpoint, at which point it enters a different *perspective* as shown in figure 5.2,

Perspective: An Eclipse layout showing certain views that are related to each other.

The program is now in the debug perspective, and is stopped at line 7 where we placed a breakpoint. The blue margin contains the current execution point, shown as an arrow, partly obscured by the breakpoint which is also on line 7 (label "1"). The call stack is in the Debug view and shows the currently executing method, in our case the `main` method (label "2"). The Variables view shows local variables in the current stack frame, `args` being the only variable currently shown here (label "3"). Finally, the toolbar sports buttons useful in debug mode, such as Step Into, Step Over and Resume (label "4").

Figure 5.2: Eclipse in the debug perspective.

Using the Step Over button on the toolbar will execute the current Java statement, after which the debugger stops again at the next statement. At each point, you're able to hover the mouse over variables to examine their values. In figure 5.3, we've repeatedly used the Step Over command to advance execution to line 13, entering 'No' in the console in answer to the prompt at line 12. Once at line 13, we've hovered the mouse over the `answer` variable to see its value,

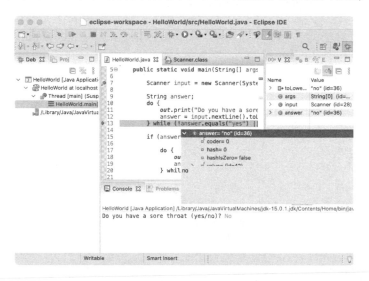

Figure 5.3: Stopped at a breakpoint to examine the value of `answer`.

We've entered the value "No", but hovering over the variable `answer` shows its value as "no", the result of calling `toLowerCase()`. `answer`'s value can also be seen in the Variables view at this point.

We can also open the Expressions view, which initially is a tab to the right of the Variables view, and enter expressions of our choosing to evaluate them in real-time. Figure 5.4 shows the Expressions tab, which I've made wider for illustration, and I've entered a couple of expressions including the `while` loop's condition, to see their results,

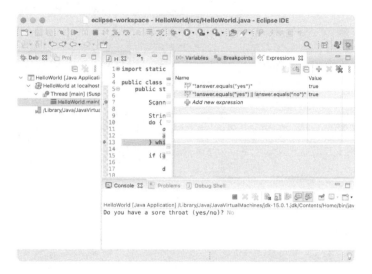

Figure 5.4: Evaluating expressions in the Expressions view of the debugger.

Stepping through the program and looking at variables' values, it doesn't take long for us to realize what's wrong with the `while` loop's condition and fix it. Once you're done with the debugger, you can switch back to the Java perspective using the "Window → Perspective → Open Perspective → Java" command.

> **Technique 7. Use the debugger to locate bugs at runtime**
>
> Use the debugger to locate bugs at runtime—it has a variety of features that allow you to control your program's execution, examine variables, navigate the call stack, and much more.

Chapter Summary

- The `while` statement executes a block of code repeatedly until a boolean expression evaluates to false. It's suitable for repetition when the number of iterations isn't known in advance.

- The **for** statement executes a block of code repeatedly until a boolean expression evaluates to false, while also maintaining a loop counter. It's useful for repeating a specific number of times.
- The **break** statement causes execution to exit from a loop immediately.
- The **continue** statement causes execution to skip the rest of the current iteration.
- Common debugging techniques include using log messages as well as stepping through code using the debugger in Eclipse.

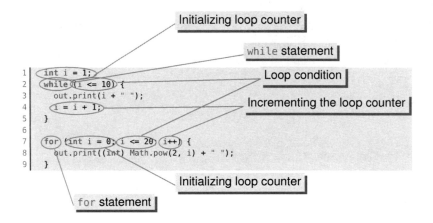

Exercise Solutions

5.1
```
1   out.print("Enter a number: ");
2   int number = input.nextInt();
3   input.nextLine();
4
5   while (number > 0) {
6     out.println(number % 10);
7     number = number / 10;
8   }
```

```
Enter a number: 431
1
3
4
```

5.2
```
1   String answer;
2   do {
3     out.print("Do you have a sore throat (yes/no)? ");
4     answer = input.nextLine().toLowerCase();
```

```
 5    } while (!answer.equals("yes") && !answer.equals("no"));
 6
 7    if (answer.equals("yes")) {
 8      do {
 9        out.print("Do you have a fever? ");
10        answer = input.nextLine().toLowerCase();
11      } while (!answer.equals("yes") && !answer.equals("no"));
12      if (answer.equals("yes"))
13        out.print("Possibly the flu.");
14      else
15        out.print("Possibly strep throat.");
16    }
17    else {
18      do {
19        out.print("are you in pain? ");
20        answer = input.nextLine().toLowerCase();
21      } while (!answer.equals("yes") && !answer.equals("no"));
22      if (answer.equals("yes"))
23        out.print("Try Advil.");
24      else
25        out.print("You appear to be fine.");
26    }
```

```
Do you have a sore throat (yes/no)? nope
Do you have a sore throat (yes/no)? no
are you in pain? no
You appear to be fine.
```

5.3
```
1    for (int i = 2; i <= 20; i = i + 2)
2      out.print(i + " ");
```

```
2 4 6 8 10 12 14 16 18 20
```

5.4
```
1    for (int i = 1; i <= 10; i++)
2      out.printf("%.3f ", Math.sqrt(i));
```

```
1.000 1.414 1.732 2.000 2.236 2.449 2.646 2.828 3.000 3.162
```

5.5
```
1    int sum = 0;
2    while (sum <= 100) {
3      int number = (int) (Math.random() * 10 + 1);
4      sum += number;
5      out.print (number + " ");
6    }
```

```
8 5 2 7 1 10 1 5 1 4 6 8 10 8 3 5 3 2 5 3 8
```

5.6
```
1    out.print("How many random numbers do you want? ");
2    int count = input.nextInt();
3    input.nextLine();
4    int sum = 0;
5    for (int i = 1; i <= count; i++) {
6      int number = (int) (Math.random() * 100 + 1);
7      sum += number;
```

```
 8     out.print(number + " ");
 9     if (i % 20 == 0)
10       out.println();
11   }
12   out.printf("\nThe average is: %.2f", (float) sum / count);
```

```
How many random numbers do you want? 30
12 74 69 79 47 23 100 97 30 60 5 41 26 89 88 77 41 41 6 32
14 25 60 59 32 86 15 93 25 67
The average is: 50.43
```

5.7
```
 1   int sum = 0;
 2   for (int i = 1; i <= 10; i++) {
 3     int number = (int) (Math.random() * 100 + 1);
 4     out.print(number + " ");
 5     sum += number;
 6   }
 7   out.printf("\nThe sum of the above random numbers is %d", sum);
```

```
10 78 30 70 88 28 10 55 18 7
The sum of the above random numbers is 394
```

5.8
```
 1   out.print("Do you have a sore throat (yes/no)? ");
 2   String answer = input.nextLine().toLowerCase();
 3   while (true) {
 4     out.print("Do you have a sore throat (yes/no)? ");
 5     answer = input.nextLine().toLowerCase();
 6     if (answer.equals("yes") || answer.equals("no"))
 7       break;
 8   }
```

```
Do you have a sore throat (yes/no)? a little bit
Do you have a sore throat (yes/no)? yes
```

5.9
```
 1   int sum = 0;
 2   for (int i = 1; ; i++) {
 3     int number = (int) (Math.random() * 100 + 1);
 4     sum += number;
 5     out.print(number + " ");
 6     if (i % 20 == 0)
 7       out.println();
 8     if (i == 100)
 9       break;
10   }
11   out.println("The average is: " + sum / 100);
```

```
16 29 37 78 12 84 41 26 18 78 46 10 27 77 56 94 18 16 51 86
97 18 53 8 80 87 1 80 59 13 36 82 88 62 47 18 91 8 92 45
38 50 23 50 3 12 68 35 69 11 93 44 76 89 35 36 58 36 36 79
52 83 34 32 84 94 47 41 47 93 86 94 37 73 59 33 16 25 87 37
29 32 31 73 95 80 51 18 25 65 54 37 5 60 53 47 26 56 66 45
The average is: 50
```

5.10
```
 1   out.print("         ");
 2   for (int j = 1; j <= 5; j++)
 3     out.printf("%5d", j);
```

```
 4   out.println();
 5   out.println();
 6   for (int i = 1; i <= 5; i++) {
 7     out.printf("%5d   ", i);
 8     for (int j = 1; j <= 5; j++)
 9       out.printf("%5d", (int) Math.pow(i, j));
10     out.println();
11   }
```

```
         1    2    3    4    5

    1    1    1    1    1    1
    2    2    4    8   16   32
    3    3    9   27   81  243
    4    4   16   64  256 1024
    5    5   25  125  625 3125
```

5.11

```
 1   out.println("Sun  Mon  Tue  Wed  Thu  Fri  Sat");
 2   out.println();
 3   for (int day = 1; day <= 31; day++) {
 4     out.printf("%?d   ", day);
 5     if (day % 7 == 0)
 6       out.println();
 7   }
```

```
Sun  Mon  Tue  Wed  Thu  Fri  Sat

  1    2    3    4    5    6    7
  8    9   10   11   12   13   14
 15   16   17   18   19   20   21
 22   23   24   25   26   27   28
 29   30   31
```

5.12

```
 1   for (int i = 0; i <= 8; i++) {
 2     for (int j = 0; j <= 8; j++)
 3       if ((j >= i && 8-j >= i) || (j <= i && 8-j <= i))
 4         out.print("*");
 5       else
 6         out.print(" ");
 7     out.println();
 8   }
```

```
*********
 *******
  *****
   ***
    *
   ***
  *****
 *******
*********
```

Arrays | **6**

6.1 Creating Arrays

Arrays are collections of variables of the same type, and each member of the array can be referenced using its sequence number, which we call its *index*. The items in an array are called its *elements*, and they all have unique indexes, starting with zero and ending with one less than the array size. For example, in an array of five integers, the individual integers have indexes 0 through 4. An array itself is a variable, and has to be declared and initialized before you use it.

The syntax to declare an array is

type[] *arrayname*;

where *type* is the type of each element of the array, and *arrayname* is the array variable's name. The syntax to initialize an array is

arrayname = new *type*[*count*];

where *count* is the size of the array. Once you've initialized an array, you can access (that is, read from or write to) each element of the array using the syntax

arrayname[*index*]

Let's look at this in action,

Arrays in Java are *zero-based*.

Example 6.1. Array syntax.

```
1   String[] names;
2   names = new String[7];
3   names[0] = "Ronald";
4   out.println("The first name is " + names[0]);
```

```
The first name is Ronald
```

Example 6.1 declares an array of strings called `names`, assigns the string `"Ronald"` to the first element of the array, the first element having index 0, and then prints the value of the first element of the array. The elements of an array can't be accessed before the array is initialized, since the array's elements haven't been created yet.

Let's suppose you want a program that stores student names and ID numbers. Without using an array, you could do something like this,

```
1    String student1 = "Ronald";
2    String student2 = "Mike";
3    String student3 = "Cindy";
4    String student4 = "Tammy";
5    String student5 = "Blake";
6    String student6 = "Martha";
7    String student7 = "Sam";
8
9    int id1 = 7103;
10   int id2 = 4933;
11   int id3 = 6548;
12   int id4 = 6830;
13   int id5 = 711;
14   int id6 = 8937;
15   int id7 = 2002;
16
17   out.println("The first student is " + student1 + " with ID " + id1);
18   out.println("The second student is " + student2 + " with ID " + id2);
19   out.println("The third student is " + student3 + " with ID " + id3);
20   out.println("The fourth student is " + student4 + " with ID " + id4);
21   out.println("The fifth student is " + student5 + " with ID " + id5);
22   out.println("The sixth student is " + student6 + " with ID " + id6);
23   out.println("The seventh student is " + student7 + " with ID " + id7);
```

```
The first student is Ronald with ID 7103
The second student is Mike with ID 4933
The third student is Cindy with ID 6548
The fourth student is Tammy with ID 6830
The fifth student is Blake with ID 711
The sixth student is Martha with ID 8937
The seventh student is Sam with ID 2002
```

Arrays allow us to simplify this and organize our data in a much more manageable way. Using a string array for student names, and an integer array for student ID numbers, we can rewrite the above example as follows,

```
1   String[] students;
2   students = new String[7];
3   students[0] = "Ronald";
4   students[1] = "Mike";
5   students[2] = "Cindy";
6   students[3] = "Tammy";
7   students[4] = "Blake";
8   students[5] = "Martha";
9   students[6] = "Sam";
10
11  int[] IDs;
12  IDs = new int[7];
13  IDs[0] = 7103;
14  IDs[1] = 4933;
15  IDs[2] = 6548;
16  IDs[3] = 6830;
17  IDs[4] = 711;
18  IDs[5] = 8937;
19  IDs[6] = 2002;
20
21  for (int i = 0; i < 7; i++)
22    out.println("Student " + (i+1) + " is " + students[i] + " with ID " + IDs[i
       ]);
```

Example 6.2. Using arrays to store student names and ID numbers.

```
Student 1 is Ronald with ID 7103
Student 2 is Mike with ID 4933
Student 3 is Cindy with ID 6548
Student 4 is Tammy with ID 6830
Student 5 is Blake with ID 711
Student 6 is Martha with ID 8937
Student 7 is Sam with ID 2002
```

Putting our student names and IDs in arrays has allowed us to simplify the code that prints the data. We've replaced all seven `println` statements with just one `println` statement within a loop. Note that the number of array elements is 7, and the indexes are 0 through 6. We've used the array accessor syntax students[] and IDs[] for both writing to the arrays, and reading from them. Note that we use *(i+1)* in the `println` statement to print the sequence number starting at 1.

There's an alternate syntax that can be used to initialize arrays, as shown in the following example (6.3),

```
1   String[] students = new String[] { "Ronald", "Mike", "Cindy", "Tammy", "Blake
       ", "Martha", "Sam" };
2   int[] IDs = new int[] {7103, 4933, 6548, 6830, 711, 8937, 2002};
3
4   for (int i = 0; i < 7; i++)
5     out.println("Student " + (i+1) + " is " + students[i] + " with ID " + IDs[i
       ]);
```

Example 6.3. Array initializer syntax.

```
Student 1 is Ronald with ID 7103
Student 2 is Mike with ID 4933
Student 3 is Cindy with ID 6548
Student 4 is Tammy with ID 6830
Student 5 is Blake with ID 711
Student 6 is Martha with ID 8937
Student 7 is Sam with ID 2002
```

Using the alternate initializer syntax shown in example 6.3, the array size isn't provided between the square brackets in the new statement, and the new statement ends with a list of values within curly braces. This syntax is useful when the initial values of the array's elements are known at compile time. Java also allows you to omit the new operator if you're initializing the array when declaring it. Thus, the following is acceptable,

$$int[] \; IDs = \{7103, 4933, 6548, 6830, 711, 8937, 2002\}$$

Null: An array reference has the value null prior to the array being created.

Null reference exception: Dereferencing an array reference before the array is created results in a null reference exception.

Once an array is created, its size can't be changed. The array variable is just a reference to the actual array, and it's initially null. The "new" statement is what actually creates the array. Using the array accessor syntax ([ ]) with the array variable is called *dereferencing* the array. If an array variable is dereferenced before an array is created, a null reference exception occurs.

Exercises

6.1   Modify example 6.3. Add an array of seven student grades, and print the grades along with the students' names and IDs.

6.2   Modify the loop in example 6.3. Put an if statement in the loop, to print only students with an ID number under 6000.

6.2 Looping Through Arrays

In example 6.3, we used a loop to print the student names and ID numbers. We'll add a new array for student grades, and print those as well,

```
1  String[] students = new String[] { "Ronald", "Mike", "Cindy", "Tammy", "Blake
     ", "Martha", "Sam" };
2  int[] IDs = new int[] {7103, 4933, 6548, 6830, 711, 8937, 2002};
3  int[] grades = new int[] {95, 98, 100, 71, 89, 75, 90};
4
5  for (int i = 0; i < 7; i++)
6    out.printf("%s (%d): %d\n", students[i], IDs[i], grades[i]);
```

Example 6.4. Looping through an array.

```
Ronald (7103): 95
Mike (4933): 98
Cindy (6548): 100
Tammy (6830): 71
Blake (711): 89
Martha (8937): 75
Sam (2002): 90
```

We've replaced `println` on line 6 with `printf`, since it's easier to read what is being output. The "\n" at the end of the format string causes the output to advance to the next line.

Combining this with the code in example 5.10, we can print the average grade by keeping a running total of the grades, and dividing the total by the number of students after the loop completes,

```
1  String[] students = new String[] { "Ronald", "Mike", "Cindy", "Tammy", "Blake
     ", "Martha", "Sam" };
2  int[] IDs = new int[] {7103, 4933, 6548, 6830, 711, 8937, 2002};
3  int[] grades = new int[] {95, 98, 100, 71, 89, 75, 90};
4
5  int total = 0;
6  for (int i = 0; i < 7; i++) {
7    out.printf("%s (%d): %d\n", students[i], IDs[i], grades[i]);
8    total += grades[i];
9  }
10 out.println("The average grade is " + (total / 7));
```

Example 6.5. Computing an average.

```
Ronald (7103): 95
Mike (4933): 98
Cindy (6548): 100
Tammy (6830): 71
Blake (711): 89
Martha (8937): 75
Sam (2002): 90
The average grade is 88
```

Note in example 6.5 that the literal number 7 occurs in two places, on lines 6 and 10. If we add a student to this program, we would have to update that number on both lines 6 and 10 to account for the new array size, which is error-prone because we may forget to do it in one or both of those places. An important improvement is to replace the hardcoded 7 with the size of the array, as in example 6.6,

Example 6.6. Removing hardcoded array lengths.

```
1   String[] students = new String[] { "Ronald", "Mike", "Cindy", "Tammy", "Blake
        ", "Martha", "Sam" };
2   int[] IDs = new int[] {7103, 4933, 6548, 6830, 711, 8937, 2002};
3   int[] grades = new int[] {95, 98, 100, 71, 89, 75, 90};
4
5   int total = 0;
6   for (int i = 0; i < students.length; i++) {
7     out.printf("%s (%d): %d\n", students[i], IDs[i], grades[i]);
8     total += grades[i];
9   }
10  out.println("The average grade is " + (total / students.length));
```

```
Ronald (7103): 95
Mike (4933): 98
Cindy (6548): 100
Tammy (6830): 71
Blake (711): 89
Martha (8937): 75
Sam (2002): 90
The average grade is 88
```

An array's size can be obtained at runtime by using the `length` property of the array using the syntax `students.length`. Replacing the hardcoded array size with that expression makes our program more resilient to change.

Technique 8. Avoid hardcoded values when they can be replaced by computed values

Avoiding hardcoded values can make your program more resilient to change.

Let's update example 6.6 to also print the maximum and minimum grade. To compute the maximum grade, we need a new variable to hold the largest grade seen so far. Within the loop, if the student being processed has a bigger grade than the largest so far, we replace the largest so far with the current grade. Similar logic is used for the minimum grade except that its initial value needs to be large.

Example 6.7. Computing maximum and minimum.

```
1   String[] students = new String[] { "Ronald", "Mike", "Cindy", "Tammy", "Blake
        ", "Martha", "Sam" };
2   int[] IDs = new int[] {7103, 4933, 6548, 6830, 711, 8937, 2002};
3   int[] grades = new int[] {95, 98, 100, 71, 89, 75, 90};
4
5   int total = 0;
6   int maxGrade = 0;
7   int minGrade = 100;
8   for (int i = 0; i < students.length; i++) {
9     out.printf("%s (%d): %d\n", students[i], IDs[i], grades[i]);
10    total += grades[i];
11    if (grades[i] > maxGrade)
```

```
12        maxGrade = grades[i];
13      if (grades[i] < minGrade)
14        minGrade = grades[i];
15    }
16    out.println("The average grade is " + (total / students.length));
17    out.println("The maximum grade is " + maxGrade);
18    out.println("The minimum grade is " + minGrade);
```

```
Ronald (7103): 95
Mike (4933): 98
Cindy (6548): 100
Tammy (6830): 71
Blake (711): 89
Martha (8937): 75
Sam (2002): 90
The average grade is 88
The maximum grade is 100
The minimum grade is 71
```

Our next example is a program that reverses the contents of an array. Before we can do this, we need to know how to swap the values of two variables. To do that, we use a temporary variable to hold the value of the first, copy the value in the second to the first, then replace the value of the second with the temporary variable's value. For example, the following code swaps the values in `number1` and `number2`,

```
1    int temp;
2    temp = number1;
3    number1 = number2;
4    number2 = temp;
```

To reverse the contents of an array, we loop from the start of the array to its midpoint. Each time through the loop, we swap the current array element with its counterpart in the second half of the array, which is the array element in the second half of the array that has equal distance to the midpoint,

```
1    int[] numbers = new int[] { 23, 87, 55, 9, 53, 27 };
2
3    out.print("Array before reversing: ");
4    for (int i = 0; i < numbers.length; i++)
5      out.print(numbers[i] + " ");
6    out.println();
7
8    for (int i = 0; i < numbers.length / 2; i++) {
9      int temp = numbers[i];
10     numbers[i] = numbers[numbers.length - 1 - i];
11     numbers[numbers.length - 1 - i] = temp;
12   }
13
14   out.print("Array after reversing: ");
15   for (int i = 0; i < numbers.length; i++)
16     out.print(numbers[i] + " ");
```

Example 6.8. Reversing the contents of an array.

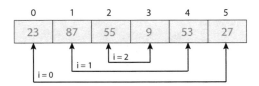

```
Array before reversing: 23 87 55 9 53 27
Array after reversing: 27 53 9 55 87 23
```

The first time through the loop, "i" is 0, and "numbers.length - 1 - i" is 5. The second time through the loop, "i" is 1, and "numbers.length - 1 - i" is 4. You can see the pairs in the below diagram. Since the array has six elements, the loop executes three times, reversing each of the three pairs.

Pairs of array elements that are processed each time through the loop.

	0	1	2	3	4	5
	23	87	55	9	53	27

i = 0 i = 1 i = 2

Tip 4. Pay special attention to array indexes and loop limits.

The code in example 6.8 is worth studying, since it exemplifies many situations you will encounter in the future. Pay special attention to the loop's upper limit, the code to swap two values, and array indexes on lines 10 and 11. If you have to, use the debugger to step through the code and examine the values of variables and expressions within the loop.

Note that this code works without any changes when the length of the array is odd, since the loop's upper limit is "numbers.length / 2", which performs integer division. For example, an array of size 5 would cause the loop to have an upper limit of 2, looping twice with "i" having values 0 and 1.

Our last example shows how to sort an array. In example 6.9, we've modified example 6.8 to sort the array instead of reversing it. Sorting is accomplished by calling the **sort** method of the **Arrays** class,

Example 6.9. Sorting an array.

```java
String[] teams = new String[] { "Red Sox", "Yankees", "White Sox", "Vikings",
    "Jaguars", "Patriots", "Cowboys" };

out.print("Teams before sorting the array: ");
for (int i = 0; i < teams.length; i++)
  out.print(teams[i] + " ");
out.println();

java.util.Arrays.sort(teams);

out.print("Teams after sorting the array: ");
for (int i = 0; i < teams.length; i++)
  out.print(teams[i] + " ");
```

```
Teams before sorting the array: Red Sox Yankees White Sox Vikings Jaguars Patriots Cowboys
Teams after sorting the array: Cowboys Jaguars Patriots Red Sox Vikings White Sox Yankees
```

Exercises

6.3 Write a program that prompts the user for high temperatures for seven days (Sunday through Saturday). Store those temperatures in an array, and use a loop to find the highest temperature of the week.

6.4 Create an array of city names. Write a loop that goes through the array and tells whether it's sorted.

- Hint 1: You'll have to compare each element of the array to the one before it.
- Hint 2: You can compare two strings using this syntax: str1.compareTo(str2). This method returns a positive number if str1 is after str2 alphabetically, a negative number if str1 is before str2 alphabetically, and zero if they're equal.

6.5 Combine the code from examples 6.8 and 6.9 to sort the team names, then reverse them so that the output shows the team names in reverse alphabetical order.

6.3 Two-Dimensional Arrays

You can think of a two-dimensional array as an array of arrays. The syntax to declare it reflects that. A 2-D array is declared as "(type)[][]". Allocating a two-dimensional array with three rows and four columns is done with this syntax,

```
1   int[][] array;
2   array = new int[3][4];
```

The initializer syntax also works for two-dimensional arrays. Example 6.10 declares a 2-D array of integers that contains student grades, six grades per student. After creating the array, it prints them all out.

Example 6.10. 2-D array of student grades.

```
1   int[][] grades = new int[][] {
2     { 65, 100, 82, 97, 100, 75 },
3     { 99, 50, 100, 89, 71, 95 },
4     { 81, 85, 93, 99, 84, 85 }
5   };
6
7   for (int i = 0; i < grades.length; i++) {
8     out.print("Student " + i + ": ");
9     for (int j = 0; j < grades[i].length; j++)
10      out.print(grades[i][j] + " ");
11    out.println();
12  }
```

```
Student 0: 65 100 82 97 100 75
Student 1: 99 50 100 89 71 95
Student 2: 81 85 93 99 84 85
```

There is a duality between arrays and loops. Loops are the fundamental way that we process arrays. In the same way, nested loops are the algorithmic counterpart of multidimensional arrays.

Just as we used the `new` keyword to define a one-dimensional array, we use it to define a two-dimensional array, and in example 6.10 we use the same initializer syntax, except that the array elements are themselves arrays (lines 2-4). The nested loops are reminiscent of example 5.15, where we printed a multiplication table. Each iteration of the outer loop prints one row, while the inner loop prints one cell at a time, thus the outer loop corresponds to rows and the inner loop corresponds to columns. The row header is printed within the outer loop, before the inner loop is invoked, and we use a `println` statement after the inner loop to advance the output to the next line.

As we've seen in prior examples, example 6.10 uses the customary "i" and "j" variable names for the loop counters. More appropriate names would have been "student" and "assignment". Along with changing these loop counter names, our next example adds an array containing the student names, and uses the student names as the row headers,

Example 6.11. Adding student names to the grade output.

```
1   String[] students = new String[] { "Paul", "Tabatha", "Elaine" };
2   int[][] grades = new int[][] {
3     { 65, 100, 82, 97, 100, 75 },
4     { 99, 50, 100, 89, 71, 95 },
5     { 81, 85, 93, 99, 84, 85 }
6   };
7
8   for (int student = 0; student < grades.length; student++) {
9     out.print(students[student] + ": ");
10    for (int assignment = 0; assignment < grades[student].length; assignment++)
11      out.print(grades[student][assignment] + " ");
12    out.println();
13  }
```

```
Paul: 65 100 82 97 100 75
Tabatha: 99 50 100 89 71 95
Elaine: 81 85 93 99 84 85
```

The code is a bit longer using "student" and "assignment" as loop counters, but the change was worthwhile, since the code is clearer that way. Identifiers should help document the code as much as possible.

> **Technique 9. Use descriptive names for identifiers**
>
> Use descriptive names for variables, classes, and other identifiers. This helps make your code self-documenting, and helps you to quickly understand the code when you return to it later.

Next we enhance our example so that it prints out the average of grades for each student, and the overall average grade. For this, we use similar code to that in example 6.6, by keeping a running total of the grades and dividing the total by the number of grades to get the average,

```
1   String[] students = new String[] { "Paul", "Tabatha", "Elaine" };
2   int[][] grades = new int[][] {
3     { 65, 100, 82, 97, 100, 75 },
4     { 99, 50, 100, 89, 71, 95 },
5     { 81, 85, 93, 99, 84, 85 }
6   };
7
8   int overallSum = 0;
9   int overallCount = 0;
10  for (int student = 0; student < grades.length; student++) {
11    out.print(students[student] + ": ");
12    int sum = 0;
13    for (int assignment = 0; assignment < grades[student].length; assignment++)
        {
14      out.print(grades[student][assignment] + " ");
15      sum += grades[student][assignment];
16    }
17    out.println(". Average: " + sum / grades[student].length);
18    overallSum += sum;
19    overallCount += grades[student].length;
20  }
21  out.println("Class average is " + overallSum / overallCount);
```

Example 6.12. Adding grade averages.

```
Paul: 65 100 82 97 100 75 . Average: 86
Tabatha: 99 50 100 89 71 95 . Average: 84
Elaine: 81 85 93 99 84 85 . Average: 87
Class average is 86
```

In example 6.12 we compute the student's average by adding up the grades for the student, that is, the grades on the student's row, and then divide the sum by the number of grades on that row. The number of grades on the row is the upper limit of the inner loop's counter, `grades[student].length`. Similarly, the overall average is computed on line 21 by dividing the overall sum of grades by the total number of grades.

The rows in a two-dimensional array don't have to have the same number of columns. That's because the two-dimensional array is technically an array of arrays, each having its own length. This is called a *jagged* array, sometimes also called a *ragged* array. Exercise 6.8 shows an example of an array with a different number of columns in each row. Because Java allows jagged arrays, you should be careful to use the length of each row in an inner loop's upper limit, instead of the length of the first row in all iterations of the inner loop.

Jagged array: A two-dimensional array in which different rows have different lengths.

Your programs can have multi-dimensional arrays beyond two dimensions, if needed, and the syntax is similar, for example, "int[][][] a = new int[2][2][2]" defines a 2x2x2 array of integers.

Table 6.1 shows some of the common loop patterns.

Table 6.1: Some common loop patterns.

Pattern	Example
`for`	Reversing the contents of an array (example 6.8)
`for` `if`	Finding the biggest item in an array (example 6.7)
`for` `for`	Print a 2-D array (example 6.10)

`for`
   `for`
     `if`
	Finding the biggest item in a 2-D array

Exercises

6.6   Write a program that computes airline revenue. It should have a two-dimensional array of integers, each row being one flight on a particular day and each cell containing the price that a particular passenger paid. Iterate through the array to compute the total revenue for the day.

6.7   Create a two-dimensional array of strings. Each row should represent a state, and contains a list of cities. Use **Arrays.sort** as in example 6.9 to sort the cities of each state alphabetically. After sorting the contents of each row, print out the cities.

6.8   Fix the logic error in the following program, and test it to make sure it works,

```
1    // each row is a class containing an array of student IDs
2    int[][] classEnrollments = new int[][] {
3      { 101, 2101, 412, 625, 420, 5561, 823, 99 },
4      { 72, 518, 602, 3097, 421 },
5      { 809, 393, 521, 345, 299, 711 }
6    };
7
8    int overallCount = 0;
9    for (int i = 0; i < classEnrollments.length; i++) {
10     int count = 0;
11     for (int student = 0; student < classEnrollments[i].length; student
         ++) {
12       out.print(classEnrollments[i][student] + " ");
13       count += classEnrollments[i][student];
14     }
15     out.println(". Students in this class: " + count);
16     overallCount += count;
17   }
18   out.println("Total number of enrollments is " + overallCount);
```

6.4 Garbage Collection

As noted in section 6.1, the new keyword is what we use to allocate memory for an array, and the variable we use to refer to the array is merely a reference, initially having the null value. An array that has been allocated resides in an area of memory called the *heap*. An array's size can't change once it's been allocated, and it remains in the heap until it's no longer needed, at which time its memory is deallocated and can be reused for another purpose. An array can have more than one reference. For example, consider the following code,

```
1    String[] staff = new String[30];
2    String[] fullTimeStaff = staff;
```

Line 1 in the above code allocates space for an array of thirty strings, and points the variable **staff** at that array. The variable **staff** is merely a reference that we use to read from and write to the array. Line 2 creates a new variable of type **String[]** and points it to the existing array. Both **staff** and **fullTimeStaff** are *references* to the same array.

Garbage collection occurs automatically at certain intervals throughout the lifetime of your program.

An array can have any number of references pointing to it. A reference in your code is a variable that points to the actual memory holding the array's contents. In the above section of code, we have two references pointing to one array. Can an array have no references pointing to it? Yes, and that's what occurs when the block of code defining the reference finishes executing. The reference, like any variable, is limited in *scope* to the block of code in which it's defined. Once all references to an array are out of scope, the array can no longer be accessed, and Java deallocates the array through a process called garbage collection. Java keeps a running count of references that are pointing to a given array, and garbage collection is performed at certain intervals throughout the lifetime of your program. You don't need to worry about cleaning up the memory that you allocate using the `new` keyword—Java does that for you automatically.

A variable's scope is limited to the block of code in which it's defined.

6.5 Comments

Comments start with two slashes, //.

Our examples have reached a level of complexity that warrants adding clarifying comments. Comments in Java start with a double forward-slash (//), and are meant for the software developer to leave notes to him- or herself. These aid him or her when going over the code at a later date to make changes or perform other types of maintenance. The Java compiler ignores a comment, starting with the forward slashes, up to the end of the line that it occurs on. Comments should be used to label sections of code, or clarify code sections whose functions aren't immediately obvious. When deciding whether a comment is needed, ask yourself whether it's faster to read the code to understand its purpose, or read the comment associated with that code. This is highly subjective, so every developer will have a different style with regard to comments. Furthermore, you'll find that your own commenting habits change over time. In example 6.13 we have added comments to the code from example 6.12,

Example 6.13. Adding comments.

```java
String[] students = new String[] { "Paul", "Tabatha", "Elaine" };

// each row has one student's grades
int[][] grades = new int[][] {
  { 65, 100, 82, 97, 100, 75 },
  { 99, 50, 100, 89, 71, 95 },
  { 81, 85, 93, 99, 84, 85 }
};

// print grades for each student
```

```
11   int overallSum = 0, overallCount = 0;
12   for (int student = 0; student < grades.length; student++) {
13     out.print(students[student] + ": "); // row header
14     int sum = 0;
15     for (int assignment = 0; assignment < grades[student].length; assignment++)
         {
16       out.print(grades[student][assignment] + " ");
17       sum += grades[student][assignment];
18     }
19     out.println(". Average: " + sum / grades[student].length); // student's
           average
20     overallSum += sum;
21     overallCount += grades[student].length;
22   }
23   out.println("Class average is " + overallSum / overallCount);
```

```
Paul: 65 100 82 97 100 75 . Average: 86
Tabatha: 99 50 100 89 71 95 . Average: 84
Elaine: 81 85 93 99 84 85 . Average: 87
Class average is 86
```

In example 6.13, we've also merged the declaration of overallSum and overallCount into one line, on line 11. Java lets us do this if the types are the same. The two variables are separated by a comma, and can still be initialized individually. Note that comments are used sparingly—not every section of code needs a comment. Remember that the comments are there to help you when you look at your code later, and only need to be there if they help you read the code faster, or if they help you locate a certain section of code faster. Comments are also often used to document formulas or algorithms.

Technique 10. Add comments to help you navigate your code later

Comments should help you locate a section of code faster when you later read your code. They're also used to help someone else understand your code.

Before moving on, I want to show a different **for** loop syntax, one that is often used when you don't need to use the array index within the loop (e.g., to modify the array). Example 6.14 has the rewritten code with the new loop syntax,

```
1   String[] students = new String[] { "Paul", "Tabatha", "Elaine" };
2
3   // each row has one student's grades
4   int[][] grades = new int[][] {
5     { 65, 100, 82, 97, 100, 75 },
6     { 99, 50, 100, 89, 71, 95 },
```

Example 6.14. Using the enhanced for loop syntax.

```
 7      { 81, 85, 93, 99, 84, 85 }
 8    };
 9
10    // print grades for each student
11    int overallSum = 0, overallCount = 0;
12    for (int student = 0; student < grades.length; student++) {
13      out.print(students[student] + ": "); // row header
14      int sum = 0;
15      for (int grade : grades[student]) {
16        out.print(grade + " ");
17        sum += grade;
18      }
19      out.println(". Average: " + sum / grades[student].length); // student's
           average
20      overallSum += sum;
21      overallCount += grades[student].length;
22    }
23    out.println("Class average is " + overallSum / overallCount);
```

```
Paul: 65 100 82 97 100 75 . Average: 86
Tabatha: 99 50 100 89 71 95 . Average: 84
Elaine: 81 85 93 99 84 85 . Average: 87
Class average is 86
```

The modified code is on lines 15-17. This syntax is clearer but doesn't provide the actual index, which we didn't need in the inner **for**-loop. Instead of "for (int assignment = 0; assignment < grades[student].length; assignment++)", we have "for (int grade : grades[student])". This declares the integer variable `grade`, and assigns it in turn to each integer element of the `grades[student]` array. Within the loop, we use `grade` in the call to `print`, as well as to increment `sum`. Note that we can't use this enhanced **for** syntax in the outer loop since we need the index in order to access the student name from the `students` array.

Our last example uses a two-dimensional array of floating point numbers to hold coordinates of a list of destinations. Each row contains the latitude and longitude of one city. We loop through the cities and compute the distance from each city to the next. This time, we don't want to process each row, but rather we want to process each *pair* of rows. So, the number of loop iterations is *one less* than the number of rows, and the code in the loop looks at the current row and the next row,

Example 6.15. Showing distances between cities on a trip.

```
1  double[][] points = new double[][] {
2    { 28.53, -81.38 },   // Orlando
3    { 29.75, -95.39 },   // Houston
4    { 32.21, -110.93 },  // Tucson
5    { 32.71, -117.15 },  // San Diego
6    { 40.71, -74.00 },   // New York
7    { 42.35, -71.07 }    // Boston
```

```
 8    };
 9
10    double tripLength = 0;
11    for (int i = 0; i < points.length - 1; i++) {
12      double[] point1 = points[i];
13      double[] point2 = points[i+1];
14
15      // distance between two points = square root of (latitude difference
            squared + longitude difference squared)
16      double leg = Math.sqrt(
17        Math.pow(point1[0] - point2[0], 2) +
18        Math.pow(point1[1] - point2[1], 2));
19
20      /* Convert degrees to miles. 69 miles per degree longitude,
21       * and 55 miles per degree latitude (approximate for the
22       * United States). So we'll use 62 miles per degree as a
23       * very approximate average */
24      leg *= 62;
25
26      out.printf("Next leg: %.2f miles\n", leg);
27      tripLength += leg;
28    }
29    out.printf("Trip length = %.2f miles", tripLength);
```

```
Next leg: 871.91 miles
Next leg: 975.48 miles
Next leg: 386.88 miles
Next leg: 2720.89 miles
Next leg: 208.18 miles
Trip length = 5163.34 miles
```

Note the use of comments in three places, where they're necessary to clarify the programmer's intent:

- Each latitude/longitude pair has a comment containing the city's name.
- The formula for distance between two points.
- The conversion of degrees to miles, with explanation of how the formula was derived. Here we use a different comment notation which starts with /* and ends with */, and can span multiple lines.

A common practice when a developer wants to remove code from the program, but keep it around for use later, is to convert it into a comment by surrounding it with the /* and */ delimiters, or preceding each line with //. This is often because the code isn't working yet and the developer wants to focus on other parts of the program, or because the code is complicating a test case that he or she is working on. A quick way to comment out a block of code is to select it and use the Ctrl+/ shortcut (Cmd+/ on Mac). The same action will uncomment a block of code.

Colloquially, converting a section of code into a comment is known as *commenting out* the code.

Note in example 6.15 the `double` type which we're seeing for the first time. `double` works like `float`, except that it uses twice as many bits, resulting in more precise calculations. That's not why we've used it here in place of `float`. We're using it because `Math.pow()` and `Math.sqrt()` take parameters of type `double` and return a `double` value, and it would entail more code to cast values between the `float` and `double` types.

Chapter Summary

- An array is a sequence of variables that are accessed by index. Arrays are allocated with a specific number of elements, and an array's size can't be changed after it's been allocated.
- An array's elements all have the same type.
- Loops are commonly used to iterate through arrays, to performa an operation on each array element, or find an array element with a certain property.
- A two-dimensional array corresponds to a grid of items, all of the same type.

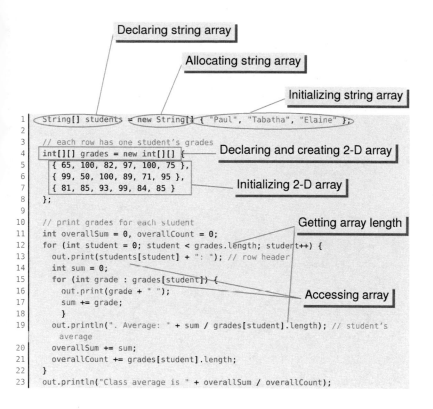

```
1   String[] students = new String[] { "Paul", "Tabatha", "Elaine" };
2
3   // each row has one student's grades
4   int[][] grades = new int[][] {
5       { 65, 100, 82, 97, 100, 75 },
6       { 99, 50, 100, 89, 71, 95 },
7       { 81, 85, 93, 99, 84, 85 }
8   };
9
10  // print grades for each student
11  int overallSum = 0, overallCount = 0;
12  for (int student = 0; student < grades.length; student++) {
13      out.print(students[student] + ": "); // row header
14      int sum = 0;
15      for (int grade : grades[student]) {
16          out.print(grade + " ");
17          sum += grade;
18      }
19      out.println(". Average: " + sum / grades[student].length); // student's
        average
20      overallSum += sum;
21      overallCount += grades[student].length;
22  }
23  out.println("Class average is " + overallSum / overallCount);
```

Labels in figure:
- Declaring string array
- Allocating string array
- Initializing string array
- Declaring and creating 2-D array
- Initializing 2-D array
- Getting array length
- Accessing array

Exercise Solutions

6.1
```
1   String[] students = new String[] { "Ronald", "Mike", "Cindy", "
        Tammy", "Blake", "Martha", "Sam" };
2   int[] IDs = new int[] {7103, 4933, 6548, 6830, 711, 8937, 2002};
3   char[] grades = new char[] {'C', 'A', 'A', 'B', 'A', 'C', 'A'};
4
5   for (int i = 0; i < 7; i++)
6       out.println("Student " + (i+1) + " is " + students[i] + " with
            ID " + IDs[i] + " and grade " + grades[i]);
```

```
Student 1 is Ronald with ID 7103 and grade C
Student 2 is Mike with ID 4933 and grade A
Student 3 is Cindy with ID 6548 and grade A
Student 4 is Tammy with ID 6830 and grade B
Student 5 is Blake with ID 711 and grade A
Student 6 is Martha with ID 8937 and grade C
Student 7 is Sam with ID 2002 and grade A
```

6.2
```
1   String[] students = new String[] { "Ronald", "Mike", "Cindy", "
        Tammy", "Blake", "Martha", "Sam" };
2   int[] IDs = new int[] {7103, 4933, 6548, 6830, 711, 8937, 2002};
```

```
3
4    for (int i = 0; i < 7; i++)
5      if (IDs[i] < 6000)
6        out.println("Student " + (i+1) + " is " + students[i] + " with
           ID " + IDs[i]);
```

```
Student 2 is Mike with ID 4933
Student 5 is Blake with ID 711
Student 7 is Sam with ID 2002
```

6.3
```
1    int[] temps = new int[7];
2    for (int i = 0; i < 7; i++) {
3      out.print("Enter high temperature for day " + (i+1) + ": ");
4      temps[i] = input.nextInt();
5    }
6
7    int high = Integer.MIN_VALUE;
8    for (int i = 0; i < 7; i++)
9      if (temps[i] > high)
10       high = temps[i];
11   out.println("Highest temperature of the week: " + high);
```

```
Enter high temperature for day 1: 81
Enter high temperature for day 2: 83
Enter high temperature for day 3: 88
Enter high temperature for day 4: 75
Enter high temperature for day 5: 79
Enter high temperature for day 6: 80
Enter high temperature for day 7: 81
Highest temperature of the week: 88
```

6.4
```
1    String[] cities = new String[] { "Atlanta", "Baltimore", "DC", "
         Buffalo", "Phoenix" };
2    boolean sorted = true;
3    for (int i = 1; i < cities.length; i++)
4      if (cities[i-1].compareTo(cities[i]) > 0) {
5        sorted = false;
6        break;
7      }
8
9    if (sorted)
10     out.println("City names are sorted");
11   else
12     out.println("City names are not sorted");
```

```
City names are sorted
```

6.5
```
1    String[] teams = new String[] { "Red Sox", "Yankees", "White Sox",
         "Vikings", "Jaguars", "Patriots", "Cowboys" };
2
3    java.util.Arrays.sort(teams);
4    for (int i = 0; i < teams.length / 2; i++) {
5      String temp = teams[i];
6      teams[i] = teams[teams.length - 1 - i];
7      teams[teams.length - 1 - i] = temp;
8    }
9
10   out.print("Teams in reverse alphabetical order: ");
```

```
11    for (int i = 0; i < teams.length; i++)
12      out.print(teams[i] + " ");
```

```
Teams in reverse alphabetical order: Yankees White Sox Vikings Red Sox Patriots Jaguars Cowboys
```

6.6
```
1    int[][] prices = {
2        { 294, 279, 288, 164, 186, 217, 202, 237, 273, 107 },
3        { 109, 214, 111, 157, 208, 142 },
4        { 84, 65, 58, 130, 77, 67, 135, 163, 76 },
5    };
6
7    int sum = 0;
8    for (int flight = 0; flight < prices.length; flight++)
9      for (int passenger = 0; passenger < prices[flight].length;
         passenger ++)
10        sum += prices[flight][passenger];
11
12    out.println("Total revenue is $" + sum);
```

```
Total revenue is $4043
```

6.7
```
1    String[][] cities = {
2        { "Cupertino", "Pasadena", "Los Angeles", "San Diego" },
3        { "Buffalo", "NYC", "Albany" },
4        { "Tampa", "Orlando", "Miami", "Jacksonville" },
5    };
6
7    for (int state = 0; state < cities.length; state++) {
8      java.util.Arrays.sort(cities[state]);
9      for (int city = 0; city < cities[state].length; city++)
10        out.print(cities[state][city] + " ");
11      out.println();
12    }
```

```
Cupertino Los Angeles Pasadena San Diego
Albany Buffalo NYC
Jacksonville Miami Orlando Tampa
```

6.8
```
1    // each row is a class containing an array of student IDs
2    int[][] classEnrollments = new int[][] {
3      { 101, 2101, 412, 625, 420, 5561, 823, 99 },
4      { 72, 518, 602, 3097, 421 },
5      { 809, 393, 521, 345, 299, 711 }
6    };
7
8    int overallCount = 0;
9    for (int i = 0; i < classEnrollments.length; i++) {
10     int count = 0;
11     for (int student = 0; student < classEnrollments[i].length;
         student++) {
12        out.print(classEnrollments[i][student] + " ");
13        count++;
14        }
15     out.println(". Students in this class: " + count);
16     overallCount += count;
17   }
18   out.println("Total number of enrollments is " + overallCount);
```

```
101 2101 412 625 420 5561 823 99 . Students in this class: 8
72 518 602 3097 421 . Students in this class: 5
809 393 521 345 299 711 . Students in this class: 6
Total number of enrollments is 19
```

Methods | 7

7.1 Methods

Methods are simply blocks of code that you can execute from other parts of your program. Consider the following example,

```
1  public static void main(String[] args) {
2      sayHello();
3  }
4
5  public static void sayHello () {
6      out.println("Hello, User!");
7  }
```

```
Hello, User!
```

Lines 5-7 define the method `sayHello`. This method contains one line which prints the greeting. A method's name conforms to the same rules as variable names, and by convention is in camel case. The sayHello definition resembles that of `main`, with the keywords `public static void`. We'll get to `public` and `static` in chapter 8. The `void` keyword is the return type, and indicates no return value. Invoking the `sayHello` method is done in the `main` method by using its name followed by a pair of parentheses. When a method is called, the calling code is suspended, and will resume when the called method returns. We can invoke the method repeatedly using a loop,

```
1  public static void main(String[] args) {
2      for (int i = 0; i < 10; i++)
3          sayHello();
4  }
5
6  public static void sayHello () {
7      out.println("Hello, User!");
8  }
```

```
Hello, User!
Hello, User!
Hello, User!
Hello, User!
Hello, User!
Hello, User!
Hello, User!
Hello, User!
Hello, User!
Hello, User!
```

If `sayHello` contained more than one line, say a ten-line sequence of code, we would save a significant number of lines by calling it from multiple places rather than pasting its code into those places. This brings us to the first main benefit of using methods—they allow us to consolidate repeated segments of code, an application of technique 5 on page 75. Organizing your code to group related functionality takes practice. Methods are one of the main tools you have to keep your code organized and maintainable, and you'll see examples of this throughout the rest of the book.

Reorganizing a program's code so that it's more maintainable is sometimes called *refactoring*.

7.2 Parameters

The code that invokes a method can pass information into the method in the form of parameters. These are given between the opening and closing parentheses. In example 7.1, we modify the above program to pass a string into the `sayHello` method, which is used in the greeting message,

Example 7.1. Passing a parameter.

```
1   public static void main(String[] args) {
2       sayHello("Grumpy");
3       sayHello("Dopey");
4       sayHello("Happy");
5       sayHello("Bashful");
6       sayHello("Sneezy");
7       sayHello("Sleepy");
8       sayHello("Doc");
9   }
10
11  public static void sayHello (String name) {
12      out.println("Hello, " + name + "!");
13  }
```

```
Hello, Grumpy!
Hello, Dopey!
Hello, Happy!
Hello, Bashful!
Hello, Sneezy!
Hello, Sleepy!
Hello, Doc!
```

A method's definition can contain any number of parameters between the parentheses, separated by commas. The `sayHello` method requires one parameter called name, of type `String`. Each call to the method (lines 2 through 8) contains the required name parameter between the parentheses. Calls to a method must pass the correct number of parameters, and the parameter types must match the method's definition, or you'll get a compile error.

A parameter is the variable in the method's declaration, whereas an argument is the *value* passed in to the parameter.

In example 7.2, the methods `printMax` and `printAverage` each take two numbers as parameters, and print the larger one and their average, respectively,

```
1    public static void main(String[] args) {
2      printMax(5, 15);
3      printAverage(5, 15);
4      printMax(37, -11);
5      printAverage(37, -11);
6    }
7
8    public static void printMax (int number1, int number2) {
9      if (number1 > number2)
10       out.println(number1);
11     else
12       out.println(number2);
13   }
14
15   public static void printAverage (int number1, int number2) {
16     out.println((double) (number1 + number2) / 2);
17   }
```

Example 7.2. Passing multiple parameters.

```
15
10.0
37
13.0
```

7.3 Return Types

The point of having methods is to make code reusable. Having a method that takes two parameters and prints the average is not very reusable, so we'll fix that in example 7.3,

Example 7.3. Methods with return values.

```java
public static void main(String[] args) {
  printStatistics(5, 15);
  printStatistics(37, -11);
}

public static void printStatistics (int number1, int number2) {
  int maxNumber = getMax(number1, number2);
  out.println(maxNumber);
  double average = getAverage(number1, number2);
  out.println(average);
}

public static int getMax (int number1, int number2) {
  if (number1 > number2)
    return number1;
  else
    return number2;
}

public static double getAverage (int number1, int number2) {
  return (double) (number1 + number2) / 2;
}
```

```
15
10.0
37
13.0
```

The `printMax` and `printAverage` methods have been changed to `getMax` and `getAverage`, and they don't actually print anything. Rather, they return the results of the calculations. That way, they're much more reusable, for two reasons,

- The code that calls each of them may want the output to have a different format.
- The code that calls each of them may want to use the results (maximum or average) in different ways.

Stack Frame: The memory space containing a method's parameters and local variables.

Call Stack: The memory space where stack frames are allocated.

Stack Overflow: When the call stack runs out of memory because of too many nested method invocations.

A method can call another one, and the second method can in turn call a third. This nesting of method invocations can be arbitrarily deep as long as your program doesn't run out of memory. In our example, `main` calls `printStatistics`, which in turn calls `getMax` and `getAverage`. When a method calls another, Java allocates memory for the new method's local variables including parameters, and this memory block is called the stack frame. When the invoked method returns, the stack frame is deallocated. It's called a stack frame because these frames are stacked on one another when methods call each other (this is called pushing a frame onto the stack), and when methods return, their frames are deallocated (this is called popping the frame from the stack). If too many nested method invocations are made, the stack's memory runs out, and this is known as stack overflow. You shouldn't worry about stack overflows as the stack memory is large, and it doesn't run out unless a bug in your code caused an infinite recursion situation, where a bug causes a method to call itself repeatedly without breaking out of that loop.

Recursion is when a method calls itself. We'll discuss recursion in detail in chapter 15

Each method can return a value of a particular type, or may not return a value at all if its return type is declared as `void`. The return type is declared in the *method declaration* right before the method name. In the above example, `getMax` returns an integer, and `getAverage` returns a double precision floating point number. The `return` statement actually causes the method to terminate and return the value specified. Note that a `void` method can also use the return statement to return to the caller, but may not specify a value to return.

return statement.

Our final version of this example will prompt the user for two integers, then call the `printStatistics` method to print the maximum and average,

```java
public static void main(String[] args) {
    Scanner input = new Scanner(System.in);
    out.print("Enter two numbers separated by spaces: ");
    int first = input.nextInt();
    int second = input.nextInt();
    printStatistics(first, second);
    input.close();
}

public static void printStatistics (int number1, int number2) {
    int maxNumber = getMax(number1, number2);
    out.println(maxNumber);
    double average = getAverage(number1, number2);
    out.println(average);
}

public static int getMax (int number1, int number2) {
    if (number1 > number2)
        return number1;
    else
        return number2;
}

public static double getAverage (int number1, int number2) {
    return (double) (number1 + number2) / 2;
}
```

Example 7.4. Calculating statistics from user input.

```
Enter two numbers separated by spaces: 21 42
The maximum is 42
The average is 31.5
```

Now that we know how to pass parameters into methods and return results from methods, we have a powerful tool to simplify our programs. Let's look back at examples 5.1 and 5.3 which we combine now as example 7.5,

Example 7.5. Medical diagnosis program before simplification.

```java
String answer;

do {
  out.print("Do you have a sore throat (yes/no)? ");
  answer = input.nextLine().toLowerCase();
} while (!answer.equals("yes") && !answer.equals("no"));

if (answer.equals("yes")) {

  do {
    out.print("Do you have a fever? ");
    answer = input.nextLine().toLowerCase();
  } while (!answer.equals("yes") && !answer.equals("no"));

  if (answer.equals("yes"))
    out.print("Possibly the flu.");
  else
    out.print("Possibly strep throat.");
}
else {

  do {
    out.print("Are you in pain? ");
    answer = input.nextLine().toLowerCase();
  } while (!answer.equals("yes") && !answer.equals("no"));

  if (answer.equals("yes"))
    out.print("Try Advil.");
  else
    out.print("You appear to be fine.");
}
```

```
Do you have a sore throat (yes/no)? Yes
Do you have a fever? No
Possibly strep throat.
```

The repeated sections (lines 3-6, 10-13 and 22-25) can be moved out into a new method that takes two parameters, the `Scanner` object and the question to ask, and returns the user's answer,

```java
public static void main(String[] args) {

  Scanner input = new Scanner(System.in);

  String answer = askQuestion(input, "Do you have a sore throat (yes/no)? ");
  if (answer.equals("yes")) {

    answer = askQuestion(input, "Do you have a fever? ");
    if (answer.equals("yes"))
      out.print("Possibly the flu.");
    else
      out.print("Possibly strep throat.");
```

```
13     }
14     else {
15
16       answer = askQuestion(input, "Are you in pain? ");
17       if (answer.equals("yes"))
18         out.print("Try Advil.");
19       else
20         out.print("You appear to be fine.");
21     }
22
23     input.close();
24   }
25
26   public static String askQuestion(Scanner input, String question) {
27     String answer = "";
28     do {
29       out.print(question);
30       answer = input.nextLine().toLowerCase();
31     } while (!answer.equals("yes") && !answer.equals("no"));
32     return answer;
33   }
```

```
Do you have a sore throat (yes/no)? Yes
Do you have a fever? No
Possibly strep throat.
```

This hasn't saved us too many lines of code, but the repeated sections are gone and adding more questions will cause us to add far fewer lines to the program as opposed to the previous version. But, we shouldn't stop there, as we can simplify the program further. We don't need to return the actual user's input, which is a string. We can simply return true or false. In fact, we really should make this change because these are yes/no questions and true/false is the natural representation of the user's answer. So, our next version is as follows,

```
 1   public static void main(String[] args) {
 2
 3     Scanner input = new Scanner(System.in);
 4
 5     if (askQuestion(input, "Do you have a sore throat (yes/no)? ")) {
 6       if (askQuestion(input, "Do you have a fever? "))
 7         out.print("Possibly the flu.");
 8       else
 9         out.print("Possibly strep throat.");
10     }
11     else {
12       if (askQuestion(input, "Are you in pain? "))
13         out.print("Try Advil.");
14       else
15         out.print("You appear to be fine.");
16     }
17
18     input.close();
19   }
20
```

```
21  public static boolean askQuestion(Scanner input, String question) {
22    String answer = "";
23    do {
24      out.print(question);
25      answer = input.nextLine().toLowerCase();
26    } while (!answer.equals("yes") && !answer.equals("no"));
27    return answer.equals("yes");
28  }
```

```
Do you have a sore throat (yes/no)? Yes
Do you have a fever? No
Possibly strep throat.
```

Since the `askQuestion` method now returns a boolean, we were able to call it within the *if* statement, saving space and making the program easier to read. In addition, we could also use the question-mark-colon operator to combine the inner `if` statements, as follows,

Example 7.6. Medical diagnosis program after simplification.

```
1   public static void main(String[] args) {
2
3     Scanner input = new Scanner(System.in);
4
5     if (askQuestion(input, "Do you have a sore throat (yes/no)? "))
6       out.print(askQuestion(input, "Do you have a fever? ") ? "Possibly the flu.
        " : "Possibly strep throat.");
7     else
8       out.print(askQuestion(input, "Are you in pain? ") ? "Try Advil." : "You
        appear to be fine.");
9
10    input.close();
11  }
12
13  public static boolean askQuestion(Scanner input, String question) {
14    String answer = "";
15    do {
16      out.print(question);
17      answer = input.nextLine().toLowerCase();
18    } while (!answer.equals("yes") && !answer.equals("no"));
19    return answer.equals("yes");
20  }
```

This is a worthwhile change, as it reduces the number of lines of code, and doesn't affect the clarity or runtime efficiency.

7.4 Variable Scope

When a method is called from another, variables in the calling method aren't visible in the method that was called. For example, when `printStatistics` is called from `main` in example 7.4,

Tip 5. You should get used to the kind of code simplification that we performed to get from example 7.5 to example 7.6, and make it part of your routine.

the variables "first" and "second" in `main` aren't available to the `printStatistics` method. That is, their scope is limited to the method in which they're defined.

Furthermore, even if we renamed the parameters `number1` and `number2` in `printStatistics` to be `first` and `second` instead, they would be unrelated to the variables `first` and `second` in `main`. Each variable in Java has a distinct scope, and can only be referenced within that scope. In general, the scope of a variable begins at the line on which it's defined and ends at the end of the block in which it's defined. So the variable `first` in example 7.4 is accessible only between lines 4 and 8. `second` is accessible only between lines 5 and 8, and the variable `args` is accessible only between lines 1 and 8.

7.5 Modifying Parameters

In Java, parameters are passed *by value*. This means that the parameter received by the method is a `copy` of the parameter passed in by the caller. So modifying the parameter within the method doesn't change the variable specified in the method call, as example 7.7 shows,

```
1   public static void main(String[] args) {
2       int number = 26;
3       out.println("Before calling the method, the number is " + number);
4       method(number);
5       out.println("After calling the method, the number is " + number);
6   }
7
8   public static void method (int parameter) {
9       out.println("  Before changing the parameter, its value is " + parameter);
10      parameter = 0;
11      out.println("  After changing the parameter, its value is " + parameter);
12  }
```

Example 7.7. Parameters are passed by value.

```
Before calling the method, the number is 26
  Before changing the parameter, its value is 26
  After changing the parameter, its value is 0
After calling the method, the number is 26
```

As you can see from the output, changing the value of `parameter` within `method` doesn't change the value of the variable `number` which is passed into `method` as a parameter. Java copied the value contained within `number`, assigning that value to a new variable named `parameter` within the method.

When a reference type is passed in to a method as a parameter, a copy of the *reference* is passed in, meaning the parameter is pointing to the same structure that the caller is. To understand this, consider example 7.8,

Example 7.8. Modifying an array parameter's contents.

```
1    public static void main(String[] args) {
2      int[] numbers = { 1, 2, 3 };
3      out.print("Before calling the method, the numbers are ");
4      printNumbers(numbers);
5      method(numbers);
6      out.print("After calling the method, the numbers are ");
7      printNumbers(numbers);
8    }
9
10   public static void method (int[] numbers) {
11     out.print("  Before changing the parameter, its value is ");
12     printNumbers(numbers);
13     numbers[0] = 999;
14     out.print("  After changing the parameter, its value is ");
15     printNumbers(numbers);
16   }
17
18   public static void printNumbers(int[] numbers) {
19     for (int number : numbers)
20       out.print(number + " ");
21     out.println();
22   }
```

```
Before calling the method, the numbers are 1 2 3
  Before changing the parameter, its value is 1 2 3
  After changing the parameter, its value is 999 2 3
After calling the method, the numbers are 999 2 3
```

As you can see from the output, the array belonging to the *caller* has been modified by *called* method. This illustrates the nature of reference variables. The variable "numbers" defined in `main` is a reference, or a *pointer* to the real location of the array. The array's location (the reference) has been copied into the `numbers` parameter, and used to modify the contents of the array belonging to the caller. In Java, arrays and classes (discussed in chapter 8) are reference types, in other words, any variable that is assigned a value by the "new" operator contains a reference to data, not actual data.

7.6 Overloading

In Java, as with many other languages, different methods can have the same name as long as they have a different number of parameters, or parameters of different types. To illustrate this, example 7.9 shows a program that computes the largest among a group of numbers,

```
 1   public static void main(String[] args) {
 2
 3       out.println("The maximum of 31 and 35 is " + getMax(31, 35));
 4
 5       int[] numbers = new int[] { 70, 75, 90 };
 6       out.println("The maximum number in the array is " + getMax(numbers));
 7   }
 8
 9   public static int getMax(int number1, int number2) {
10       return number1 > number2 ? number1 : number2;
11   }
12
13   public static int getMax(int[] numbers) {
14       int result = Integer.MIN_VALUE;
15       for (int number : numbers)
16           if (number > result)
17               result = number;
18       return result;
19   }
```

Example 7.9. Overloading a method.

```
The maximum of 31 and 35 is 35
The maximum number in the array is 90
```

Example 7.9 has two different methods with the same name, `getMax`. In this situation, we say that `getMax` is overloaded. This isn't a syntax error because the two methods have different numbers of parameters, so Java can tell which one is being called by the number of parameters supplied. The call to `getMax` on line 3 refers to the instance having two parameters, and the call on line 6 refers to the instance having one parameter. Similarly, we could have defined a third `getMax` method with two parameters of type `float`, which would be allowed because the new method's parameters have different types from the existing method's parameters' types.

Method overloading: two or more methods having the same name.

The combination of a method's name, the number of parameters that it has, and the *types* of its parameters is called a method's *signature*. Java allows multiple methods with the same name in the same class as long as they all have different signatures. Note that the names of the parameters doesn't matter. It's the *types* of the parameters that make up its signature. Also note that the method's return type isn't part of its signature. Overloading is a common technique, and you will find yourself using it occasionally.

Method signature: the combination of a method's name and the types of each parameter that it takes.

Note how we've simplified the code in example 7.9. The `getMax` method that takes two parameters uses the ternary operator to keep the code brief, and the `getMax` method that takes one parameter uses a for-if pattern to get the largest number in the array using a minimal set of lines while keeping the code clear and without sacrificing runtime efficiency. The `result` variable starts with the value `Integer.MIN_VALUE` so that the answer is correct even when the input array contains only negative numbers. `Integer.MIN_VALUE` is a constant provided by Java's `Integer` class, having the smallest possible integer value. Note that the method returns `Integer.MIN_VALUE` if the input array is empty.

`Integer.MIN_VALUE` has the value $-2,147,483,648$ as shown in table 2.1.

Our examples have grown to a nontrivial size. If you're thinking at this point that it's taking a long time to type them in, you might consider using a typing tutor to increase your speed. There are many good free typing tutors online, and anyone can increase his or her typing speed. Use a typing tutor until your speed is at least 60 words per minute for standard English practice phrases. You can't be a top performing software developer without this skill, as it will help you in more than one way:

Tip 6. Use a typing tutor to increase your typing speed.

- It will significantly increase your productivity.
- More importantly, it will buy you time. As a software developer, your multiple commitments and deadlines will often be out of your control. Being a fast coder gives you time to improve your code before you have to move on to the next project, thus improving the quality of your code and helping you to improve as a developer.

7.7 `main` Method Arguments

An **Argument** is the value passed in to a method's parameter.

The "args" parameter of the `main` method passes in command-line arguments. Many command-line programs use arguments that modify their behavior in different ways. Depending on what your program does, it may or may not use these command-line arguments. If it does, it reads them from the `args` parameter, a string array. In Eclipse, you can pass in arguments to your program via the run configuration mentioned in section 3.1. The second tab of the Run Configurations dialog contains the Program Arguments text field where arguments are specified, as shown in figure 7.1.

Having specified "-a" as the command-line argument in the Run Configuration dialog, we can modify our program to read this argument in the `main` method, and act on it,

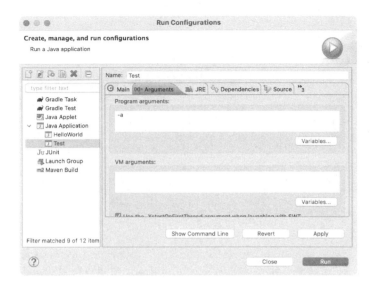

Figure 7.1: Specifying command line arguments.

```
1   public static void main(String[] args) {
2     if (args.length > 0 && args[0].equals("-a"))
3       out.println("HELLO FROM main()");
4     else
5       out.println("Hello from main()");
6   }
```

Example 7.10. Using `args` parameter in `main` method.

```
HELLO FROM main()
```

Note that we've used the shortcut-and operator (`&&`) to ensure there is at least one argument, then read the first argument and if it's a dash followed by lowercase "a", we print the greeting in all-uppercase.

7.8 Variable-Length Arguments

In Java, a method can accept a variable number of parameters. This feature is not used too often, but we'll put it to good use in chapter 15. The notation "(type) ... (variable)" in the parameter list means that the caller can pass in an arbitrary number of arguments of the specified type. Within the method, they appear as an array of the specified type. Example 7.11 shows this in action,

Example 7.11. Using variable-length arguments.

```
1   public static void main(String[] args) {
2     out.println("The product of 1, 3, 5 and 7 is " + productOf(1, 3, 5, 7));
3   }
4
5   public static int productOf(int... numbers) {
6     int result = 1;
7     for (int number : numbers)
8       result *= number;
9     return result;
10  }
```

```
The product of 1, 3, 5 and 7 is 105
```

We've defined a method called `productOf` that accepts a variable number of parameters, all of type `int`, and returns their product. Note that we initialize the result with the value 1, and 1 is returned if no arguments are passed in to the method. Also note that we're using the `*=` operator which works like `+=` but does multiplication instead of addition. A method can have other parameters as well, but if it takes a variable number of parameters, the varargs parameter has to be the last one.

Exercises

7.1   Rewrite example 6.8 to use a method that swaps two elements in the array. It should receive the array and the indexes of the two elements to be swapped as parameters.

7.2   Rewrite example 6.12 to use a method that prints the grades for one student. It should receive as parameters the student's name and the student's grades (an array). It should print the student's grades and then return their sum.

7.3   Rewrite example 6.15 to use a method that calculates the distance between two points. It should receive two parameters, each representing one latitude/longitude coordinate pair, and should return the distance between the two points.

7.4   Fix the syntax errors in the following program, and test it to make sure it works,

```
1   public static void main(String[] args) {
2     int[] grades = new int[] { 70, 75, 90 };
3     out.println("The average of 70, 75, 90 is " +
4       getAverage(grades));
5   }
```

```
 6
 7    public static float getAverage(int[] numbers) {
 8        int sum = 0;
 9        for (int number : grades)
10            sum += number;
11        return sum / grades.length;
12    }
```

Chapter Summary

- A method is a block of code that is identified by name, and can be invoked from other places in your program.
- A method can receive parameters, which are local variables that have types. These parameters are passed into the method by the calling code.
- A method can optionally return a value to the calling code, representing the result of some computation that the method performs.
- Parameters are passed by value and not by reference. This means that when the method modifies its parameter's value, the corresponding parameter passed in by the caller isn't changed.

```
 1    public static void main(String[] args) {                    Method call
 2
 3        Scanner input = new Scanner(System.in);                 Passing parameters
 4
 5        if (askQuestion(input, "Do you have a sore throat (yes/no)? "))
 6            out.print(askQuestion(input, "Do you have a fever? ") ? "Possibly the flu.
             " : "Possibly strep throat.");
 7        else
 8            out.print(askQuestion(input, "Are you in pain? ") ? "Try Advil." : "You
             appear to be fine.");                               Method definition
 9
10        input.close();
11    }                                                          Parameter definitions
12
13    public static boolean askQuestion(Scanner input, String question) {
14        String answer = "";
15        do {
16            out.print(question);
17            answer = input.nextLine().toLowerCase();
18        } while (!answer.equals("yes") && !answer.equals("no"));
19        return answer.equals("yes");
20    }                                                          Return statement
```

Exercise Solutions

7.1
```
 1  public static void main(String[] args) {
 2
 3      Scanner input = new Scanner(System.in);
 4
 5      int[] numbers = new int[] { 23, 87, 55, 9, 53, 27 };
 6
 7      out.print("Array before reversing: ");
 8      for (int i = 0; i < numbers.length; i++)
 9        out.print(numbers[i] + " ");
10      out.println();
11
12      for (int i = 0; i < numbers.length / 2; i++)
13        swap(numbers, i, numbers.length - 1 - i);
14
15      out.print("Array after reversing: ");
16      for (int i = 0; i < numbers.length; i++)
17        out.print(numbers[i] + " ");
18
19      input.close();
20  }
21
22  public static void swap(int[] array, int index1, int index2) {
23      int temp = array[index1];
24      array[index1] = array[index2];
25      array[index2] = temp;
26  }
```

```
Array before reversing: 23 87 55 9 53 27
Array after reversing: 27 53 9 55 87 23
```

7.2
```
 1  public static void main(String[] args) {
 2
 3      String[] students = new String[] { "Paul", "Tabatha", "Elaine"
          };
 4      int[][] grades = new int[][] {
 5        { 65, 100, 82, 97, 100, 75 },
 6        { 99, 50, 100, 89, 71, 95 },
 7        { 81, 85, 93, 99, 84, 85 }
 8      };
 9
10      int overallSum = 0;
11      int overallCount = 0;
12      for (int student = 0; student < grades.length; student++) {
13        int sum = processStudent(students[student], grades[student]);
14        overallSum += sum;
15        overallCount += grades[student].length;
16      }
17      out.println("Class average is " + overallSum / overallCount);
18  }
19
20  public static int processStudent(String name, int[] studentGrades)
          {
21      out.print(name + ": ");
22      int sum = 0;
```

```
23      for (int assignment = 0; assignment < studentGrades.length;
          assignment++) {
24        out.print(studentGrades[assignment] + " ");
25        sum += studentGrades[assignment];
26        }
27      out.println(". Average: " + sum / studentGrades.length);
28      return sum;
29    }
```

```
Paul: 65 100 82 97 100 75 . Average: 86
Tabatha: 99 50 100 89 71 95 . Average: 84
Elaine: 81 85 93 99 84 85 . Average: 87
Class average is 86
```

7.3

```
1    public static void main(String[] args) {
2
3      double[][] points = new double[][] {
4        { 28.53, -81.38 },  // Orlando
5        { 29.75, -95.39 },  // Houston
6        { 32.21, -110.93 }, // Tucson
7        { 32.71, -117.15 }, // San Diego
8        { 40.71, -74.00 },  // New York
9        { 42.35, -71.07 }   // Boston
10     };
11
12     double tripLength = 0;
13     for (int i = 0; i < points.length - 1; i++) {
14       double leg = distance(points[i], points[i+1]);
15       out.printf("Next leg: %.2f miles\n", leg);
16       tripLength += leg;
17     }
18     out.printf("Trip length = %.2f miles", tripLength);
19   }
20
21   public static double distance(double[] point1, double[] point2) {
22
23     // distance between two points = square root of (latitude
          difference squared + longitude difference squared)
24     double distance = Math.sqrt(
25         Math.pow(point1[0] - point2[0], 2) +
26         Math.pow(point1[1] - point2[1], 2));
27
28     /* Convert degrees to miles. 69 miles per degree longitude,
29      * and 55 miles per degree latitude (approximate for the
30      * United States). So we'll use 62 miles per degree as a
31      * very approximate average */
32     distance *= 62;
33
34     return distance;
35   }
```

```
Next leg: 871.91 miles
Next leg: 975.48 miles
Next leg: 386.88 miles
Next leg: 2720.89 miles
Next leg: 208.18 miles
Trip length = 5163.34 miles
```

7.4

```
1    public static void main(String[] args) {
2      int[] grades = new int[] { 70, 75, 90 };
```

```
3       out.println("The average of 70, 75, 90 is " +
4         getAverage(grades));
5   }
6
7   public static float getAverage(int[] numbers) {
8     int sum = 0;
9     for (int number : numbers)
10      sum += number;
11    return sum / numbers.length;
12  }
```

```
The average of 70, 75, 90 is 78.0
```

Classes | 8

8.1 Defining a Class

Classes are a way to group related data and functionality. Let's suppose you're writing a program to keep track of inventory. Each product in inventory has a name, a price, quantity on hand, and so on. Using a class allows us to group all these attributes together, along with code that performs computations related to inventory items.

Encapsulation refers to the bundling of an object's data and methods that operate on that data in a single place.

We'll start with example 8.1 by creating a new class, `Test`, in a new file, Test.java. Within this same java file, we add the new class, `Inventory`, which contains its data elements.

By convention, class names start with a capital letter.

```
1   public class Test {
2     public static void main(String[] args) {
3       InventoryItem item = new InventoryItem();
4       item.product = "Jenga Classic Game";
5       item.price = 9.50;
6       item.quantityOnHand = 80;
7     }
8   }
9
10  class InventoryItem {
11    String product;
12    double price;
13    int quantityOnHand;
14  }
```

Example 8.1. Inventory class.

The inventory class is in the same file as the `Test` class, but it can have its own file—we have them in the same file for convenience. The three data elements are defined, each with its own type. The `Test` class's `main` method creates a new instance of `InventoryItem`, and assigns values to each of its data members.

A class's data elements are variables declared within the class. They're variously known as class variables, instance variables, data elements, attributes or data members.

A class defines a new type, and objects (*instances*) of that type are created using the "new" keyword. As with arrays, variables of a class's type are references, and start out having the `null` value. Dereferencing an object reference without assigning an object instance to it results in a null pointer exception.

Creating a class instance.

To **dereference** is to access an object or array instance using a reference to that object or array.

As with arrays, an object created using the "new" keyword is stored in a special area of memory called the heap, and Java maintains a count of active references to it. Java also frees its memory once the number of references to an object reaches zero, through the garbage collection process that runs periodically throughout the lifetime of a Java program.

Data members of a class instance can be accessed using the dot notation. In example 8.1 we used the syntax "item.price = 9.50" to assign a value to the `price` data member of the `item` class instance.

The next example (8.2) defines a class to represent a car, with make, model, tankCapacity and mpg (miles per gallon) data members. The `main` method creates a `Car` instance, initializes its data and computes the vehicle's range in miles.

Example 8.2. Car class.

```
1  public class Test {
2    public static void main(String[] args) {
3      Car car = new Car();
4      car.mpg = 34;
5      car.make = "Honda";
6      car.model = "Civic";
7      car.tankCapacity = 21;
8      double range = car.tankCapacity * car.mpg;
9      out.println("The range is " + range + " miles.");
10   }
11 }
12
13 class Car {
14   double mpg;
15   String make;
16   String model;
17   double tankCapacity;
18 }
```

```
The range is 714.0 miles.
```

Note that the `main` method writes to the `car` object's instance variables on lines 4-7, and reads from them on line 8.

Exercises

8.1　Create a class that represents a television program, with data members for title, genre, production year, actors' names (an array) and director's name.

8.2   Create a class that represents a news story, with data members for title, summary, author and publication year.

8.2 Class Methods

A class not only contains data members, but also methods that operate on those data members. Consider example 8.3 which revises example 8.2 by adding the `printRange` instance method to the `Car` class, which computes and prints the vehicle's range in miles. The `main` method uses `printRange` to calculate and output the vehicle's range, instead of performing that computation itself.

```
 1  public class Test {
 2    public static void main(String[] args) {
 3      Car car = new Car();
 4      car.mpg = 34;
 5      car.make = "Honda";
 6      car.model = "Civic";
 7      car.tankCapacity = 21;
 8      car.printRange();
 9    }
10  }
11
12  class Car {
13    double mpg;
14    String make;
15    String model;
16    double tankCapacity;
17
18    void printRange() {
19      double range = tankCapacity * mpg;
20      out.println("The range is " + range + " miles.");
21    }
22  }
```

Example 8.3. Instance methods.

```
The range is 714.0 miles.
```

The printRange() method is called using the class instance and dot notation, the same way you would access its instance variables. An instance's methods have direct access to its data members, so the dot notation isn't used within `printRange` when accessing `tankCapacity` and `mpg`.

The implementation in example 8.3 is better than that in example 8.2, because it's preferable to calculate the range within the "Car" class than in the `main` method of the "Test" class. In general, performing calculations related to the entity represented by a class should be within the class's code. This causes the code related to the class to be localized within the class, and makes it easier to maintain the application. If the vehicle's range was needed in two different places, each would call `printRange`, and the needed calculations would only exist in on place, within `printRange`. This is a special case of technique 2 on page 53, but deserves to be called out as its own technique:

Technique 11. Keep computations related to a class within the class

Keeping computations related to a class's functionality within the class promotes maintainability and modularity.

Example 8.3 is further refined in example 8.4, where `printRange` is replaced with `getRange`. The `main` method gets the range by calling `getRange` and then prints out the range instead of allowing an instance method of `Car` to print the range.

Example 8.4. User interaction in high-level code.

```
 1  public class Test {
 2    public static void main(String[] args) {
 3      Car car = new Car();
 4      car.mpg = 34;
 5      car.make = "Honda";
 6      car.model = "Civic";
 7      car.tankCapacity = 21;
 8      out.println("The range is " + car.getRange() + " miles.");
 9    }
10  }
11
12  class Car {
13    double mpg;
14    String make;
15    String model;
16    double tankCapacity;
17
18    double getRange() {
19      return tankCapacity * mpg;
20    }
21  }
```

```
The range is 714.0 miles.
```

Printing the range in `main` is better than printing it within a method belonging to the `Car` class. The reason has to do with reusability. Having a `getRange` method that returns the range allows more than one caller to get the range and print it out, or use it in other ways. In contrast, the `printRange` method of example 8.3 isn't as useful because it doesn't give the calling method the option of printing the range in a different way. In general, performing input and output within a class's instance methods makes code less reusable. Instead, input and output functionality should gravitate to high-level code, and algorithms should gravitate to low-level code. Low-level code is within classes, and should be more generic in nature, so that it can be more useful to a variety of callers. High-level code, in contrast, is code that utilizes classes to implement the high-level objectives of an application.

Caller: Colloquially, the code that calls a method.

Tip 7. As you work on your application, always maintain an awareness of which part of your code is high-level and which is low-level. As you gain experience, keeping your code organized will get easier.

Technique 12. Don't perform input or output in low-level code

A class's instance methods should allow the calling code to retrieve or change the class's data. User interaction (input and output) shouldn't be done at a low level, but rather at a higher level such as the `main` method. This makes a class's methods more reusable.

Exercises

8.3　Create a class that represents a baseball game. Add data elements for the two team names, number of innings, the first team's total runs and the second team's total runs. Add a method that returns the name of the winning team. Test the method to make sure it works.

8.4　Create a class that represents a calendar event. It should contain the event's name and the event's date (day, month and year). Add a method that tells the user how many days remain until the event occurs.

- Hint 1: Create two instances of the `java.time.LocalDate` class, one representing today's date, and one representing the calendar event's date.
- Hint 2: Get today's date with `LocalDate.now()`.

- Hint 3: Convert the event's date to a `LocalDate` using `LocalDate.of(year, month, day)`.
- Hint 4: You can get the number of days between two `LocalDate`s with the syntax `java.time.temporal.ChronoUnit.DAYS.between(date1, date2)`, which returns a long integer.

8.3 Constructors

A class in Java can be initialized more easily using a constructor, which is a special method that has the same name as the class and has no return type, not even `void`. The constructor's parameters provide initial data that is used by the constructor to initialize the instance data. Next, we revise example 8.4 by adding a constructor to the `Car` class, and using it to initialize the data instead of initializing each piece of data separately within the `main` method,

Example 8.5. Class constructors.

```java
public class Test {
  public static void main(String[] args) {
    Car car = new Car(34, "Honda", "Civic", 21);
    out.println("The range is " + car.getRange() + " miles.");
  }
}

class Car {
  double mpg;
  String make;
  String model;
  double tankCapacity;

  public Car(double mpg, String make, String model, double tankCapacity) {
    this.mpg = mpg;
    this.make = make;
    this.model = model;
    this.tankCapacity = tankCapacity;
  }

  double getRange() {
    return tankCapacity * mpg;
  }
}
```

```
The range is 714.0 miles.
```

The constructor is called when an object is created using the "new" keyword, as on line 3 of example 8.5, and the parameters provided in the object creation must match the parameters that the constructor expects.

Line 15 shows the initialization of the instance variable mpg using the parameter having the same name. Since the parameter mpg has the same name as the instance variable mpg, it *hides* it. All references to mpg within the constructor will refer to the parameter instead of the instance variable. But, the instance variable can still be accessed using the "this.mpg" notation. Thus, we initialize the instance variable with the syntax "this.mpg = mpg".

Identifier hiding: when an identifier from an enclosing scope isn't accessible because another variable having the same name is declared in an inner scope.

In the same way, the other three data members are initialized on lines 16-18. Thus, the `Car` constructor initializes all four instance variables using the data passed into the constructor as parameters. If needed, additional initialization can be performed within constructors, although we didn't need to do that in this example.

A constructor that takes no parameters is called the default constructor. It's called when you create an object with the syntax "new Car()". If you don't declare any constructors, a default constructor is implicitly created for you, which is why the code in example 8.1 is able to create a new `InventoryItem` object in the statement "InventoryItem item = new InventoryItem()".

Default constructor: The constructor that takes no parameters. If no constructors are defined, Java creates an implicit default constructor.

Multiple constructors can be declared when you want to provide different ways of creating objects of a class. Consider example 8.6 where the class allows a caller to create a `Car` object by specifying all four attributes, or just the make and model,

```
1  public class Test {
2    public static void main(String[] args) {
3      Car car1 = new Car(34, "Honda", "Civic", 21);
4      out.println("The " + car1.model + "'s range is " + car1.getRange() + "
         miles.");
5      Car car2 = new Car("Ford", "Fiesta");
6      out.println("The " + car2.model + "'s range is " + car2.getRange() + "
         miles.");
7    }
8  }
9
10 class Car {
11   double mpg;
12   String make;
13   String model;
14   double tankCapacity;
15
16   public Car(double mpg, String make, String model, double tankCapacity) {
17     this.mpg = mpg;
18     this.make = make;
19     this.model = model;
20     this.tankCapacity = tankCapacity;
```

Example 8.6. Multiple constructors.

```
21    }
22
23    public Car(String make, String model) {
24      this.mpg = 20; // default mpg is 20 miles per gallon
25      this.make = make;
26      this.model = model;
27      this.tankCapacity = 15; // default tank capacity is 15 gallons
28    }
29
30    double getRange() {
31      return tankCapacity * mpg;
32    }
33 }
```

```
The Civic's range is 714.0 miles.
The Fiesta's range is 300.0 miles.
```

When the caller (the `main` method in this case) uses the constructor that accepts only make and model, the mpg and tankCapacity attributes are initialized to default values.

It's good practice to declare values that don't change, such as the default mpg and tankCapacity, as named constants. Example 8.7 does just that,

Example 8.7. Using named constants.

```
1  class Car {
2    double mpg;
3    String make;
4    String model;
5    double tankCapacity;
6
7    final double DEFAULT_MPG = 20;
8    final double DEFAULT_TANK_CAPACITY = 15;
9
10   public Car(double mpg, String make, String model, double tankCapacity) {
11     this.mpg = mpg;
12     this.make = make;
13     this.model = model;
14     this.tankCapacity = tankCapacity;
15   }
16
17   public Car(String make, String model) {
18     this.mpg = DEFAULT_MPG;
19     this.make = make;
20     this.model = model;
21     this.tankCapacity = DEFAULT_TANK_CAPACITY;
22   }
23
24   double getRange() {
25     return tankCapacity * mpg;
26   }
27 }
```

```
The Civic's range is 714.0 miles.
The Fiesta's range is 300.0 miles.
```

Note the use of the `final` keyword, which indicates that the default values are *constants*, that is, they can't be changed after being assigned a value in the initialization on lines 7 and 8 of example 8.7. When a constant value is used in more than one place within a program, having it declared as a named constant helps by ensuring that its value is only specified in one place, an application of technique 5 on page 75.

Constants in Java are in uppercase with underscores by convention.

Technique 13. Use named constants

Use named constants for values that don't change.

The next example (8.8) further simplifies the code in example 8.7 by consolidating the repeated code within the two constructors of the `Car` class,

Example 8.8. Constructor chaining.

```
 1  class Car {
 2      double mpg;
 3      String make;
 4      String model;
 5      double tankCapacity;
 6
 7      static final double DEFAULT_MPG = 20;
 8      static final double DEFAULT_TANK_CAPACITY = 15;
 9
10      public Car(double mpg, String make, String model, double tankCapacity) {
11          this.mpg = mpg;
12          this.make = make;
13          this.model = model;
14          this.tankCapacity = tankCapacity;
15      }
16
17      public Car(String make, String model) {
18          this(DEFAULT_MPG, make, model, DEFAULT_TANK_CAPACITY);
19      }
20
21      double getRange() {
22          return tankCapacity * mpg;
23      }
24  }
```

```
The Civic's range is 714.0 miles.
The Fiesta's range is 300.0 miles.
```

There are two things to note about example 8.8,

- The constructor that accepts only make and model has *called* the constructor that accepts all four attributes as parameters. To call one constructor from another, the `this` keyword is used as the method name. By passing the default values for mpg and tank capacity on line 18, we've consolidated the repeated code in the two constructors by having the first constructor do the second constructor's work. This is another application of technique 5 on page 75.
- To use the named constants `DEFAULT_MPG` and `DEFAULT_TANK_-CAPACITY` as parameters to another constructor, we've had to add the `static` keyword to the two constants. The `static` keyword associates the constant with the class, and not the instance of the class. We'll explain the `static` keyword in detail later on, in section 9.6.

Constructor chaining: Having one constructor call another to increase code reuse and decrease code duplication.

This way of consolidating code within constructors by having one constructor call another is called *constructor chaining*. Any number of constructors can be chained, typically where each constructor calls the one that's slightly more specific.

> **The `this` keyword**
>
> Code within a class's methods can use the `this` keyword to refer to the object whose context the method is running in. Using "this." is like using the dot qualifier on an object reference. Thus, "car.mpg" in `main` is similar to using "this.mpg" in an instance method belonging to the `Car` class. The "this" keyword isn't needed except in certain situations,
>
> - The identifier being referenced is hidden by another identifier of the same name, as in "mpg" in the constructor on line 15 of example 8.5.
> - A constructor needs to call another constructor, as in example 8.8.

Exercises

8.5   Use example 8.8 as a starting point. Create an array of four cars in the `main` method. Add a method that takes an array of cars as a parameter, and returns the average miles per gallon for all of them. Print the average in the `main` method.

8.4 UML

The Unified Modeling Language (UML) Provides many types of diagrams that help document software programs. Its class diagram is a standard way to visually represent a class. It depicts the class's name, its attributes and their types, and its methods along with each method's return type and its parameters with the type of each parameter. Figure 8.1 shows a UML diagram of the `Car` class in example 8.8. The class name is at the top of the diagram. The next section shows the class's attributes, each with a name and a type. The final section of the diagram shows the class's methods, each with the method's name, return type, parameter names and the type of each parameter. The two constructors don't have a return type.

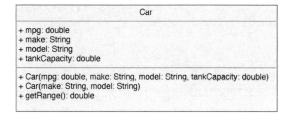

Figure 8.1: UML diagram of the `Car` class.

UML diagrams are commonly used to document a class so that consumers of that class know what it offers as far as attributes and methods. They can also be used to provide specifications for classes that a system requires, as documentation for the programmer who is tasked with implementing the class.

The excellent and free `https://diagrams.net` website supports various UML diagram types.

Chapter Summary

- A class encapsulates the data elements and code that relate to a particular domain entity. A class defines a type, and instances of that class can be created using the `new` keyword.
- A class can contain data elements and methods that operate on the data elements.

- A class's constructor is a special method that allows it to initialize its data. The caller can provide initial data values as arguments to the constructor.

```
1  public class Test {
2    public static void main(String[] args) {
3      Employee susan = new Employee(1001, "Susan");
4      out.println("Susan's information is: " + susan);
5    }
6  }
7
8  class Employee {
9
10   int id;
11   String name;
12
13   public Employee (int id, String name) {
14     this.id = id;
15     this.name = name;
16   }
17
18   @Override
19   public String toString() {
20     return name + " (ID " + id + ")";
21   }
22 }
```

Creating class instance

Class declaration

Class variables

Constructor

Exercise Solutions

8.1
```
1  class TelevisionProgram {
2    String title;
3    String genre;
4    int productionYear;
5    String[] actors;
6    String director;
7  }
```

8.2
```
1  class NewsStory {
2    String title;
3    String summary;
4    String author;
5    int publicationYear;
6  }
```

8.3
```
1  import static java.lang.System.out;
2
3  public class Test {
4    public static void main(String[] args) {
5      BaseballGame game = new BaseballGame();
6      game.team1Name = "Red Sox";
7      game.team2Name = "Yankees";
8      game.numberOfInnings = 11;
9      game.team1Runs = 3;
```

```
10      game.team2Runs = 4;
11
12      out.print("The winning team is: " + game.winningTeam());
13    }
14  }
15
16  class BaseballGame {
17    String team1Name, team2Name;
18    int numberOfInnings;
19    int team1Runs, team2Runs;
20
21    String winningTeam() {
22      if (team1Runs > team2Runs)
23        return team1Name;
24      else
25        return team2Name;
26    }
27  }
```

The winning team is: Yankees

8.4
```
1  import static java.lang.System.out;
2
3  import java.time.LocalDate;
4
5  public class Test {
6    public static void main(String[] args) {
7      Event event = new Event();
8      event.day = 1;
9      event.month = 1;
10     event.year = 2025;
11
12     out.print("Days until New Year's day 2025: " + event.daysUntil()
         );
13    }
14  }
15
16  class Event {
17    String name;
18    int day, month, year;
19
20    int daysUntil() {
21      LocalDate today = LocalDate.now();
22      LocalDate date = LocalDate.of(year, month, day);
23      return (int) java.time.temporal.ChronoUnit.DAYS.between(today,
         date);
24    }
25  }
```

Days until New Year's day 2025: 1419

8.5
```
1    public static void main(String[] args) {
2
3      Car[] carArray = {
4          new Car(34, "Honda", "Civic", 15),
5          new Car(39, "Toyota", "Corola", 16),
6          new Car(32, "Ford", "F350", 25),
7          new Car(26, "Jeep", "Cherokee", 21)
```

```
8      };
9      out.println("Average miles per gallon = " + AverageMpg (carArray
       ));
10  }
11
12  private static double AverageMpg (Car[] cars)
13  {
14    double total = 0;
15    for (Car car : cars)
16      total += car.getMpg();
17    return total / cars.length;
18  }
```

```
Average miles per gallon = 32.75
```

Inheritance | 9

9.1 Enumerations

An important Java feature we haven't seen yet is enumerations. An enumeration is a way to define a type whose instances can only have a certain set of possible values. For example, we could define an enumeration to represent a color,

```
enum Color { BLUE, RED, GREEN, YELLOW, MAGENTA, BLACK,
                 WHITE, GRAY };
```

By convention, enumeration values are uppercase, since they're essentially constants.

Having defined the Color enumeration, we can use it as a type,

```
Color backgroundColor = Color.GREEN;
```

This defines a variable called backgroundColor of type Color, and initializes its value to Color.GREEN. We would further be able to test an enum variable's value with an if or switch statement,

```
if (backgroundColor == Color.RED)
```

We could have used String as the type of this variable, but that wouldn't constrain the variable's possible values. By using an enumeration as the color variable's type, we guard against accidentally mistyping the color, and that reduces the number of bugs in the long run.

To show enumerations in action, the next example (9.1) has a class representing different types of employees,

Example 9.1. Using an enumeration.

```java
import static java.lang.System.out;

public class Test {
  public static void main(String[] args) {

    Employee susan = new Employee(1001, "Susan", EmployeeType.FULL_TIME, 52000,
      0, 0);
    Employee irene = new Employee(1002, "Irene", EmployeeType.FULL_TIME, 36000,
      0, 0);
    Employee phil = new Employee(1003, "Phil", EmployeeType.CONTRACT, 0, 40,
      45);
    Employee william = new Employee(1004, "William", EmployeeType.PART_TIME, 0,
      15, 28);

    out.printf("Susan's weekly salary is $%.2f\n", susan.getWeeklySalary());
    out.printf("Irene's weekly salary is $%.2f\n", irene.getWeeklySalary());
    out.printf("Phil's weekly salary is $%.2f\n", phil.getWeeklySalary());
    out.printf("William's weekly salary is $%.2f\n", william.getWeeklySalary())
      ;
  }
}

enum EmployeeType { FULL_TIME, PART_TIME, CONTRACT };

class Employee {

  EmployeeType type;
  int id;
  String name;
  int yearlySalary;   // for full-time employees
  int hourlySalary;   // for part-time and contract employees
  int hoursPerWeek;   // for part-time and contract employees
  double taxRate = 0.205; // for full-time and part-time employees

  public Employee (int id, String name, EmployeeType type, int yearlySalary,
      int hoursPerWeek, int hourlySalary) {
    this.id = id;
    this.name = name;
    this.type = type;
    this.yearlySalary = yearlySalary;
    this.hoursPerWeek = hoursPerWeek;
    this.hourlySalary = hourlySalary;
  }

  double getWeeklySalary () {
    switch (type) {
    case FULL_TIME:
      return (double) yearlySalary / 52 * (1 - taxRate);
    case PART_TIME:
      return (double) hoursPerWeek * hourlySalary * (1 - taxRate);
    case CONTRACT:
      return (double) hoursPerWeek * hourlySalary;
    default:
      return 0;
    }
  }
}
```

```
Susan's weekly salary is $795.00
Irene's weekly salary is $550.38
Phil's weekly salary is $1800.00
William's weekly salary is $333.90
```

The `Employee` class encapsulates data related to employees, such as ID and name, as well as algorithms such as the code that calculates weekly salary in `getWeeklySalary()`. In the example, only full-time and part-time employees have taxes deducted from their pay. In addition, only part-time and contract employees are paid by the hour. This is a good example of how to isolate code related to an entity (an employee in this case) within the class representing that entity.

The `EmployeeType` enumeration is defined on line 18 of example 9.1. Note the role that this enumeration plays in the example. It's used by the `Employee` class to define the employee's type, and to calculate weekly salaries appropriately for each type of employee. An invalid employee type, e.g., as a parameter to the `Employee` constructor on line 6, or in a case clause of the switch statement on line 40, will result in a compile-time error, so the syntactic support that enumerations provides is significant.

Finally, note the `default` clause of the `switch` statement within `getWeeklySalary`. Without it, Java generates a compile error because it's doesn't recognize that all possible enumeration values have been handled by the `switch`. It's awkward, but the only obvious alternatives are to add a "return 0;" after the `switch` or replace the `switch` statement with a series of `if` statements.

> **Object Oriented Programming**
>
> Java supports object oriented programming, as do many other languages including C++, from which Java is derived. Object oriented programming refers to arranging code in classes that represent real-world entities, which helps to keep related code together in the same area of a program.

9.2 Inheritance

A Java class can extend another, and when it does, it inherits all of the base class's data members and instance methods. This allows

Creating a new class by extending another is sometimes called *subclassing*. The new class is the subclass, and the class that has been extended is called the *superclass*, the *base class* or the *parent class*.

you to extend the functionality of a class without modifying that class. This is usually used to create a new class that represents a more specific entity than the entity that the parent class represents. For example, a class representing a vehicle can be extended by a class representing a sedan. Extending a class is accomplished with the following syntax,

```
class Sedan extends Vehicle { }
```

We'll demonstrate inheritance by transforming example 9.1 so that each of the employee types has its own class,

Example 9.2. Using inheritance.

```
1  import static java.lang.System.out;
2
3  public class Test {
4    public static void main(String[] args) {
5
6      FullTimeEmployee susan = new FullTimeEmployee(1001, "Susan", 52000);
7      FullTimeEmployee irene = new FullTimeEmployee(1002, "Irene", 36000);
8      ContractEmployee phil = new ContractEmployee(1003, "Phil", 40, 45);
9      PartTimeEmployee william = new PartTimeEmployee(1004, "William", 15, 28);
10
11     out.printf("Susan's weekly salary is $%.2f\n", susan.getWeeklySalary());
12     out.printf("Irene's weekly salary is $%.2f\n", irene.getWeeklySalary());
13     out.printf("Phil's weekly salary is $%.2f\n", phil.getWeeklySalary());
14     out.printf("William's weekly salary is $%.2f\n", william.getWeeklySalary())
         ;
15   }
16  }
17
18  class Employee {
19
20    int id;
21    String name;
22
23    public Employee (int id, String name) {
24      this.id = id;
25      this.name = name;
26    }
27  }
28
29  class FullTimeEmployee extends Employee {
30
31    int yearlySalary;
32    double taxRate = 0.205;
33
34    public FullTimeEmployee (int id, String name, int yearlySalary) {
35      super(id, name);
36      this.yearlySalary = yearlySalary;
37    }
38
39    double getWeeklySalary () {
40      return (double) yearlySalary / 52 * (1 - taxRate);
41    }
42  }
43
```

```
44  class PartTimeEmployee extends Employee {
45
46    int hourlySalary;
47    int hoursPerWeek;
48    double taxRate = 0.205;
49
50    public PartTimeEmployee (int id, String name, int hoursPerWeek, int
          hourlySalary) {
51      super(id, name);
52      this.hoursPerWeek = hoursPerWeek;
53      this.hourlySalary = hourlySalary;
54    }
55
56    double getWeeklySalary () {
57      return (double) hoursPerWeek * hourlySalary * (1 - taxRate);
58    }
59  }
60
61  class ContractEmployee extends Employee {
62
63    int hourlySalary;
64    int hoursPerWeek;
65
66    public ContractEmployee (int id, String name, int hoursPerWeek, int
          hourlySalary) {
67      super(id, name);
68      this.hoursPerWeek = hoursPerWeek;
69      this.hourlySalary = hourlySalary;
70    }
71
72    double getWeeklySalary () {
73      return (double) hoursPerWeek * hourlySalary;
74    }
75  }
```

```
Susan's weekly salary is $795.00
Irene's weekly salary is $550.38
Phil's weekly salary is $1800.00
William's weekly salary is $333.90
```

Note the following details concerning the class inheritance in example 9.2,

- There are three types that each extend `Employee`. The `Employee` base class contains data and functionality that is common to all employee types (in this case, the employee's ID and name).
- Each of the three derived types, `FullTimeEmployee`, `Part-TimeEmployee` and `ContractEmployee` inherit the `Employee` base class's data members (employee ID and name), and add their own data members, for example the yearly salary in the case of `FullTimeEmployee`.
- Each derived type's constructor calls the `Employee` constructor using the keyword `super`, passing it the parameters relevant

to the superclass. This is similar to the constructor chaining we saw earlier in chapter 8.

- Each derived type implements its own `getWeeklySalary` method, which is called from the `main` method.

Let us contrast examples 9.1 and 9.2 with respect to the distribution of data and code. When we switched to subclassing, the data and code specific to each type of employee migrated into the respective subclasses. This consolidated the data and code related to each subclass, but also broke apart the code which previously had computed weekly salaries for all employee types. We know from technique 2 on page 53 that related code should be together, so from first principles, it's not entirely clear that the move to subclassing is the better approach. There are pros and cons, as you can see, but on the whole it's better in example 9.2. It all depends on whether the new arrangement of data and code is more readable and more maintainable.

Exercises

9.1 Create classes for Animal, Dog, Cat and Mouse. The Dog, Cat and Mouse classes should extend Animal. Add a name variable to Animal. Add a method named speak() to each animal's class, which print out its sound. Create one object of each animal type, and make it speak.

9.3 The `Object` Class

You can have a class extend another, which itself extends a third class, and so on. Each subclass inherits all the data elements and methods in its direct superclass and each of its indirect superclasses.

In Java, all classes are ultimately derived from the built-in `Object` class, either directly or indirectly. If your class doesn't explicitly extend another class, it automatically extends the `Object` class. `Object` implements a small number of methods. A few of these are noteworthy:

- `toString()` returns a string representing the object, which is useful if you want to print the object to the console.

- `hashCode()` returns an integer that represents the object's data, and is meant to distinguish objects that contain different data. It's used internally in certain situations, and we'll deal with it in chapter 14.
- `equals()` returns true or false depending on whether the object's data is identical to the data within another object of the same type. For example, two strings should be compared for equality using the `equals()` method instead of the equality operator (==). We'll deal with `equals()` in chapter 14 as well.

Since every class extends `Object`, either directly or indirectly, every class inherits its methods, which includes `toString`. To see `toString` in action, let's print an employee's information,

```
1   ...
2     FullTimeEmployee susan = new FullTimeEmployee(1001, "Susan", 52000);
3     out.printf("Susan's information is: " + susan.toString());
4   ...
```

Example 9.3. Default `toString()`.

```
Susan's information is: FullTimeEmployee@4b1210ee
```

The output from example 9.3 shows the object's class name followed by its location in memory, which is the string that the `Object` class's `toString` implementation returns. The return value from the `toString` method is concatenated with the literal string by the + operator, after which the concatenated string is output by `printf`. Since the expression on the left of the + operator is a string, the operator converts the expression on its right to a string, so the explicit call to `toString` isn't actually necessary. If `susan.toString()` is replaced with `susan`, the `toString` method is invoked implicitly to convert the object to a string,

Calling `toString` implicitly.

```
1   ...
2     FullTimeEmployee susan = new FullTimeEmployee(1001, "Susan", 52000);
3     out.printf("Susan's information is: " + susan);
4   ...
```

Example 9.4. Implicitly calling `toString()`.

```
Susan's information is: FullTimeEmployee@4b1210ee
```

A class can choose to *override* a method that's defined by its superclass. In example 9.5, the `Employee` class overrides `toString` to provide a more appropriate representation of the object,

Overriding a method.

Example 9.5. Overriding `toString()`.

```
1  ...
2    FullTimeEmployee susan = new FullTimeEmployee(1001, "Susan", 52000);
3    out.printf("Susan's information is: " + susan);
4  ...
5  class Employee {
6
7    int id;
8    String name;
9
10   public Employee (int id, String name) {
11     this.id = id;
12     this.name = name;
13   }
14
15   @Override
16   public String toString() {
17     return name + " (ID " + id + ")";
18   }
19 }
20 ...
```

```
Susan's information is: Susan (ID 1001)
```

By providing its own implementation of the `toString` method, the `Employee` class has hidden the base class's implementation. When `printf` calls `toString`, the implementation within `Employee` is called, instead of the implementation in `Object`. Note the `@Override` keyword before the `toString` implementation, which tells Java that it's meant to override a method that's defined in the base class. The code will work without this `@Override` keyword, but in the presence of `@Override`, the compiler generates an error if there is no such method in the base class, which guards against a mistyped method name.

This isn't quite enough, as we want to add the data contained in `FullTimeEmployee`, not just `Employee`, so we must override `toString` in the `FullTimeEmployee` class, which is done in the next example (9.6),

Example 9.6. Chaining `toString()`.

```
1  ...
2  class FullTimeEmployee extends Employee {
3
4    int yearlySalary;
5    double taxRate = 0.205;
6
7    public FullTimeEmployee (int id, String name, int yearlySalary) {
8      super(id, name);
9      this.yearlySalary = yearlySalary;
10   }
11
12   double getWeeklySalary () {
13     return (double) yearlySalary / 52 * (1 - taxRate);
```

```
14    }
15
16    @Override
17    public String toString() {
18      return super.toString() + " [$" + yearlySalary + "/year]";
19    }
20 }
21 ...
```

```
Susan's information is: Susan (ID 1001) [$52000/year]
```

Note the new `toString` implementation in `FullTimeEmployee`, which calls its superclass's `toString` implementation, and adds its own information to it. Calling the superclass's `toString` implementation is done using the `super` keyword, just as we do in the constructor to call the base class's constructor. Without the `super` keyword, calling `toString` won't call the implementation within `Employee`, but rather will call the `toString` method in the `FullTimeEmployee` class. This is because defining `toString` in `Full-TimeEmployee` hides the base class's implementation of that same method.

Note that we could have output all the data items within the `toString` method of the `FullTimeEmployee` class, including data items defined in `Employee`. But it's better to structure our code as in the above example, so that code related to the `Employee`'s data is within the `Employee` class, in keeping with technique 11 on page 140.

After making a similar change in the other two classes, `PartTimeEmployee` and `ContractEmployee` to include hourly salary, our example is as follows,

```
1  import static java.lang.System.out;
2
3  public class Test {
4    public static void main(String[] args) {
5
6      FullTimeEmployee susan = new FullTimeEmployee(1001, "Susan", 52000);
7      FullTimeEmployee irene = new FullTimeEmployee(1002, "Irene", 36000);
8      ContractEmployee phil = new ContractEmployee(1003, "Phil", 40, 45);
9      PartTimeEmployee william = new PartTimeEmployee(1004, "William", 15, 28);
10
11     out.println("Susan's information is: " + susan);
12     out.println("Irene's information is: " + irene);
13     out.println("Phil's information is: " + phil);
14     out.println("William's information is: " + william);
15   }
16 }
17
```

Example 9.7. `Employee` example using `toString()`.

```
18  class Employee {
19
20    int id;
21    String name;
22
23    public Employee (int id, String name) {
24      this.id = id;
25      this.name = name;
26    }
27
28    @Override
29    public String toString() {
30      return name + " (ID " + id + ")";
31    }
32  }
33
34  class FullTimeEmployee extends Employee {
35
36    int yearlySalary;
37    double taxRate = 0.205;
38
39    public FullTimeEmployee (int id, String name, int yearlySalary) {
40      super(id, name);
41      this.yearlySalary = yearlySalary;
42    }
43
44    double getWeeklySalary () {
45      return (double) yearlySalary / 52 * (1 - taxRate);
46    }
47
48    @Override
49    public String toString() {
50      return super.toString() + " [$" + yearlySalary + "/year]";
51    }
52  }
53
54  class PartTimeEmployee extends Employee {
55
56    int hourlySalary;
57    int hoursPerWeek;
58    double taxRate = 0.205;
59
60    public PartTimeEmployee (int id, String name, int hoursPerWeek, int
        hourlySalary) {
61      super(id, name);
62      this.hoursPerWeek = hoursPerWeek;
63      this.hourlySalary = hourlySalary;
64    }
65
66    double getWeeklySalary () {
67      return (double) hoursPerWeek * hourlySalary * (1 - taxRate);
68    }
69
70    @Override
71    public String toString() {
72      return super.toString() + " [$" + hourlySalary + "/hour]";
73    }
74  }
75
76  class ContractEmployee extends Employee {
77
78    int hourlySalary;
```

```
79    int hoursPerWeek;
80
81    public ContractEmployee (int id, String name, int hoursPerWeek, int
          hourlySalary) {
82      super(id, name);
83      this.hoursPerWeek = hoursPerWeek;
84      this.hourlySalary = hourlySalary;
85    }
86
87    double getWeeklySalary () {
88      return (double) hoursPerWeek * hourlySalary;
89    }
90
91    @Override
92    public String toString() {
93      return super.toString() + " [$" + hourlySalary + "/hour]";
94    }
95 }
```

```
Susan's information is: Susan (ID 1001) [$52000/year]
Irene's information is: Irene (ID 1002) [$36000/year]
Phil's information is: Phil (ID 1003) [$45/hour]
William's information is: William (ID 1004) [$28/hour]
```

Figure 9.1 shows the UML diagram for the four classes in example 9.7. Inheritance is depicted with an arrow from the derived class to the extended class.

Exercises

9.2   Extend your solution to exercise 9.1 on page 156. Add a constructor that initializes the name, and override the toString method in Animal to print the animal's name. Create one object of each animal type, and print them out.

9.3   Extend your solution to exercise 9.2. Print the animal type along with the animal's name, and make each animal speak.

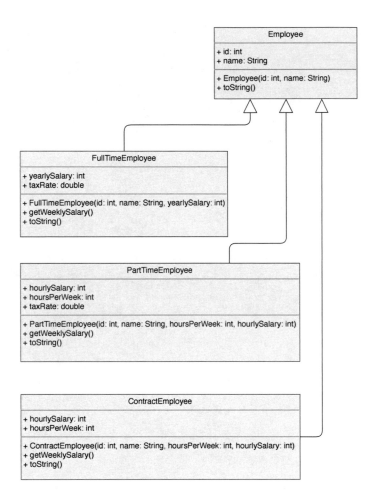

Figure 9.1: UML diagram of the Employee class and the classes that extend it.

9.4 Access Modifiers

Three common levels of access are provided by Java: `public`, `private` and `protected`. They're optionally used in the declaration of data elements and methods of a class.

- `public`: allows any code to access the data element or method.
- `private`: allows only code within the class itself to access the data element or method.
- `protected`: allows only code within the class or its subclasses to access the data element or method.

These access modifiers are meant to restrict access to certain data and functionality within a class in order to enforce a particular way of using the class or enforce rules imposed by the problem domain. The following example (9.8) illustrates this,

```
1   public static void main(String[] args) {
2      PartTimeEmployee william = new PartTimeEmployee(1004, "William", 15, 12);
3      out.println("William's information is: " + william);
4   }
5   ...
6   class PartTimeEmployee extends Employee {
7
8     final int MINIMUM_WAGE = 15;
9
10    private int hourlySalary;
11    private int hoursPerWeek;
12    private double taxRate = 0.205;
13
14    public PartTimeEmployee (int id, String name, int hoursPerWeek, int
          hourlySalary) {
15       super(id, name);
16       setHoursPerWeek(hoursPerWeek);
17       setHourlySalary(hourlySalary);
18    }
19
20    public int getHourlySalary () {
21       return hourlySalary;
22    }
23
24    public void setHourlySalary (int hourlySalary) {
25       if (hourlySalary < MINIMUM_WAGE)
26          hourlySalary = MINIMUM_WAGE;
27       this.hourlySalary = hourlySalary;
28    }
29
30    public int getHoursPerWeek () {
31       return hoursPerWeek;
32    }
33
34    public void setHoursPerWeek (int hoursPerWeek) {
35       this.hoursPerWeek = hoursPerWeek;
36    }
37
38    double getWeeklySalary () {
39       return (double) hoursPerWeek * hourlySalary * (1 - taxRate);
40    }
41
42    @Override
43    public String toString() {
44       return super.toString() + " [$" + hourlySalary + "/hour]";
45    }
46 }
```

Example 9.8. Defining getters and setters.

```
William's information is: William (ID 1004) [$15/hour]
```

Example 9.8 adds four new methods to the `PartTimeEmployee` class, two for each of the class variables `hourlySalary` and `hoursPer-Week`. For each of those variables, *get* and *set* methods have been defined. The *get* methods return the respective variables, and the

Defining *getters* and *setters*.

set methods modify the variables by assigning new values. For example, `getHourlySalary` returns the value of `hourlySalary` and `setHourlySalary` sets the value of `hourlySalary` to a new value. These methods are commonly known as *getters* and *setters*.

Also note in example 9.8 that the variables `hourlySalary` and `hoursPerWeek` are now `private`, while the getters and setters are `public`. The getters and setters can be used from outside the class, while code outside the class can't directly access the class variables. Thus, the getters and setters manage access to these variables. This is useful for two reasons,

This is an example of how object oriented techniques are meant to minimize the effects of future changes in the code.

- If the internal implementation of a particular algorithm changes, and a class's variables change as a result, the getters and setters can often be adjusted without changing their signatures. Since calling code, that is, code that uses the class, can't directly access the class variables and only uses the getters and setters, the programmer is guaranteed that his or her internal changes to the class won't result in external code having to be adjusted.

Depending on the problem domain, these domain rules are sometimes called *business rules*.

- If the particular problem domain has rules that the program needs to enforce, setters provide a place to consolidate the enforcement of those rules, and that way the programmer doesn't need to enforce the rules in each section of code where the relevant data value is changed. In the above example, `setHourlySalary` checks to make sure that the hourly salary is at least equal to the minimum wage.

Note that the constructor also calls the two setters. That way, each class variable is only modified directly in one place, the setter.

> **Technique 14. Use getters and setters to manage access to class variables**
>
> Getters and setters don't have to be used for every class variable, but they should be used when either of the above two benefits applies. This is subjective, and involves anticipating the future needs of your program.

UML diagrams document access levels. The plus or minus sign to the left of each attribute and method indicate a public or private access level, respectively.

9.5 Abstract Classes

An abstract class is one that represents a real-world entity that has multiple flavors, such as the `Employee` class in example 9.7. In example 9.7, Instances of the `Employee` class itself aren't created directly. We only create instances of the subclasses of `Employee`. Thus, `Employee` is only there to define the common attributes that its subclasses share. We'll illustrate how abstract classes are defined in Java with example 9.9,

```java
1   import static java.lang.System.out;
2
3   public class Test {
4     public static void main(String[] args) {
5
6       FullTimeEmployee susan = new FullTimeEmployee(1001, "Susan", 52000);
7       FullTimeEmployee irene = new FullTimeEmployee(1002, "Irene", 36000);
8       ContractEmployee phil = new ContractEmployee(1003, "Phil", 40, 45);
9       PartTimeEmployee william = new PartTimeEmployee(1004, "William", 15, 28);
10
11      out.println("Susan's information is: " + susan);
12      out.println("Irene's information is: " + irene);
13      out.println("Phil's information is: " + phil);
14      out.println("William's information is: " + william);
15    }
16  }
17
18  abstract class Employee {
19
20    int id;
21    String name;
22
23    public Employee (int id, String name) {
24      this.id = id;
25      this.name = name;
26    }
27
28    @Override
29    public String toString() {
30      return name + " (ID " + id + ")";
31    }
32
33    abstract double getWeeklySalary();
34  }
35
36  class FullTimeEmployee extends Employee {
37
38    int yearlySalary;
39    double taxRate = 0.205;
40
41    public FullTimeEmployee (int id, String name, int yearlySalary) {
42      super(id, name);
43      this.yearlySalary = yearlySalary;
44    }
45
46    double getWeeklySalary () {
47      return (double) yearlySalary / 52 * (1 - taxRate);
48    }
```

Example 9.9. Abstract classes.

```
49
50    @Override
51    public String toString() {
52      return super.toString() + " [$" + yearlySalary + "/year]";
53    }
54  }
55
56  class PartTimeEmployee extends Employee {
57
58    final int MINIMUM_WAGE = 15;
59
60    private int hourlySalary;
61    private int hoursPerWeek;
62    private double taxRate = 0.205;
63
64    public PartTimeEmployee (int id, String name, int hoursPerWeek, int
           hourlySalary) {
65      super(id, name);
66      setHoursPerWeek(hoursPerWeek);
67      setHourlySalary(hourlySalary);
68    }
69
70    public int getHourlySalary () {
71      return hourlySalary;
72    }
73
74    public void setHourlySalary (int hourlySalary) {
75      if (hourlySalary < MINIMUM_WAGE)
76        hourlySalary = MINIMUM_WAGE;
77      this.hourlySalary = hourlySalary;
78    }
79
80    public int getHoursPerWeek () {
81      return hoursPerWeek;
82    }
83
84    public void setHoursPerWeek (int hoursPerWeek) {
85      this.hoursPerWeek = hoursPerWeek;
86    }
87
88    double getWeeklySalary () {
89      return (double) hoursPerWeek * hourlySalary * (1 - taxRate);
90    }
91
92    @Override
93    public String toString() {
94      return super.toString() + " [$" + hourlySalary + "/hour]";
95    }
96  }
97
98  class ContractEmployee extends Employee {
99
100   int hourlySalary;
101   int hoursPerWeek;
102
103   public ContractEmployee (int id, String name, int hoursPerWeek, int
           hourlySalary) {
104     super(id, name);
105     this.hoursPerWeek = hoursPerWeek;
106     this.hourlySalary = hourlySalary;
107   }
108
```

```
109   double getWeeklySalary () {
110     return (double) hoursPerWeek * hourlySalary;
111   }
112
113   @Override
114   public String toString() {
115     return super.toString() + " [$" + hourlySalary + "/hour]";
116   }
117 }
```

```
Susan's information is: Susan (ID 1001) [$52000/year]
Irene's information is: Irene (ID 1002) [$36000/year]
Phil's information is: Phil (ID 1003) [$45/hour]
William's information is: William (ID 1004) [$28/hour]
```

Note that the `Employee` class now has the **abstract** keyword (line 18), and has the new `getWeeklySalary` method definition with the abstract keyword and no body (line 33). We say that the method `getWeeklySalary` is *abstract*, as it has no body defined, thus each non-abstract class derived from `Employee` must define it (otherwise, the compiler will generate an error). We also say that the `Employee` class is abstract, as it can't be instantiated directly. The main benefit of abstract classes is to declare the methods that must be implemented by concrete classes that extend the abstract class.

Concrete class: a class that is not abstract.

9.6 The Static Keyword

A static variable is a variable that doesn't belong to an *instance* of the class. Rather, it belongs to the class itself. The class doesn't need to have any instances defined in order for a static variable of that class to exist and hold a value. This is useful, for example, to define constants, such as `Math.PI`, which is a constant defined in the built-in `Math` class. To use `Math.PI`, we didn't have to create an instance of the `Math` class. Instead, to reference a static variable, constant or method in a class, we use the class name followed by a dot, then the name of the variable, constant or method.

Declaring a static variable or constant is done by adding the **static** keyword before the type of that variable or constant. Initialization of static variables or constants is accomplished with the usual initialization syntax. Note that static variables or constants are initialized when the program starts, as opposed to class variables which are initialized when each instance of the class is created.

Static methods are defined by adding the `static` keyword before the return type. Static methods can't refer to instance variables, since a static method isn't defined in the context of an instance, but rather in the context of the class itself. Static methods allow a class to offer functionality that doesn't require instance data. An example of this is the `Math.random()` method that we used in chapters 4 and 5. Here again, it's not necessary to create an instance of the `Math` class in order to use its static methods. We just prefix the static method's name with the class name. Example 9.10 defines a static method that converts miles per hour to kilometers per hour,

Example 9.10. Static methods.

```java
1  import static java.lang.System.out;
2  import java.util.Scanner;
3
4  public class Test {
5    public static void main(String[] args) {
6
7      Scanner input = new Scanner(System.in);
8      out.print("Enter miles per hour: ");
9      double milesPerHour = input.nextDouble();
10
11     out.printf("%.2f miles per hour is equal to %.2f kilometers per hour",
12         milesPerHour, Car.kmPerHour(milesPerHour));
13
14     input.close();
15   }
16  }
17
18  class Car {
19
20    public static double KM_PER_MILE = 1.60934;
21
22    public static double kmPerHour(double milesPerHour) {
23      return milesPerHour * KM_PER_MILE;
24    }
25  }
```

```
Enter miles per hour: 80
80.00 miles per hour is equal to 128.75 kilometers per hour
```

Chapter Summary

- Classes can extend one another. A class that extends another class inherits its data elements and functionality, and can override the base class's functionality with its own implementation.
- All classes ultimately extend the built-in `Object` class, either directly or indirectly.

- A class's data elements and methods can have access modifiers that prevent code outside the class from accessing them.

```
1  public class Test {
2    public static void main(String[] args) {
3      FullTimeEmployee susan = new FullTimeEmployee(1001, "Susan", 52000);
4      out.println("Susan's information is: " + susan);
5    }
6  }
7
8  class Employee {
9
10   int id;
11   String name;
12
13   public Employee (int id, String name) {
14     this.id = id;
15     this.name = name;
16   }
17
18   @Override
19   public String toString() {
20     return name + " (ID " + id + ")";
21   }
22 }
23
24 class FullTimeEmployee extends Employee {
25
26   int yearlySalary;
27   double taxRate = 0.205;
28
29   public FullTimeEmployee (int id, String name, int yearlySalary) {
30     super(id, name);
31     this.yearlySalary = yearlySalary;
32   }
33
34   double getWeeklySalary () {
35     return (double) yearlySalary / 52 * (1 - taxRate);
36   }
37
38   @Override
39   public String toString() {
40     return super.toString() + " [$" + yearlySalary + "/year]";
41   }
42 }
```

Labels: Creating class instance · Class declaration · Class variables · Constructor · Overriding base class method · One class extending another · Constructor chaining · Calling base class method

Exercise Solutions

9.1

```
1  ...
2    public static void main(String[] args) {
3      Cat cat = new Cat();
4      Mouse mouse = new Mouse();
5      Dog dog = new Dog ();
6
7      cat.speak();
8      mouse.speak();
9      dog.speak();
```

```
10   }
11 ...
12
13 class Animal {
14   String name;
15 }
16
17 class Cat extends Animal {
18   public void speak() {
19     out.println("meow!");
20   }
21 }
22
23 class Dog extends Animal {
24   public void speak() {
25     out.println("bark!");
26   }
27 }
28
29 class Mouse extends Animal {
30   public void speak() {
31     out.println("squeak!");
32   }
33 }
```

```
meow!
squeak!
bark!
```

9.2

```
 1 ...
 2   public static void main(String[] args) {
 3     Cat cat = new Cat("Skip");
 4     Mouse mouse = new Mouse("Flash");
 5     Dog dog = new Dog ("Trick");
 6
 7     out.println(cat);
 8     out.println(mouse);
 9     out.println(dog);
10   }
11 ...
12
13 class Animal {
14   String name;
15
16   public Animal (String name) {
17     this.name = name;
18   }
19
20   @Override
21   public String toString() {
22     return "name=" + name;
23   }
24 }
25
26 class Cat extends Animal {
27   public Cat (String name) {
28     super (name);
29   }
30
31   public void speak() {
32     out.println("meow!");
```

```
33        }
34      }
35
36      class Dog extends Animal {
37        public Dog (String name) {
38          super (name);
39        }
40
41        public void speak() {
42          out.println("bark!");
43        }
44      }
45
46      class Mouse extends Animal {
47        public Mouse (String name) {
48          super (name);
49        }
50
51        public void speak() {
52          out.println("squeak!");
53        }
54      }
```

```
name=Skip
name=Flash
name=Trick
```

9.3

```
 1      ...
 2        public static void main(String[] args) {
 3          Cat cat = new Cat("Skip");
 4          Mouse mouse = new Mouse("Flash");
 5          Dog dog = new Dog ("Trick");
 6
 7          out.println(cat);
 8          cat.speak();
 9          out.println(mouse);
10          mouse.speak();
11          out.println(dog);
12          dog.speak();
13        }
14      ...
15
16      class Animal {
17        String name;
18
19        public Animal (String name) {
20          this.name = name;
21        }
22
23        @Override
24        public String toString() {
25          return "name=" + name;
26        }
27      }
28
29      class Cat extends Animal {
30        public Cat (String name) {
31          super (name);
32        }
33
34        @Override
```

```
35    public String toString() {
36      return "Cat: " + super.toString();
37    }
38
39    public void speak() {
40      out.println("meow!");
41    }
42  }
43
44  class Dog extends Animal {
45    public Dog (String name) {
46      super (name);
47    }
48
49    @Override
50    public String toString() {
51      return "Dog: " + super.toString();
52    }
53
54    public void speak() {
55      out.println("bark!");
56    }
57  }
58
59  class Mouse extends Animal {
60    public Mouse (String name) {
61      super (name);
62    }
63
64    @Override
65    public String toString() {
66      return "Mouse: " + super.toString();
67    }
68
69    public void speak() {
70      out.println("squeak!");
71    }
72  }
```

```
Cat: name=Skip
meow!
Mouse: name=Flash
squeak!
Dog: name=Trick
bark!
```

10.1 The `ArrayList` Class

The size of a native array in Java can't be changed after it's been created. An array is allocated with a particular size, and any attempt to read or write past the end of the array results in an `ArrayIndex-OutOfBoundsException`. This can be seen in example 10.1,

```java
import static java.lang.System.out;

public class Test {
  public static void main(String[] args) {

    String[] names = new String[3];
    names[0] = "Corrine";
    names[1] = "Steph";
    names[2] = "Zoe";
    names[3] = "Krich";

    out.print("The first name is: " + names[0]);
  }
}
```

Example 10.1. Writing past the end of an array.

```
Exception in thread "main" java.lang.ArrayIndexOutOfBoundsException: Index 3 out of bounds for length 3
        at Test.main(Test.java:10)
```

Example 10.1 creates an array of three strings. After writing the three strings, it attempts to write a fourth string, which causes the exception on line 10, as seen in the output. The string `names` in the example is a *native* Java array. Java provides a collection class called `ArrayList` which is more convenient than native arrays when the size of the data can change at runtime. This class contains a native array internally, and the class resizes that native array when needed, so that the array can grow dynamically. It resizes the native array by allocating a new, larger, native array and copying the contents of the existing array to the new one. Using an `ArrayList` is slightly different than using a native array because different syntax is required, but most of the concepts involved are the same. Example 10.1 can be rewritten as in example 10.2 to use the `ArrayList` class,

Example 10.2. Using `ArrayList`.

```
1  import static java.lang.System.out;
2  import java.util.ArrayList;
3
4  public class Test {
5    public static void main(String[] args) {
6
7      ArrayList<String> names = new ArrayList<>();
8      names.add("Corrine");
9      names.add("Steph");
10     names.add("Zoe");
11     names.add("Krich");
12
13     out.print("The first name is: " + names.get(0));
14   }
15 }
```

```
The first name is: Corrine
```

`ArrayList` is one of Java's collection classes, and we'll have more to say about the rest of the collection classes later. The `names` variable is now a collection, that is, it's a reference to an object of the `ArrayList` class. Note the following differences between examples 10.1 and 10.2,

- The native array and the collection are declared differently:
  - The native array is declared with the syntax

    `String[] names`

    This declares `names` as a reference to an array of `String` objects.
  - The collection is declared with the syntax

    `ArrayList<String> names`

    This declares `names` as a reference to an object of type `ArrayList<String>`. This is read as "array list of strings", where `ArrayList` is a parameterized class, and `String` is the parameter. We'll explain parameterized classes later in this chapter.
- The native array and the collection are created differently:
  - The native array is created with the syntax

    `new String[3]`

    This allocates an array of three `String` references.
  - The collection is created with the syntax

```
new ArrayList<>()
```

This creates an object of type `ArrayList<String>`.

- The native array is created with a specific size of 3, and can't grow beyond that. The collection is created with an initial size of zero, and can grow to an unlimited size, constrained only by the available memory space.
- We write to the native array with the syntax `names[0] = "Corrine"`, using the index to specify the array element that we want to write to. In contrast, we add items to the collection using the `add` method.
- We read from the native array with the syntax `names[0]`. In contrast, we read from the collection using the `get` method.

As you see, declaring a collection, allocating it, writing to it and reading from it all use syntax that is different from the syntax you use when working with arrays, but conceptually the two are similar in that we allocate a variable to hold strings, and then write strings and read them. The main difference is that we don't need to track the maximum size of a collection, since it will grow as needed. But, we still need to take into account the *current* size of a collection, and if we attempt to read beyond the current size, a runtime exception will occur.

The current size of an `ArrayList` is retrieved with the `size` method (as opposed to using `.length` for arrays). Consider the following example (10.3) which reads an arbitrary number of integers from the user, and then outputs the sum of those numbers,

```
1   Scanner input = new Scanner(System.in);
2   ArrayList<Integer> numbers = new ArrayList<>();
3   int number = 0;
4   do {
5     out.print("Enter a number (-1 to exit): ");
6     number = input.nextInt();
7     input.nextLine();
8     if (number != -1)
9       numbers.add(number);
10  } while (number != -1);
11
12  int sum = 0;
13  for (int i = 0; i < numbers.size(); i++)
14    sum += numbers.get(i);
15  out.println("The sum is " + sum);
16
17  input.close();
```

Example 10.3. Processing an arbitrary number of integers.

```
Enter a number (-1 to exit): 13
Enter a number (-1 to exit): 14
Enter a number (-1 to exit): 15
Enter a number (-1 to exit): -1
The sum is 42
```

Example 10.3 creates a collection of integers then asks the user to enter numbers one after another. The user can enter −1 to terminate the loop, after which the sum of all numbers that were entered will be displayed. Note that the loop on lines 13 and 14 looks the same as many looping examples we've already seen, except that the collection's size is retrieved using the `size` method, and the elements of the collection are retrieved with the `get` method. However, the loop's essence remains the same as loops we've already written, and we track and use array indexes in the same way.

Writing to an existing index in a collection.

We saw how to add new items to the end of a collection using the `add` method. We haven't yet seen how to modify existing elements of a collection. That's easy to do with the `set` method, which takes two parameters, the index to write to, and the data to write to that index in the collection.

Exercises

10.1   Create an `ArrayList` of strings and try to add an integer to it. Does this result in a compile-time error, or run-time error?

10.2   Create an `ArrayList` of ten random numbers between 1 and 50. Then, iterate over the `ArrayList` and compute their average.

10.2 Generics

Generic classes, or *generics* for short, are classes that accept one or more parameters, the parameters themselves being classes. Java's collection classes are examples of such parameterized types. As seen in the previous section, `ArrayList` accepts a type as a parameter, which is the type of item to be held in the collection. The parameter must be a class, and can't be a native type, thus `ArrayList<Integer>` is a valid type definition, but `ArrayList<int>` is not. `Integer` is what we call a wrapper class. It's a class that encapsulates an integer value and provides additional useful functionality, such as the

`Integer.parseInt` method that we used in chapter 2. Table 10.1 shows some of the available wrapper classes that Java provides,

Native Type	Wrapper Class
`int`	`Integer`
`long`	`Long`
`float`	`Float`
`double`	`Double`
`char`	`Character`
`boolean`	`Boolean`

Table 10.1: Wrapper classes.

When creating an instance of a generic class, the syntax is `new ArrayList<Integer>()`, but `new ArrayList<>()` is also permitted, since the compiler can infer the parameter's type from the type of reference the collection will be assigned to. Thus the statement:

```
ArrayList<Integer> numbers = new ArrayList<>();
```

creates a new `ArrayList<Integer>` and assigns it to `numbers`, which is a reference to an `ArrayList<Integer>`.

Java uses the type's parameter (`Integer` in the above example) to enforce at compile time the parameter types for the collection's `add` and `set` methods, and the return type of the `get` method. In the case of an `ArrayList<Integer>`, the `add` method accepts a parameter of type `Integer`, and the `get` method returns a value of type `Integer`. Looking at the UML class definition for `ArrayList` in figure 10.1, you can see the type parameter is referred to simply as `E`.

`E` and `T` are common placeholders for the class parameter.

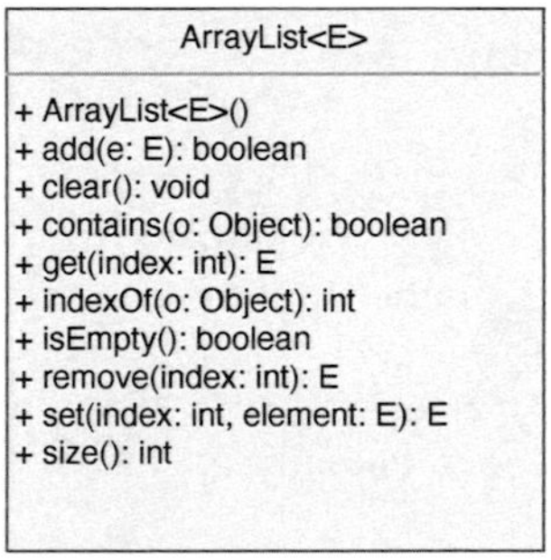

```
ArrayList<E>
─────────────────────────────
+ ArrayList<E>()
+ add(e: E): boolean
+ clear(): void
+ contains(o: Object): boolean
+ get(index: int): E
+ indexOf(o: Object): int
+ isEmpty(): boolean
+ remove(index: int): E
+ set(index: int, element: E): E
+ size(): int
```

Figure 10.1: `ArrayList`'s partial class diagram.

While the class diagram for `ArrayList` has the placeholder `E` in place of the actual type parameter, your code will specify an actual type for the parameter and Java reflects that in the compilation and the editor's autocompletion support, which you can see in figure 10.2, where Eclipse shows that **add** accepts one parameter of type `Integer`,

```
8       Scanner input = new Scanner(System.in);
9       ArrayList<Integer> numbers = new ArrayList<>();
10      int number = 0;
11      do {
12          out.print("Enter a number (-1 to exit): ");
13          number = input.nextInt();
14          input.nextLine();
15          if (number != -1)
16              numbers.add(number);
17      } while (number    ● add(Integer e) : boolean - ArrayList
18                         ● add(int index, Integer element) : void - ArrayList
19      int sum = 0;        ● addAll(Collection<? extends Integer> c) : boolean - ArrayL
20      for (int i = 0;    ● addAll(int index, Collection<? extends Integer> c) : boolea
21          sum += numbe   ● clear() : void - ArrayList
22      out.println("The   ● clone() : Object - ArrayList
23                         ● contains(Object o) : boolean - ArrayList
24      input.close();
25      }
```

Figure 10.2: Eclipse's autocompletion helper shows the declared parameter type.

Figure 10.1 shows some of `ArrayList`'s most important methods. Let's take a closer look at them,

You don't need to memorize these, but you should remember that they are there, so you can look up their details later when you need to use them. You will eventually use all of these methods.

- **add** takes one parameter, the new element to add to the list. It appends the item to the end of the list, increasing the list's size by one, and returns `true`.
- **clear** removes all items from the list.
- **contains** returns true or false depending on whether a specific item is in the list or not.
- **get** takes an index, and returns the element at that index in the list.
- **indexOf** takes an item and returns the first index at which that item occurs in the list, or -1 if the item isn't in the list.
- **isEmpty** returns `true` or `false` depending on whether the list is empty or not.
- **remove** takes an index and removes the element at that index, returning it.
- **set** takes an index and an item to insert at that index. It returns the element that was previously at that index.
- **size** returns the number of elements currently in the list.

You can create your own generic classes if you need to. Example 10.4 is a generic class that remembers the last three items that it's given,

Example 10.4. Defining your own generic class.

```
1  class LimitedMemory <E> {
2    private E item1 = null, item2 = null, item3 = null;
3
4    public void remember(E newItem) {
5      item3 = item2;
6      item2 = item1;
```

```
 7      item1 = newItem;
 8    }
 9
10    public ArrayList<E> getLastThree() {
11      ArrayList<E> result = new ArrayList<>();
12      result.add(item3);
13      result.add(item2);
14      result.add(item1);
15      return result;
16    }
17  }
```

The class definition **class LimitedMemory** is followed by the type
parameter **<E>**, and the type **E** is used within the class as the type of
three data items that this class can remember. The caller can keep
sending it new items to remember, but it will only remember the last
three items it has been given. The method **getLastThree** returns
these three in an **ArrayList**. Now we can use this class to remember
items of different types, as in example 10.5,

```
 1   Scanner input = new Scanner(System.in);
 2
 3   LimitedMemory<Integer> memory = new LimitedMemory<>();
 4   int number = 0;
 5   do {
 6     out.print("Enter a number (-1 to exit): ");
 7     number = input.nextInt();
 8     input.nextLine();
 9     if (number != -1)
10       memory.remember(number);
11   } while (number != -1);
12   out.println("The last three are: " + memory.getLastThree());
13   out.println();
14
15   LimitedMemory<String> memory2 = new LimitedMemory<>();
16   String name = "";
17   do {
18     out.print("Enter a name ('exit' to exit): ");
19     name = input.nextLine();
20     if (!name.equals("exit"))
21       memory2.remember(name);
22   } while (!name.equals("exit"));
23   out.println("The last three are: " + memory2.getLastThree());
24
25   input.close();
```

Example 10.5. Using your own
generic class.

```
Enter a number (-1 to exit): 91
Enter a number (-1 to exit): 24
Enter a number (-1 to exit): -3
Enter a number (-1 to exit): 75
Enter a number (-1 to exit): 200
Enter a number (-1 to exit): -1
The last three are: [-3, 75, 200]

Enter a name ('exit' to exit): Larry
Enter a name ('exit' to exit): Bill
Enter a name ('exit' to exit): Nitro
Enter a name ('exit' to exit): Wolf
Enter a name ('exit' to exit): Yuri
Enter a name ('exit' to exit): exit
The last three are: [Nitro, Wolf, Yuri]
```

There are some things you aren't allowed to do within generic types, such as creating a new instance of the generic type E, and creating an array of the generic type E.

You probably won't need to define your own generic types often. Rather, you'll use them mostly by consuming the generic collection classes. Still, you should know that it's possible to create your own generics if you need to.

10.3 Iterating Over an ArrayList

There are several ways to iterate over an ArrayList collection.

for Loop

We saw in example 10.3 how to use a for-loop to get the sum of numbers in a list. Example 10.6 creates ten random numbers between 1 and 100, adds them to a list, then uses a for loop to print them out, followed by another for loop to compute the sum,

Example 10.6. Iterating over a list using a for loop.

```java
1   import static java.lang.System.out;
2   import java.util.ArrayList;
3
4   public class Test {
5     public static void main(String[] args) {
6
7       // generate 10 random numbers, each between 1 and 100
8       ArrayList<Integer> numbers = new ArrayList<>();
9       for (int i = 0; i < 10; i++)
10        numbers.add((int) (Math.random() * 100) + 1);
11
12      printNumbers(numbers);
13      out.println("The sum is " + getSum(numbers));
14    }
```

```
15
16    public static void printNumbers(ArrayList<Integer> numbers) {
17      out.print("The list is ");
18      for (int i = 0; i < numbers.size(); i++)
19        out.print(numbers.get(i) + " ");
20      out.println();
21    }
22
23    public static int getSum(ArrayList<Integer> numbers) {
24      int sum = 0;
25      for (int i = 0; i < numbers.size(); i++)
26        sum += numbers.get(i);
27      return sum;
28    }
29 }
```

```
The list is 8 23 69 34 62 48 43 44 19 44
The sum is 394
```

Enhanced `for` Loop Syntax

The alternate `for` syntax that we first saw in example 6.14 can also be used to iterate through lists. This is called the *enhanced* for-loop syntax. Example 10.7 revises example 10.6 to use the enhanced `for` syntax,

```
1    public static void printNumbers(ArrayList<Integer> numbers) {
2      out.print("The list is ");
3      for (int number : numbers)
4        out.print(number + " ");
5      out.println();
6    }
7
8    public static int getSum(ArrayList<Integer> numbers) {
9      int sum = 0;
10     for (int number : numbers)
11       sum += number;
12     return sum;
13   }
```

Example 10.7. Iterating over a list using the enhanced `for` syntax.

```
The list is 34 24 87 7 55 74 79 60 26 54
The sum is 500
```

Using Iterators

An iterator is a class that helps us to iterate over the contents of a collection. The `iterator` method of the `ArrayList` class returns an object that is used to do the iteration. The iterator class has a `next` method that returns the next item in the collection, and a `hasNext` method that returns "true" as long as there are items remaining to be processed. Using an iterator is illustrated in the next example (10.8),

Example 10.8. Iterating over a list using an iterator class.

```
1  import java.util.Iterator;
2  ...
3    public static void printNumbers(ArrayList<Integer> numbers) {
4      out.print("The list is ");
5      Iterator<Integer> iterator = numbers.iterator();
6      while (iterator.hasNext())
7        out.print(iterator.next() + " ");
8      out.println();
9    }
10
11   public static int getSum(ArrayList<Integer> numbers) {
12     int sum = 0;
13     Iterator<Integer> iterator = numbers.iterator();
14     while (iterator.hasNext())
15       sum += iterator.next();
16     return sum;
17   }
```

```
The list is 85 20 84 56 99 98 28 22 21 79
The sum is 592
```

Note that the iterator class is generic. Since `numbers` is of type `ArrayList<Integer>`, its `iterator` method on lines 5 and 13 each return an iterator of type `Iterator<Integer>`. The `while` loops continue calling `iterator.next()` until `iterator.hasNext()` returns false. The `next` method returns the next element of the list, in this case an `Integer` value.

Using `forEach`

The last way that we'll show to iterate over a list is to use its `forEach` method. This method takes a single parameter which contains a method. `forEach` will call this method once for each item contained in the list. The method receives the data item (of type `Integer` in this case) as a parameter, and can perform operations on that parameter. Example 10.9 shows this in action,

```
1   public static void printNumbers(ArrayList<Integer> numbers) {
2     out.print("The list is ");
3     numbers.forEach((e) -> { out.print(e + " "); });
4     out.println();
5   }
6
7   private static int sum = 0;
8   public static int getSum(ArrayList<Integer> numbers) {
9     numbers.forEach((e) -> { sum += e; });
10    return sum;
11  }
```

Example 10.9. Iterating over a list using `forEach`.

```
The list is 38 68 41 33 50 74 58 82 44 63
The sum is 551
```

As mentioned above, the parameter to `forEach` contains a method. The syntax `(e) -> { out.print(e + " "); }` is called a *lambda expression*, or *lambda* for short, which is code that is passed around like data. The syntax is shorthand for a method that takes a single parameter called `e`, and executes the statements contained within the curly braces. It's important for you to eventually be comfortable with lambda expressions, but it's more important for us at this point to focus on the basics. For that reason, this technique should be considered less important than the above three iteration techniques.

Lambda expression: a piece of code that's passed around like data.

The way `forEach` is being used to print the list is fine, but there's a problem with the way it's being used to compute the sum. The sum variable is declared as static because it can't be a local variable within `getSum`. If declared as a local variable in `getSum`, we get a compile-time error stating that accessing a variable declared in an enclosing scope from within this lambda expression requires it to be declared as `final`, which wouldn't work in our case because we need to increment the `sum` variable. Having `sum` as static at the class level lets us access it from within the lambda expression, because it technically wouldn't be in an enclosing scope. But the problem with using a static variable in this way is that there's only one instance of this variable, effectively making it a global variable. Unless you are using global variables as a place to store global settings, they're undesirable for two reasons,

Global variable: A variable that's available to all the code within a program. Using global variables tends to make tracing code dependencies more difficult.

Local variable: A variable that's defined in a local scope, such as a method.

- Global variables can be accessed from anywhere, so they can create a situation with subtle dependencies between different parts of a program. To reduce complexity and increase maintainability, we want different parts of the program to be self contained and independent, to the extent possible.

- If the `getSum` method was running more than once in parallel, it wouldn't work because all running instances share the same sum value. A single method can run multiple times in parallel if your code is multithreaded, such as code running on a web server with multiple web requests being processed simultaneously. A piece of code that uses a global variable in this way is called *non-reentrant*.

Technique 15. Avoid using global variables

Global variables should be avoided unless they hold data that's meant to be shared, such as global settings.

Now that we've explained why the code in example 10.9 is undesirable, we can show a slightly more complex implementation that doesn't have the drawback of using a static variable,

Example 10.10. Second attempt of iterating over a list using `forEach`.

```
1   public static void printNumbers(ArrayList<Integer> numbers) {
2       out.print("The list is ");
3       numbers.forEach((e) -> { out.print(e + " "); });
4       out.println();
5   }
6
7   public static int getSum(ArrayList<Integer> numbers) {
8       final ArrayList<Integer> sumList = new ArrayList<>();
9       sumList.add(0);
10      numbers.forEach((e) -> { sumList.set(0, sumList.get(0) + e); });
11      return sumList.get(0);
12  }
```

```
The list is 88 38 24 5 98 50 60 45 31 95
The sum is 534
```

The code in `getSum` within example 10.10 effectively uses an `ArrayList` as a container to hold the sum. It can be declared as `final` while still allowing the lambda expression's code to update its contents.

Exercises

10.3 Create an `ArrayList` of student names, and another `ArrayList` of grades, one grade per student. Iterate over both lists, and print each student's name with his or her grade on a separate line.

10.4 Modify your program from the previous exercise. Create a `Student` class that contains the student's name and grade. Create an `ArrayList` of `Student` objects and print each student's name with his or her grade on a separate line.

10.4 Example Project: Flight Database

We've got enough under our belt to attempt a slightly larger project now, putting together many of the concepts we've already learned. Along the way, we'll discuss some common practices with regard to the process of making software.

We'll write a program that allows the user to track airline flights, with features such as searching for flight by flight number or by destination. The program won't actually save the flights to a database (we'll add that in chapter 12).

It's important to keep in mind the phases of a project. First you should identify the requirements, then design the implementation, and finally implement the program.

The first thing to do is identify the list of features that your program needs. This shouldn't include technical details. It's a list of requirements. In the real world, sometimes you are given the requirements, and sometimes it's up to you to elicit them. Either way, it's important to have the requirements in writing, so that there's no ambiguity and you have a clear task to accomplish. Requirements shouldn't be too elaborate. Keep it brief and to the point. For this example project, we'll use the following list of features:

- The user can add a new flight to the flight list.
- The user can delete a flight from the flight list.
- The user can change a flight's details.

CRUD is a commonly used acronym that refers to the four basic operations offered in a software application, the ability to *create*, *read*, *update* and *delete* records.

- The user can display all flights.
- The user can look up a flight by airline and flight number.
- The user can search for flights by destination.
- Each flight record contains the airline, flight number, origin, destination, departure time, and arrival time.
- The program assumes every flight flies daily.

Just as you shouldn't start the coding before identifying the requirements, you shouldn't start coding before designing your program. The design doesn't contain requirements. Rather, it documents how each requirement will be implemented. As with the requirements, it should be brief and to the point. It's also important not to spend too much time on the design. It's just a starting point. As you write the code, your plan will often change, which is okay. The design doesn't have to conform to a specific format or list the design points in a specific order. Here's our design for implementing the above list of requirements,

- Repeatedly present a menu of choices with options for adding a flight, deleting a flight, changing a flight, displaying all flights, searching by flight number, searching by destination, and exiting from the program.
- Use three-letter airport codes for origin and destination.
- Create a class, `Flight`, to represent a flight.
- Use an `ArrayList` of `Flight` objects to contain the flights.
- The flights in the `ArrayList` aren't sorted in a particular order.
- When adding a new flight, gather the flight's data from the user and add the new `Flight` object to the `ArrayList`. Don't allow the user to add the flight if there's already a flight with the same airline and flight number.
- When deleting a flight, ask for the airline and flight number, locate the flight object's index in the `ArrayList`, then delete it using the index.
- Use hour and minute for the departure and arrival times.
- When changing a flight's details, ask for the airline and flight number, locate the flight in the `ArrayList`, then change the object's details. Don't allow the change if there's another flight in the list with the same airline and flight number.

Note that the design adds technical details, such as the class name (`Flight`) and the collection class to use (`ArrayList`). It also adds some details which may sound like requirements but weren't listed in the requirement list. For example, the design stipulates that no two flights in the list can have the same airline and flight number. It's okay to add details such as these as long as you notify the domain experts so that they can correct you if your assumption is wrong.

Although the design looks like a list of tasks, it's unordered. It also contains many details that aren't themselves tasks. So it's helpful to write down an abbreviated list of tasks in the order that you think will be easiest to implement,

- Write the `Flight` class.
- Create the application class and add a loop that displays the menu.
- Add the 'add flight' feature.
- Add the 'display all flights' feature.
- Add the 'look up by airline and flight number' feature.
- Add the 'delete flight' feature.
- Add the 'change a flight' feature.
- Add the 'search by destination' feature.

The above process is designed to help you think through the project. At this point, we have a good idea what code is needed, and a roadmap to write it. The first part is the `Flight` class, shown in example 10.11.

Getters and Setters

In most of our examples, we gloss over the use of getters and setters, to save some space. Since this is a larger example project, we will define getters and setters in the `Flight` class, and mark the instance variables as `private`.

Separate Java Files

In most of our examples, we have multiple Java classes in the same Java file, to keep things simple. Since this is a larger example project, we will put the `Flight` class in its own file, and mark it as `public`.

```
1  public class Flight {
2      public String origin;
3      public String destination;
4      public String airline;
5      public int flightNumber;
6      public int departureHour, departureMinute;
```

Example 10.11. The `Flight` class in `Flight.java`.

```
 7    public int arrivalHour, arrivalMinute;
 8
 9    public Flight (String origin, String destination, String airline,
10        int flightNumber, int departureHour, int departureMinute,
11        int arrivalHour, int arrivalMinute) {
12      this.origin = origin;
13      this.destination = destination;
14      this.airline = airline;
15      this.flightNumber = flightNumber;
16      this.departureHour = departureHour;
17      this.departureMinute = departureMinute;
18      this.arrivalHour = arrivalHour;
19      this.arrivalMinute = arrivalMinute;
20    }
21
22    public String getOrigin() {
23      return origin;
24    }
25
26    public void setOrigin(String origin) {
27      this.origin = origin;
28    }
29
30    public String getDestination() {
31      return destination;
32    }
33
34    public void setDestination(String destination) {
35      this.destination = destination;
36    }
37
38    public String getAirline() {
39      return airline;
40    }
41
42    public void setAirline(String airline) {
43      this.airline = airline;
44    }
45
46    public int getFlightNumber() {
47      return flightNumber;
48    }
49
50    public void setFlightNumber(int flightNumber) {
51      this.flightNumber = flightNumber;
52    }
53
54    public int getDepartureHour() {
55      return departureHour;
56    }
57
58    public void setDepartureHour(int departureHour) {
59      this.departureHour = departureHour;
60    }
61
62    public int getDepartureMinute() {
63      return departureMinute;
64    }
65
66    public void setDepartureMinute(int departureMinute) {
67      this.departureMinute = departureMinute;
68    }
```

```
69
70    public int getArrivalHour() {
71      return arrivalHour;
72    }
73
74    public void setArrivalHour(int arrivalHour) {
75      this.arrivalHour = arrivalHour;
76    }
77
78    public int getArrivalMinute() {
79      return arrivalMinute;
80    }
81
82    public void setArrivalMinute(int arrivalMinute) {
83      this.arrivalMinute = arrivalMinute;
84    }
85
86    @Override
87    public String toString() {
88      return String.format("%s %d (%s %02d:%02d -> %s %02d:%02d)", airline,
        flightNumber, origin, departureHour, departureMinute, destination,
        arrivalHour, arrivalMinute);
89    }
90 }
```

Note that we're using the static method `String.format` in our `toString` method, which is like `printf` in that it uses format specifiers for greater control over the format of the output, but unlike `printf`, it writes the result to a string.

Using `String.format`.

We can't run the program yet, because we need to add the menu loop before there's anything that can be tested. But, we should aim to create a minimal program so that we can start testing it. Next is the menu loop,

```
1  import static java.lang.System.out;
2  import java.util.ArrayList;
3  import java.util.Scanner;
4
5  public class Test {
6    public static void main(String[] args) {
7
8      Scanner input = new Scanner (System.in);
9      ArrayList<Flight> flights = new ArrayList<>();
10
11     boolean done = false;
12     while (!done) {
13       out.println();
14       out.println("(A)dd flight");
15       out.println("(D)elete flight");
16       out.println("(C)hange a flight");
17       out.println("(L)ist all flights");
18       out.println("(1)Search by airline and flight number");
19       out.println("(2)Search by destination");
20       out.println("(E)xit");
21
22       String choice = input.nextLine();
23       switch (choice.toLowerCase()) {
```

Example 10.12. The menu loop in Test.java.

```java
24        case "a":
25          addFlight(input, flights);
26          break;
27        case "d":
28          deleteFlight(input, flights);
29          break;
30        case "c":
31          modifyFlight(input, flights);
32          break;
33        case "l":
34          listFlights(flights);
35          break;
36        case "1":
37          showFlightDetails(input, flights);
38          break;
39        case "2":
40          searchByDestination(input, flights);
41          break;
42        case "e":
43          done = true;
44          break;
45        default:
46          out.println("Please try again");
47          break;
48      }
49    }
50
51    input.close();
52  }
53
54  private static void addFlight(Scanner input, ArrayList<Flight> flights) {
55  }
56
57  private static void deleteFlight(Scanner input, ArrayList<Flight> flights) {
58  }
59
60  private static void modifyFlight(Scanner input, ArrayList<Flight> flights) {
61  }
62
63  private static void listFlights(ArrayList<Flight> flights) {
64  }
65
66  private static void showFlightDetails(Scanner input, ArrayList<Flight>
        flights) {
67  }
68
69  private static void searchByDestination(Scanner input, ArrayList<Flight>
        flights) {
70  }
71 }
```

```
(A)dd flight
(D)elete flight
(C)hange a flight
(L)ist all flights
(1)Search by airline and flight number
(2)Search by destination
(E)xit
2

(A)dd flight
(D)elete flight
(C)hange a flight
(L)ist all flights
(1)Search by airline and flight number
(2)Search by destination
(E)xit
e
```

Note that we've added our `flights` object, of type `ArrayList<Flight>` on line 9. Note also that we've added empty placeholder methods for each option, so that we can begin testing right away. The loop looks like it's working, so we can move on to the 'add flight' and 'display all flights' features,

Example 10.13. 'Add flight' feature.

```java
private static void addFlight(Scanner input, ArrayList<Flight> flights) {
  out.print("Airline: ");
  String airline = input.nextLine();
  out.print("Flight Number: ");
  int flightNumber = input.nextInt();
  input.nextLine();
  out.print("Origin: ");
  String origin = input.nextLine();
  out.print("Destination: ");
  String destination = input.nextLine();

  out.print("Departure time (hour:minute): ");
  String departure = input.nextLine();
  int colonIndex = departure.indexOf(':');
  int departureHour = -1, departureMinute = -1;
  if (colonIndex > 0) {
    departureHour = Integer.parseInt(departure.substring(0, colonIndex));
    departureMinute = Integer.parseInt(departure.substring(colonIndex + 1));
  }

  if (departureHour == -1 || departureMinute == -1) {
    out.println("Invalid departure time");
    return;
  }

  out.print("Arrival time (hour:minute): ");
  String arrival = input.nextLine();
  colonIndex = arrival.indexOf(':');
  int arrivalHour = -1, arrivalMinute = -1;
  if (colonIndex > 0) {
    arrivalHour = Integer.parseInt(arrival.substring(0, colonIndex));
    arrivalMinute = Integer.parseInt(arrival.substring(colonIndex + 1));
  }

  if (arrivalHour == -1 || arrivalMinute == -1) {
    out.println("Invalid arrival time");
```

```
37      return;
38    }
39
40    Flight flight = new Flight(origin, destination, airline, flightNumber,
          departureHour, departureMinute, arrivalHour, arrivalMinute);
41    flights.add(flight);
42  }
43
44  private static void listFlights(ArrayList<Flight> flights) {
45    for (Flight flight : flights)
46      out.println(flight);
47  }
```

```
a
Airline: Delta
Flight Number: 1100
Origin: JFK
Destination: MCO
Departure time (hour:minute): 13:30
Arrival time (hour:minute): 16:11

(A)dd flight
(D)elete flight
(C)hange a flight
(L)ist all flights
(1)Search by airline and flight number
(2)Search by destination
(E)xit
l
Delta 1100 (JFK 13:30 -> MCO 16:11)
```

The last menu selection here is a lowercase L, not a digit 1.

We've added the `AddFlight` and `listFlights` implementations and finally were able to see some real results. When writing code, you should try to get something minimal working so that you can test it, then as you add each feature, test it before moving on to the next feature. This way of working incrementally has several benefits,

- If you have a design problem, you will discover it earlier if you work incrementally instead of trying to write everything first, and then start testing.
- Testing each feature directly after it's written allows you to more accurately predict when you will finish the implementation. You uncover and fix bugs before moving on. On the other hand, if you write a lot of code that's yet to be tested, you are far less certain of how many problems remain and how much longer you need to work before you're done.

Technique 16. Start testing as soon as you can

Try to write something that can be tested right away, so you don't write too much code before you can begin testing.

> **Technique 17. Test each feature right after you write it**
>
> After you write a feature, test it before moving on to the next feature.

As mentioned in tip 7 and technique 12 (page 141), you should always maintain an awareness of which parts of your code are higher level, and which are lower level. So far, it's pretty simple—the low-level code is in the `Flight` class, and the high-level code is in the `Test` class. All the input and output is performed in the high-level code (the `Test` class).

Keep in mind how your code is structured.

We won't add thorough error checking of the user's input until we've covered exceptions in chapter 12. We also won't be storing our data in a file until chapter 12, which means that the program won't read the flights from a saved file when it starts. So when testing each feature, we'll have to add two or three flights to the list each time we run the program. That's a little time consuming, so to avoid having to do that, we'll hardcode some test data. That way, the program will have some flights in the list when it starts, and we can save some time when testing. Near the top of our `main` method, we'll add code that adds flights after creating the flight list,

Adding test data.

```
1  ArrayList<Flight> flights = new ArrayList<>();
2  flights.add(new Flight("JFK", "MCO", "Delta", 1100, 13, 30, 16, 11));
3  flights.add(new Flight("LGA", "LAX", "United", 29, 6, 0, 9, 21));
4  flights.add(new Flight("CLE", "PDX", "Delta", 412, 9, 59, 11, 15));
5  flights.add(new Flight("SAT", "BWI", "American", 11, 20, 42, 1, 2));
6  flights.add(new Flight("LFT", "ATL", "Delta", 90, 12, 0, 15, 57));
7  flights.add(new Flight("SNA", "CVG", "Southwest", 170, 10, 30, 12, 20));
```

```
Delta 1100 (JFK 13:30 -> MCO 16:11)
United 29 (LGA 06:00 -> LAX 09:21)
Delta 412 (CLE 09:59 -> PDX 11:15)
American 11 (SAT 20:42 -> BWI 01:02)
Delta 90 (LFT 12:00 -> ATL 15:57)
Southwest 170 (SNA 10:30 -> CVG 12:28)
```

Everything looks good so far, so we're gaining confidence that we're on the right track. Since 'delete flight' and 'look up by airline and flight number' share the code that prompts for the airline and flight number, we'll add those next,

```
1  private static int findFlight(Scanner input, ArrayList<Flight> flights) {
2      out.print("Airline: ");
3      String airline = input.nextLine();
4      out.print("Flight number: ");
5      int flightNumber = input.nextInt();
```

Example 10.14. Adding features to delete a record and show a record's details.

```
6      input.nextLine();
7
8      for (int i = 0; i < flights.size(); i++)
9        if (airline.toLowerCase().equals(flights.get(i).getAirline().toLowerCase
       ()) &&
10          flightNumber == flights.get(i).getFlightNumber())
11         return i;
12
13     return -1;
14   }
15
16   private static void deleteFlight(Scanner input, ArrayList<Flight> flights) {
17     int index = findFlight(input, flights);
18     if (index == -1) {
19       out.println("Not found");
20       return;
21     }
22
23     flights.remove(index);
24     out.println("Deleted");
25   }
26
27   private static void showFlightDetails(Scanner input, ArrayList<Flight>
       flights) {
28     int index = findFlight(input, flights);
29     if (index == -1) {
30       out.println("Not found");
31       return;
32     }
33     out.println(flights.get(index));
34   }
```

```
d
Airline: united
Flight number: 29
Deleted

(A)dd flight
(D)elete flight
(C)hange a flight
(L)ist all flights
(1)Search by airline and flight number
(2)Search by destination
(E)xit
l
Delta 1100 (JFK 13:30 -> MCO 16:11)
Delta 412 (CLE 09:59 -> PDX 11:15)
American 11 (SAT 20:42 -> BWI 01:02)
Delta 90 (LFT 12:00 -> ATL 15:57)
Southwest 170 (SNA 10:30 -> CVG 12:28)
```

```
1
Airline: delta
Flight number: 90
Delta 90 (LFT 12:00 -> ATL 15:57)
```

Next is searching by destination, which bears some resemblance to searching by airline and flight number,

```
1   private static void searchByDestination(Scanner input, ArrayList<Flight>
        flights) {
2     out.print("Destination: ");
3     String destination = input.nextLine();
4
5     for (int i = 0; i < flights.size(); i++)
6       if (destination.toLowerCase().equals(flights.get(i).getDestination().
        toLowerCase()))
7         out.println(flights.get(i));
8   }
```

Example 10.15. Search by destination feature.

```
(A)dd flight
(D)elete flight
(C)hange a flight
(L)ist all flights
(1)Search by airline and flight number
(2)Search by destination
(E)xit
2
Destination: BWI
American 11 (SAT 20:42 -> BWI 01:02)
```

Next, the 'change a flight' feature,

```
1    private static void modifyFlight(Scanner input, ArrayList<Flight> flights) {
2      int index = findFlight(input, flights);
3      if (index == -1) {
4        out.println("Not found");
5        return;
6      }
7
8      Flight flight = flights.get(index);
9
10     // gather new flight data
11
12     out.print("Airline [" + flight.getAirline() + "]: ");
13     String airline = input.nextLine();
14     if (airline.isEmpty())
15       airline = flight.getAirline();
16
17     out.print("Flight Number [" + flight.getFlightNumber() + "]: ");
18     int flightNumber = 0;
19     String flightNumberString = input.nextLine();
20     if (flightNumberString.isEmpty())
21       flightNumber = flight.getFlightNumber();
22     else
23       flightNumber = Integer.parseInt(flightNumberString);
24
25     Flight foundFlight = getFlight(flights, airline, flightNumber);
26     if (foundFlight != null && foundFlight != flight) {
27       out.println("Airline and flight number already used.");
28       return;
29     }
30
31     out.print("Origin [" + flight.getOrigin() + "]: ");
32     String origin = input.nextLine();
33     if (origin.isEmpty())
34       origin = flight.getOrigin();
35
```

Example 10.16. Change flight details feature.

```
36      out.print("Destination [" + flight.getDestination() + "]: ");
37      String destination = input.nextLine();
38      if (destination.isEmpty())
39        destination = flight.getDestination();
40
41      String timeString = String.format("%02d:%02d", flight.getDepartureHour(),
          flight.getDepartureMinute());
42      out.print("Departure time (hour:minute) [" + timeString + "]: ");
43      String departure = input.nextLine();
44      int departureHour = flight.getDepartureHour(), departureMinute = flight.
          getDepartureMinute();
45      if (!departure.isEmpty()) {
46        int colonIndex = departure.indexOf(':');
47        if (colonIndex > 0) {
48          departureHour = Integer.parseInt(departure.substring(0, colonIndex));
49          departureMinute = Integer.parseInt(departure.substring(colonIndex + 1))
            ;
50        }
51        if (departureHour == -1 || departureMinute == -1) {
52          out.println("Invalid departure time");
53          return;
54        }
55      }
56
57      timeString = String.format("%02d:%02d", flight.getArrivalHour(), flight.
          getArrivalMinute());
58      out.print("Arrival time (hour:minute) [" + timeString + "]: ");
59      String arrival = input.nextLine();
60      int arrivalHour = flight.getArrivalHour(), arrivalMinute = flight.
          getArrivalMinute();
61      if (!arrival.isEmpty()) {
62        int colonIndex = arrival.indexOf(':');
63        if (colonIndex > 0) {
64          arrivalHour = Integer.parseInt(arrival.substring(0, colonIndex));
65          arrivalMinute = Integer.parseInt(arrival.substring(colonIndex + 1));
66        }
67        if (arrivalHour == -1 || arrivalMinute == -1) {
68          out.println("Invalid arrival time");
69          return;
70        }
71      }
72
73      // update flight's data
74      flight.setAirline(airline);
75      flight.setFlightNumber(flightNumber);
76      flight.setOrigin(origin);
77      flight.setDestination(destination);
78      flight.setDepartureHour(departureHour);
79      flight.setDepartureMinute(departureMinute);
80      flight.setArrivalHour(arrivalHour);
81      flight.setArrivalMinute(arrivalMinute);
82    }
83
84    private static Flight getFlight(ArrayList<Flight> flights, String airline,
          int flightNumber) {
85      for (Flight flight : flights)
86        if (flight.getAirline().toLowerCase().equals(airline) &&
87            flight.getFlightNumber() == flightNumber)
88          return flight;
89      return null;
90    }
```

```
c
Airline: delta
Flight number: 412
Airline [Delta]:
Flight Number [412]:
Origin [CLE]:
Destination [PDX]: JFK
Departure time (hour:minute) [09:59]:
Arrival time (hour:minute) [11:15]:

(A)dd flight
(D)elete flight
(C)hange a flight
(L)ist all flights
(1)Search by airline and flight number
(2)Search by destination
(E)xit
l
Delta 1100 (JFK 13:30 -> MCO 16:11)
United 29 (LGA 06:00 -> LAX 09:21)
Delta 412 (CLE 09:59 -> JFK 11:15)
American 11 (SAT 20:42 -> BWI 01:02)
Delta 90 (LFT 12:00 -> ATL 15:57)
Southwest 170 (SNA 10:30 -> CVG 12:28)
```

The code in example 10.16 allows the user to select a flight, then change any of its details. The user is able to hit the enter key to leave particular fields unchanged. The `modifyFlight` method checks to make sure the specified combination of airline and flight number aren't already used by a different flight. All that remains is to add the same checking to the `addFlight` method, which is left as an exercise for the reader.

A class can contain a collection as an attribute, in fact that's common. Table 10.2 shows some of the common patterns involving objects and collections.

Table 10.2: Some common collection patterns.

Pattern	Example
Object Object	Team object contains a Coach object

Object
  Collection
    Object
	Team object contains a collection of Player objects

Collection
  Object
    Collection
      Object
	A list of flights, each containing a list of passengers

Exercises

10.5 Create a program that manages sales at a convenience store. It should track a list of inventory items, with each inventory item containing a name, barcode, quantity available, quantity sold, and price. The user should be able to add a new inventory item to the list, delete an inventory item from the list, change an inventory item, list all inventory items, find an inventory item by barcode or find an inventory item using a partial name search.

- Hint: For the partial name search, use the `String.contains` method to determine whether the user's input is part of the product name.

10.5 Other Collection Classes

Table 10.3 shows some of the collection classes that Java provides. As you can see from the table, `ArrayList` is used far more often than the others. Each has its own pros and cons, which we'll explore in detail in chapters 13 and 14.

Table 10.3: Some of Java's collection classes.

Class	Brief Description	Usage Frequency
`ArrayList`	Encapsulates an array of objects.	Very common
`LinkedList`	Each element points to the next one, forming a chain.	Rare
`HashMap`	Maps keys to values, where the key and value are arbitrary classes.	Somewhat common
`HashSet`	Contains distinct instances of an arbitrary class.	Rare

Chapter Summary

- The Java collection classes encapsulate native data structures such as arrays.
- Java collection classes grow automatically as more data is added to them.
- `ArrayList` is the most commonly used collection class, and encapsulates a native Java array.
- Collection classes are *generic*. They require a parameter specifying the type of data that will be contained.
- Collection classes offer methods to add data, remove data, find data items, iterate over the collection, and so on.

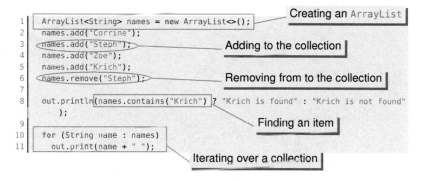

```
1   ArrayList<String> names = new ArrayList<>();        Creating an ArrayList
2   names.add("Corrine");
3   names.add("Steph");                       Adding to the collection
4   names.add("Zoe");
5   names.add("Krich");
6   names.remove("Steph");                    Removing from to the collection
7
8   out.println(names.contains("Krich") ? "Krich is found" : "Krich is not found"
    );
9                                             Finding an item
10  for (String name : names)
11      out.print(name + " ");
                                              Iterating over a collection
```

Exercise Solutions

10.1   This results in a compile-time error:

```
1   ArrayList<String> names = new ArrayList<>();
2   names.add(100);
```

```
ArrayList<String> names = new ArrayList<>();
names.add(100);
        The method add(int, String) in the type ArrayList<String> is not applicable for the arguments (int)
        3 quick fixes available:
          Add argument to match 'add(int, String)'
          Add arguments to match 'add(String, Object[], int)'
          Change to 'addAll(..)'
```

10.2
```
1   // create an ArrayList of ten random numbers
2   ArrayList<Integer> numbers = new ArrayList<>();
3   for (int i = 0; i < 10; i++)
```

```
4    numbers.add((int) (Math.random() * 50 + 1));
5
6    // get the average
7    int sum = 0;
8    for (int number : numbers)
9      sum += number;
10   out.println("The average is " + sum / numbers.size());
```

```
The average is 29
```

10.3
```
1    ArrayList<String> names = new ArrayList<>();
2    names.add("Jacob");
3    names.add("Liz");
4    names.add("Hakeem");
5
6    ArrayList<Integer> grades = new ArrayList<>();
7    grades.add(100);
8    grades.add(97);
9    grades.add(99);
10
11   for (int i = 0; i < names.size(); i++)
12     out.println(names.get(i) + ": " + grades.get(i));
```

```
Jacob: 100
Liz: 97
Hakeem: 99
```

10.4
```
1    ArrayList<Student> students = new ArrayList<>();
2    students.add(new Student("Jacob", 100));
3    students.add(new Student("Liz", 97));
4    students.add(new Student("Hakeem", 99));
5
6    for (int i = 0; i < students.size(); i++)
7      out.println(students.get(i));
8  ...
9  class Student {
10   String name;
11   int grade;
12
13   public Student (String name, int grade) {
14     this.name = name;
15     this.grade = grade;
16   }
17
18   @Override
19   public String toString() {
20     return name + ": " + grade;
21   }
22 }
```

```
Jacob: 100
Liz: 97
Hakeem: 99
```

Interfaces | 11

11.1 Abstraction

Abstraction is a powerful technique that allows us to simplify our code, making it easier to maintain and change. Suppose we want to write a program that manages a waiting list. We need a collection that holds the list of names in the waiting list. When the program adds a name to the waiting list, the name is added to the collection, and when the program removes a name from the waiting list, the name is removed from the collection. The first name added to the waiting list is the first one removed, and subsequent names are removed from the waiting list in the order in which they were added. This program implements a *queue*. Our initial version of this program is shown in example 11.1,

FIFO is a commonly used acronym describing a *first in, first out* collection of items, where the items are removed from the collection in the order in which they were added.

Example 11.1. Managing a waiting list.

```
1   ArrayList<String> queue = new ArrayList<>();
2
3   queue.add("John");
4   out.println("Added John to queue");
5
6   queue.add("George");
7   out.println("Added George to queue");
8
9   if (!queue.isEmpty()) {
10      String name = queue.remove(0);
11      out.println("Removed " + name + " from queue");
12  }
13
14  queue.add("Elizabeth");
15  out.println("Adding Elizabeth to queue");
16
17  while (!queue.isEmpty()) {
18      String name = queue.remove(0);
19      out.println("Removed " + name + " from queue");
20  }
```

```
Added John to queue
Added George to queue
Removed John from queue
Adding Elizabeth to queue
Removed George from queue
Removed Elizabeth from queue
```

The queue is implemented as an **ArrayList** of strings. Adding a name to the queue is implemented with a call to the **ArrayList**'s **add** method, which adds the new name to the end of the list. Removing a name from the queue is done with a call to the **ArrayList**'s **remove** method, passing it the index zero, which removes the first item from the list, and returns it so that it can be printed out. The queue is checked, though, before removing a name from the waiting list, to make sure that it's not empty.

Although the program works, it's better to implement the waiting list using a specialized class. So we'll rewrite example 11.1 to add a **Queue** class which has methods for adding a queue item, removing a queue item, and checking whether the queue is empty. The **Queue** class is also generic so that it can hold a queue of items of any type. This second version is shown in example 11.2,

Example 11.2. Adding a **Queue** class.

```
1  public static void main(String[] args) {
2      Queue<String> queue = new Queue<>();
3
4      queue.enqueue("John");
5      out.println("Added John to queue");
6
7      queue.enqueue("George");
8      out.println("Added George to queue");
9
10     if (!queue.isEmpty()) {
11         String name = queue.dequeue();
12         out.println("Removed " + name + " from queue");
13     }
14
15     queue.enqueue("Elizabeth");
16     out.println("Adding Elizabeth to queue");
17
18     while (!queue.isEmpty()) {
19         String name = queue.dequeue();
20         out.println("Removed " + name + " from queue");
21     }
22  }
23  ...
24  class Queue<E> {
25
26     private ArrayList<E> list = new ArrayList<>();
27
28     public void enqueue(E object) {
29         list.add(object);
30     }
31
32     public E dequeue() {
33         return list.remove(0);
34     }
35
36     public boolean isEmpty() {
37         return list.isEmpty();
38     }
39  }
```

```
Added John to queue
Added George to queue
Removed John from queue
Adding Elizabeth to queue
Removed George from queue
Removed Elizabeth from queue
```

The point of abstraction is to hide implementation details so that the interface is intuitive and easy to use. A good abstraction has several characteristics:

- Its public interface is simple and minimal. In the case of the `Queue` class, its public interface consists of only three methods, `enqueue`, `dequeue` and `isEmpty`. These methods correspond to the conceptual way that a queue works—you can add an item, you can remove an item, and you can check whether the queue is empty.
- Each item in the public interface should be named to reflect its purpose. In the case of the `Queue` class, the public methods are `enqueue`, `dequeue` and `isEmpty`. These are clear and reflect the common terminology of queues.
- The implementation details aren't available to the caller. In the case of the `Queue` class, the inner `ArrayList` object is private, so it's unavailable to the consumer of the `Queue` class. That's an advantage, not a limitation. It helps the programmer avoid missteps and makes it clear how to use the `Queue` class. If the inner `ArrayList` could be accessed by the caller, it would be distracting and confusing to the programmer consuming the `Queue` class.

Data hiding is a commonly used term referring to a class hiding its internal implementation in order to simplify its interface.

Technique 18. Use abstraction to simplify your code

Using abstraction makes your code simpler and more maintainable.

Exercises

11.1 Use example 11.2 as a starting point, and make a `Stack` class, which implements a LIFO (*last in, first out*) data structure. Use the standard stack terms *push* and *pop* for the method names.

11.2 Interfaces

An interface in Java specifies a particular set of functionality which can be implemented by a class. It contains declarations for a set of methods without their bodies. In addition, all methods in an interface are implicitly public. A class can implement any number of interfaces. When a class implements an interface, it must provide a definition for each method in that interface.

Interfaces typically define common features that are implemented by more than one class. For example, the `Comparable` interface defines the `compareTo` method which is called by Java's `sort` method. Collections of a class can be sorted if the class implements the `Comparable` interface, and we'll see an example of that later in this chapter.

To illustrate interfaces, consider example 11.3 which updates example 11.2 to add a `Queue` interface. In example 11.3, the `Queue` class is renamed `MyQueue`,

Example 11.3. The `Queue` interface.

```
 1  public class Test {
 2    public static void main(String[] args) {
 3
 4      MyQueue<String> queue = new MyQueue<>();
 5
 6      queue.enqueue("John");
 7      out.println("Added John to queue");
 8
 9      queue.enqueue("George");
10      out.println("Added George to queue");
11
12      if (!queue.isEmpty()) {
13        String name = queue.dequeue();
14        out.println("Removed " + name + " from queue");
15      }
16
17      queue.enqueue("Elizabeth");
18      out.println("Adding Elizabeth to queue");
19
20      while (!queue.isEmpty()) {
21        String name = queue.dequeue();
22        out.println("Removed " + name + " from queue");
23      }
24    }
25  }
26
27  interface Queue<E> {
28    void enqueue(E object);
29    E dequeue();
30    boolean isEmpty();
31  }
32
33  class MyQueue<E> implements Queue<E> {
34
```

```
35  private ArrayList<E> list = new ArrayList<>();
36
37  public void enqueue(E object) {
38    list.add(object);
39  }
40
41  public E dequeue() {
42    return list.remove(0);
43  }
44
45  public boolean isEmpty() {
46    return list.isEmpty();
47  }
48 }
```

```
Added John to queue
Added George to queue
Removed John from queue
Adding Elizabeth to queue
Removed George from queue
Removed Elizabeth from queue
```

The example above defines the `Queue` interface, which specifies queue functionality. Multiple classes could implement that interface, in which case we would have a choice of which queue class to use in the above example.

The UML diagram for example 11.3 is shown in figure 11.1. Note that while inheritance is denoted in UML class diagrams with an arrow and solid line, implementing an interface is denoted with an arrow and dashed line

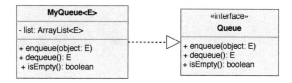

Figure 11.1: UML class diagram for example 11.3.

An interface offers a great way to implement an abstraction, since you can use it to specify needed functionality as a contract implemented by a class and utilized by code in another class.

Exercises

11.2   Create an interface called `Animal` that has a `speak` method, which prints a message to the console. Create a `Dog` class which implements the `Animal` interface. Its `speak` method should write "Bark" to the console. Create a `Cat` class which implements the `Animal` interface. Its `speak` method should write "Meow" to the console. Test the implementation with your `main` method.

11.3 Collection Class Hierarchy

Now that we know about interfaces, we can look at `ArrayList` and some of the classes and interfaces surrounding it in the hierarchy of collection classes. Figure 11.2 shows a partial UML class diagram for this hierarchy.

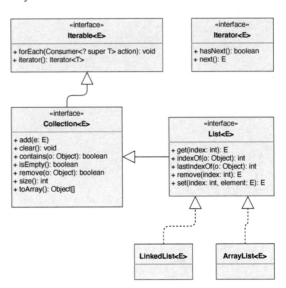

Figure 11.2: Partial collection class hierarchy in Java. For brevity, not all methods are listed.

As you can see in figure 11.2, both `ArrayList` and `LinkedList` implement the `List` interface, which extends the `Collection` interface, which in turn extends the `Iterable` interface, all of which are generic.

- `Iterator<E>` contains the methods `hasNext` and `next`, which were demonstrated in example 10.8.
- `Iterable<E>` contains the `iterator` method, which returns an object that implements `Iterator<E>` as demonstrated in example 10.8.
- `Collection<E>` contains methods that pertain to using collections, such as `add` and `contains`. A collection can contain duplicate data elements, but is inherently unordered.

- `List<E>` imposes a specific order on the elements within a collection, and adds methods that pertain to dealing with an ordered list, such as getting the data element at a specific index (`get`) and replacing the data element at a specific index (`set`).
- `ArrayList<E>` implements `List<E>` and maintains the list's data in an array. The array is initially small, but when it becomes full, the `ArrayList` class replaces it with another array that is larger than the previous one, and copies all the data to the new one. The new array is much larger than the old one, so that this time consuming operation of expanding the array isn't executed too often.
- `LinkedList<E>` implements `List<E>` by keeping each data element of type `E` in a node object. In addition to housing the data of type `E`, the node object has a pointer to the next node in the list. Thus, all elements of type `E` are kept in a specific order.

Different classes implement the same interface in different ways, and these different implementations each have their own pros and cons. For the `LinkedList` class to find the data element at a specific index, the list of node objects is walked from the beginning. This way of keeping a list within `LinkedList` has drawbacks since finding an element by index is slow, but other operations are fast, such as removing the first element of the list. We'll further discuss the performance of `ArrayList` versus `LinkedList` in chapter 13.

Example 11.4 creates two lists of numbers, one in an `ArrayList` and one in a `LinkedList`, then computes the sum of each list and prints it out,

```
1  public static void main(String[] args) {
2
3    ArrayList<Integer> arrayList = new ArrayList<Integer>();
4    for (int i = 0; i < 100; i++)
5      arrayList.add(i);
6    out.println("Sum of ArrayList is " + sumOfArrayList(arrayList));
7
8    LinkedList<Integer> linkedList = new LinkedList<Integer>();
9    for (int i = 0; i < 100; i++)
10     linkedList.add(i);
11   out.println("Sum of ArrayList is " + sumOfLinkedList(linkedList));
12 }
13
14 private static int sumOfArrayList(ArrayList<Integer> list) {
15   int sum = 0;
16   Iterator<Integer> iterator = list.iterator();
17   while (iterator.hasNext())
18     sum += iterator.next();
19   return sum;
```

Example 11.4. Computing the sum of elements in a list.

```
20 | }
21 |
22 | private static int sumOfLinkedList(LinkedList<Integer> list) {
23 |   int sum = 0;
24 |   Iterator<Integer> iterator = list.iterator();
25 |   while (iterator.hasNext())
26 |     sum += iterator.next();
27 |   return sum;
28 | }
```

```
Sum of ArrayList is 4950
Sum of LinkedList is 4950
```

Observe that `sumOfArrayList` and `sumOfLinkedList` contain the same code and only use the `list` variable to call methods that are provided by the `List` interface or interfaces that it extends. So, we can easily consolidate the two methods as in example 11.5,

Example 11.5. Using more general types.

```
1 | public static void main(String[] args) {
2 |
3 |   List<Integer> list = new ArrayList<Integer>();
4 |   for (int i = 0; i < 100; i++)
5 |     list.add(i);
6 |   out.println("Sum of ArrayList is " + sumOf(list));
7 |
8 |   list = new LinkedList<Integer>();
9 |   for (int i = 0; i < 100; i++)
10 |     list.add(i);
11 |   out.println("Sum of ArrayList is " + sumOf(list));
12 | }
13 |
14 | private static int sumOf(List<Integer> list) {
15 |   int sum = 0;
16 |   Iterator<Integer> iterator = list.iterator();
17 |   while (iterator.hasNext())
18 |     sum += iterator.next();
19 |   return sum;
20 | }
```

```
Sum of ArrayList is 4950
Sum of LinkedList is 4950
```

Notice in example 11.5 that `sumOf` now takes a parameter of type `List<Integer>`, which is an interface type, but can still be used as the type of the `list` parameter, as long as the `list` parameter is only used to access methods provided by `List` or interfaces that `List` extends.

Because the `sumOf` method's `list` parameter can refer to an `ArrayList`, a `LinkedList`, or any other class that implements the `List` interface, it can take on many forms at runtime. This is referred to as *polymorphism*.

Polymorphism is derived from the latin *poly*, meaning many, and *morph* meaning form.

Note also that `List<Integer>` is used as the `list` variable's type in `main`. `list` is assigned a reference to an `ArrayList<Integer>`, which implements `List<Integer>`. This is preferred, since the reference `list` is only used to invoke methods of the `List` interface. Later in `main`, we assigned a `LinkedList<Integer>` to the `list` variable in the same way. Holding and passing around references to a more general class or interface is preferred since this allows code to apply to more situations.

Variables can hold references to interfaces.

> **Technique 19. Hold references to more general classes or interfaces when possible**
>
> Holding and passing around references to a more general class or interface is preferred since this allows code to apply in more situations.

11.4 **Comparable** and Sorting

Sorting a list of numbers can be done with the `Collections.sort` method, as shown in example 11.6,

```
1   // Generate 20 random numbers between 1 and 20
2   List<Integer> list = new ArrayList<Integer>();
3   for (int i = 0; i < 20; i++)
4     list.add((int) (Math.random() * 20) + 1);
5
6   out.println("Before sorting: " + list);
7   Collections.sort(list);
8   out.println("After sorting: " + list);
```

Example 11.6. Sorting a list of numbers.

```
Before sorting: [5, 8, 16, 2, 7, 8, 13, 2, 17, 5, 10, 19, 20, 11, 5, 10, 3, 7, 3, 7]
After sorting: [2, 2, 3, 3, 5, 5, 5, 7, 7, 7, 8, 8, 10, 10, 11, 13, 16, 17, 19, 20]
```

The `Collections.sort` method is able to sort the list because the type of data held in the list (`Integer` in this case) implements the `Comparable` interface, which contains the `compareTo` method that allows its caller to compare two data elements. If you want your own class to support sorting, you'll have to update it to implement the `Comparable` interface. Consider example 11.7 where we define an `Employee` class and sort a list of employee objects,

Example 11.7. Sorting a list of employees.

```
 1  ...
 2    List<Employee> employees = new ArrayList<>();
 3    employees.add(new Employee("Ina", "Brown", 10121));
 4    employees.add(new Employee("John", "Forsyth", 10029));
 5    employees.add(new Employee("Laura", "Smith", 10089));
 6    employees.add(new Employee("Tim", "Edwards", 10041));
 7
 8    out.println("Before sorting: " + employees);
 9    Collections.sort(employees);
10    out.println("After sorting: " + employees);
11  ...
12  class Employee {
13    String firstName;
14    String lastName;
15    int id;
16
17    public Employee (String firstName, String lastName, int id) {
18      this.firstName = firstName;
19      this.lastName = lastName;
20      this.id = id;
21    }
22  }
```

```
out.println("Before sorting: " + employees);
Collections.sort(employees);
out.println(
          [•] The method sort(List<T>) in the type Collections is not applicable for the arguments (List<Employee>)
          1 quick fix available:
          (•) Cast argument 'employees' to 'List<T>'
ployee {
ing firstName
```

The compile error we get isn't too specific, but the reason is that we haven't implemented **Comparable** in our **Employee** class. Eclipse provides a convenient way to implement placeholder methods for an interface. First we revise the **Employee** declaration to add **implements Comparable<Employee>**,

```
 1  class Employee implements Comparable<Employee> {
```

```
 24  class Employee implements Comparable<Employee> {
 25    St
 26    St   [•] The type Employee must implement the inherited abstract method Comparable<Employee>.compareTo(Employee)
 27    in   2 quick fixes available:
 28
 29    pu      ♦ Add unimplemented methods
 30              ♦ Make type 'Employee' abstract
```

Hovering over the error message and choosing the "add unimplemented methods" option will add placeholder methods, as in example 11.8,

Tip 8. Don't use Eclipse convenience features until you're able to write the code without them.

```
 1  class Employee implements Comparable<Employee> {
 2    String firstName;
 3    String lastName;
 4    int id;
 5
 6    public Employee (String firstName, String lastName, int id) {
 7      this.firstName = firstName;
```

```
 8        this.lastName = lastName;
 9        this.id = id;
10    }
11
12    @Override
13    public int compareTo(Employee o) {
14        // TODO Auto-generated method stub
15        return 0;
16    }
17 }
```

Example 11.8. Placeholder method added by Eclipse.

The `compareTo` method is meant to compare the current object with the object passed in as a parameter, and return a positive number if the current object should be considered larger, a negative number if the current object should be considered smaller, and zero if they're equal. Our implementation of `compareTo` is shown in example 11.9 (we've also added a `toString` method),

```
 1    @Override
 2    public String toString() {
 3        return firstName + " " + lastName;
 4    }
 5
 6    @Override
 7    public int compareTo(Employee o) {
 8        if (!lastName.equals(o.lastName))
 9            return lastName.compareTo(o.lastName);
10        if (!firstName.equals(o.firstName))
11            return firstName.compareTo(o.firstName);
12        return 0;
13    }
```

Example 11.9. Custom `compareTo` implementation.

```
Before sorting: [Ina Brown, John Forsyth, Laura Smith, Tim Edwards]
After sorting: [Ina Brown, Tim Edwards, John Forsyth, Laura Smith]
```

The above implementation of `compareTo` compares the two objects' last names. If the last names aren't the same, the result of comparing the last names is returned as the result of comparing the two employees. This has the effect of sorting employees by last name. If the last names are equal, it will sort by first name, and if the last and first names are the same, the employee records are considered equal. Similar logic can be used with non-string data members.

Exercises

11.3   Update example 11.9. Add the employee's street address, city, state and zip code. Change the `compareTo` method to sort by state, then city, then street address.

Chapter Summary

- An interface specifies a set of methods that can be implemented by one or more classes.
- A variable can have an interface as its type, while referring to an instance of a class implementing the interface.
- The Java collection classes implement the generic Collection interface.
- When a class implements the `Comparable` interface, collections of that class can be sorted.

```
1   public static void main(String[] args) {
2       Dog fido = new Dog();
3       out.print("Fido says ");
4       fido.speak();
5       Cat whiskers = new Cat();
6       out.print("Whiskers says ");
7       whiskers.speak();
8   }
9   ...
10  interface Animal {
11      void speak();
12  }
13
14  class Dog implements Animal {
15      public void speak() {
16          out.println("Bark!");
17      }
18  }
19
20  class Cat implements Animal {
21      public void speak() {
22          out.println("Meow!");
23      }
24  }
```

Calling interface method

Interface definition

Declaring interface implementation

Implementing interface method

Exercise Solutions

11.1

```java
public static void main(String[] args) {

  Stack<String> stack = new Stack<>();

  stack.push("John");
  out.println("Pushed John onto the stack");

  stack.push("George");
  out.println("Pushed George onto the stack");

  if (!stack.isEmpty()) {
    String name = stack.pop();
    out.println("Popped " + name + " from the stack");
  }

  stack.push("Elizabeth");
  out.println("Pushed Elizabeth onto the stack");

  while (!stack.isEmpty()) {
    String name = stack.pop();
    out.println("Popped " + name + " from the stack");
  }
}
...
class Stack<E> {

  private ArrayList<E> list = new ArrayList<>();

  public void push(E object) {
    list.add(object);
  }

  public E pop() {
    return list.remove(list.size() - 1);
  }

  public boolean isEmpty() {
    return list.isEmpty();
  }
}
```

```
Pushed John onto the stack
Pushed George onto the stack
Popped George from the stack
Pushed Elizabeth onto the stack
Popped Elizabeth from the stack
Popped John from the stack
```

11.2

```java
public static void main(String[] args) {
  Dog fido = new Dog();
  out.print("Fido says ");
  fido.speak();
  Cat whiskers = new Cat();
  out.print("Whiskers says ");
  whiskers.speak();
```

```
 8    }
 9  ...
10  interface Animal {
11    void speak();
12  }
13
14  class Dog implements Animal {
15    public void speak() {
16      out.println("Bark!");
17    }
18  }
19
20  class Cat implements Animal {
21    public void speak() {
22      out.println("Meow!");
23    }
24  }
```

```
Fido says Bark!
Whiskers says Meow!
```

11.3
```
 1      List<Employee> employees = new ArrayList<>();
 2      employees.add(new Employee("Ina", "Brown", 10121, "100 Main St",
          "Cleveland", "OH", 44101));
 3      employees.add(new Employee("John", "Forsyth", 10029, "19
          Brookline Place", "Boston", "MA", 2109));
 4      employees.add(new Employee("Laura", "Smith", 10089, "3105 12th
          Ave", "Tucson", "AZ", 85706));
 5      employees.add(new Employee("Tim", "Edwards", 10041, "526 Gerard
          St.", "New Orleans", "LA", 70013));
 6
 7      out.println("Before sorting: " + employees);
 8      Collections.sort(employees);
 9      out.println("After sorting: " + employees);
10  ...
11  class Employee implements Comparable<Employee> {
12    String firstName;
13    String lastName;
14    int id;
15    String address;
16    String city;
17    String state;
18    int zipCode;
19
20    public Employee (String firstName, String lastName, int id, String
          address, String city, String state, int zipCode) {
21      this.firstName = firstName;
22      this.lastName = lastName;
23      this.id = id;
24      this.address = address;
25      this.city = city;
26      this.state = state;
27      this.zipCode = zipCode;
28    }
29
30    @Override
31    public String toString() {
32      return firstName + " " + lastName + " (" + address + ", " + city
          + ", " + state + ")";
33    }
34
```

```
35    @Override
36    public int compareTo(Employee o) {
37      if (!state.equals(o.state))
38        return state.compareTo(o.state);
39      if (!city.equals(o.city))
40        return city.compareTo(o.city);
41      if (!address.equals(o.address))
42        return address.compareTo(o.address);
43      return 0;
44    }
45  }
```

```
Before sorting: [Ina Brown (100 Main St, Cleveland, OH), John Forsyth
After sorting: [Laura Smith (3105 12th Ave, Tucson, AZ), Tim Edwards
```

File I/O | 12

12.1 Exceptions

As seen in section 3.3, integer division by zero at runtime causes an exception. There are a variety of runtime errors that cause different types of exceptions. When a runtime exception occurs, we say that an exception is *thrown*. Your code can handle such an occurrence, and in this case, we say that the exception is *caught*.

To do this, you would add a *try-catch* block to your code. The `try` block contains code that might throw an exception. The `catch` block is placed directly after the `try` block, and handles the exception, if it's thrown. Consider example 12.1, where we revise example 3.2 by placing the integer division within a try-catch block, and printing a warning if the code attempts to divide by zero,

```
1   Scanner input = new Scanner(System.in);
2
3   out.print("Please enter the rectangle's area: ");
4   int area = input.nextInt();
5   input.nextLine();
6   out.print("Please enter the rectangle's height: ");
7   int height = input.nextInt();
8   input.nextLine();
9
10  try {
11    int width = area / height;
12    out.print("The rectangle's width is: " + width);
13  }
14  catch (Exception ex) {
15    out.print("An error occurred: " + ex.getMessage());
16  }
17
18  input.close();
```

Example 12.1. Catching an exception.

```
Please enter the rectangle's area: 12
Please enter the rectangle's height: 0
An error occurred: / by zero
```

The `catch` block receives a parameter, the exception that was thrown. It can use this parameter to access information pertinent to the exception, such as a specific error message. In example 12.1, the `catch` block prints out the exception's error message. Execution then continues and the `Scanner` object is closed before the `main` method returns. Contrast this to the output of example 3.2 where the standard exception output was displayed, followed by the program immediately terminating. The `try-catch` statement allows us to handle exceptions in a graceful way and continue with normal program execution. How an exception is handled depends on the particular situation.

If not caught in a `catch` block, an exception causes the current method to return immediately to the calling method. The calling method, in turn, will return immediately unless it catches the exception with its own `catch` block, and so on. If no method in the call stack catches a thrown exception, the standard exception error message is displayed in the console and the program terminates.

Exception Class Hierarchy

In example 12.1, the `catch` block received a parameter of type `Exception`. In reality though, the exception thrown was an `ArithmeticException`, which indirectly extends `Exception`. Accepting an `Exception` parameter in the `catch` block works because all exception classes are ultimately derived from `Exception`. Figure 12.1 displays a partial hierarchy of the exception classes in Java.

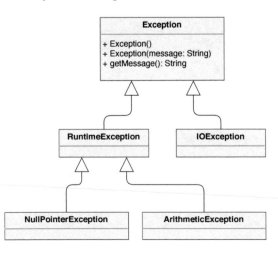

Figure 12.1: Partial exception hierarchy in Java.

Multiple `catch` Blocks

You can specify multiple `catch` blocks to catch the different types of exceptions that may be thrown in the `try` block. To do this, the `catch` blocks have to be in order from the more specific to the more general, since the first `catch` block that matches a thrown exception will be executed. This technique allows you to handle different exception types in different ways. If none of the `catch` blocks matches the type of exception thrown, it won't be caught and will proceed up the call stack to be caught at a higher level.

The `finally` Block

After all `catch` blocks, an optional `finally` block can be included to perform any needed cleanup. The code in the `finally` block is executed whether an exception is thrown within the `try` block or not. Example 12.2 illustrates this,

```
1  import static java.lang.System.out;
2  import java.util.Scanner;
3
4  public class Test {
5    public static void main(String[] args) throws Exception {
6
7      Scanner input = null;
8      try {
9        // arbitrary computation
10       int players = 3;
11       int goals = 4;
12       int goalsPerPlayer = goals / players;
13       out.println("Goals per player: " + goalsPerPlayer);
14
15       // declare Scanner
16       input = new Scanner(System.in);
17
18       // get input from user
19       out.print("Enter rectangle area: ");
20       int area = input.nextInt();
21       input.nextLine();
22
23       out.print("Enter rectangle height: ");
24       int height = input.nextInt();
25       input.nextLine();
26
27       // compute result
28       int width = area / height;
29       out.println("The rectangle's width is: " + width);
30     }
31     catch (Exception ex) {
32       int lineNumber = ex.getStackTrace()[0].getLineNumber();
33       out.println("An error occurred: " + ex.getMessage() + " at line " +
         lineNumber);
34     }
```

Example 12.2. Finally block.

```
35      finally {
36        // Scanner is closed if it has already been initialized
37        if (input != null) {
38          input.close();
39          out.println("(closed Scanner object)");
40        }
41      }
42    }
43  }
```

```
Goals per player: 1
Enter rectangle area: 12
Enter rectangle height: 3
The rectangle's width is: 4
(closed Scanner object)
```

```
Goals per player: 1
Enter rectangle area: 12
Enter rectangle height: 0
An error occurred: / by zero at line 28
(closed Scanner object)
```

The code within the `try` block has several distinct sections:

- An initial computation occurs. This is meant to illustrate some code that *may* throw an exception.
- A `Scanner` object is created. Note that the scanner is declared before the `try` block, and initialized to `null`.
- The `Scanner` is used to get input from the keyboard.
- A result is computed and output to the console. This computation may also throw an exception.

If an exception occurs, the `catch` block prints the exception's cause and the line number at which it occurred. The `finally` block closes the `Scanner` object, but only if it's already been created. The first run shown above illustrates a normal control flow where no exception occurs. But if the user entered a zero value for the rectangle's height, a divide by zero occurs. At that point, the exception's information is displayed by the `catch` block, and the `Scanner` object is closed in the `finally` block. This is shown in the second run above.

Now let's suppose that the initial code within the `try` block causes an exception. This can be simulated by changing the number of players to zero:

```
1       int players = 0;
```

```
An error occurred: / by zero at line 12
```

As you can see in the program's output, when an exception occurs in the first section of code in the `try` block, the exception is handled in the `catch` block, and the `Scanner` object isn't closed since its value was still null when the exception was thrown. The `finally` block is always executed whether an exception occurs or not, and cleanup code can be placed there to handle any cleanup no matter which path the control flow has taken. Note also that the `finally` block is executed if an exception occurs but isn't handled by any of the `catch` blocks.

Rethrowing Exceptions

After an exception is caught, it can be processed appropriately in a `catch` block and then re-thrown. This allows your `catch` block to process the error that occurred, while allowing the exception to continue in order to be caught by one of the methods further up the call stack. If a `finally` block is present, it's executed even if an exception occurs and is re-thrown. Re-throwing an exception in a `catch` block is done with the syntax "`throw ex;`", where `ex` is the exception.

Throwing Exceptions

Your code can throw an exception. When you do this, you're actually throwing an object of the `Exception` class, or one of its subclasses. Example 12.3 shows how to create and throw an exception containing a particular error message,

```
1  import static java.lang.System.out;
2  import java.util.Scanner;
3
4  public class Test {
5    public static void main(String[] args) throws Exception {
6      out.println("The result is " + compute(4507.3910));
7    }
8
9    private static double compute(double inputValue) throws Exception {
10     boolean error = true; // simulate an unexpected error
11     if (error) {
12       Exception exception = new Exception("Something unexpected happened in
         compute()");
13       throw exception;
```

Example 12.3. Throwing an exception.

```
14      }
15
16      return Math.sqrt(inputValue);
17    }
18 }
```

```
Exception in thread "main" java.lang.Exception: Something unexpected happened in compute()
        at Test.compute(Test.java:12)
        at Test.main(Test.java:6)
```

Any time a method *may* throw a particular exception type, it must append a "throws" clause to the method's declaration, as seen on lines 5 and 9 of example 12.3. While it's possible to use an exception to handle any error situation, this should only be done in exceptional error conditions. Exceptions shouldn't be used for normal flow of control, or for expected errors. There are two reasons for this,

- Since a thrown exception can skip up several levels in the call stack, it can obfuscate the flow of control.
- Exception processing is less efficient at runtime than normal control flow, so it shouldn't be a common occurrence.

Technique 20. Throw exceptions only in exceptional error situations

Exceptions should only be thrown in exceptional error situations. They shouldn't be used for normal control flow or expected errors. A method should respond to expected errors such as an invalid parameter value by returning an error code instead of throwing an exception.

You can define your own exception class, which must extend `Exception` or one of its subclasses. This can help to indicate specific error conditions and catch them easily by giving the specialized exception class its own `catch` block.

Now that we know how to catch and process exceptions, we can revise example 10.13 to handle invalid input in the entry of flight departure and arrival times. That section of code is reproduced here as example 12.4,

```
1    out.print("Departure time (hour:minute): ");
2    String departure = input.nextLine();
3    int colonIndex = departure.indexOf(':');
4    int departureHour = -1, departureMinute = -1;
5    if (colonIndex > 0) {
6      departureHour = Integer.parseInt(departure.substring(0, colonIndex));
7      departureMinute = Integer.parseInt(departure.substring(colonIndex + 1));
8    }
9
10   if (departureHour == -1 || departureMinute == -1) {
11     out.println("Invalid departure time");
12     return;
13   }
```

Example 12.4. Getting departure time from the user.

```
(A)dd flight
(D)elete flight
(C)hange a flight
(L)ist all flights
(1)Search by airline and flight number
(2)Search by destination
(E)xit
a
Airline: Delta
Flight Number: 312
Origin: JFK
Destination: LAX
Departure time (hour:minute): 10:30x
Exception in thread "main" java.lang.NumberFormatException: For input string: "30x"
        at java.base/java.lang.NumberFormatException.forInputString(NumberFormatException.java:68)
        at java.base/java.lang.Integer.parseInt(Integer.java:652)
        at java.base/java.lang.Integer.parseInt(Integer.java:770)
        at Example_Flights.addFlight(Example_Flights.java:78)
        at Example_Flights.main(Example_Flights.java:32)
```

The user's input is assigned to the **departure** string on line 2. If it doesn't contain a colon character, an error message is displayed and the **addFlight** method returns. If a colon does exist, but two valid integers don't exist before and after it, an exception is thrown and the program terminates as seen in the above screen shot. We can handle invalid input, and allow the user to re-enter the departure time by putting the code within a *try-catch* block and enclose it in a loop to allow the user to keep trying until the input's format is valid. Example 12.5 shows the revised code,

```
1    boolean valid = false;
2    int departureHour, departureMinute;
3    do {
4      out.print("Departure time (hour:minute): ");
5      String departure = input.nextLine();
6      int colonIndex = departure.indexOf(':');
7      departureHour = -1;
8      departureMinute = -1;
9      if (colonIndex > 0) {
10       try {
11         departureHour = Integer.parseInt(departure.substring(0, colonIndex));
12         departureMinute = Integer.parseInt(departure.substring(colonIndex + 1))
     ;
13         valid = true;
14       }
15       catch (NumberFormatException ex) {
16         // ignore this error
17       }
```

Example 12.5. Handling invalid user input.

```
18    }
19
20    if (departureHour == -1 || departureMinute == -1)
21      out.println("Invalid departure time");
22  } while (!valid);
```

```
a
Airline: Delta
Flight Number: 312
Origin: JFK
Destination: LAX
Departure time (hour:minute): 1030
Invalid departure time
Departure time (hour:minute): 10:30x
Invalid departure time
Departure time (hour:minute): 10:30
Arrival time (hour:minute): 13:55
```

The `while` loop and `valid` flag in example 12.5 allow repeated user input of the flight departure time until a valid time is entered. In case the numbers before or after the colon character are invalid, the `catch` block catches the exception and the loop is allowed to repeat.

12.2 Writing to a File

Now that we know about exceptions, we can learn how to write to a text file. In order to do this, we'll need to create two objects, one of the `File` class and another of the `FileWriter` class. The `File` object receives the path of the file that we want to write to as a parameter to its constructor. The `FileWriter` class receives the `File` object as a parameter to its constructor. After creating both objects, we can use the `print` method of the `FileWriter` class to write lines to the file, and when we're done we call the `FileWriter`'s `close` method. Example 12.6 shows this sequence of events, and writes the first fifteen powers of 2 to a file called `powers_of_2.txt` in the user's home directory.

```
1   import static java.lang.System.out;
2   import java.io.File;
3   import java.io.FileWriter;
4   import java.io.IOException;
5
6   public class Test {
7     public static void main(String[] args) throws IOException {
8
9       String filePath = System.getProperty("user.home") + "/powers_of_2.txt";
10      File file = new File(filePath);
11      FileWriter writer = new FileWriter(file);
12      for (int i = 0; i <= 15; i++)
13        writer.write((int) Math.pow(2, i) + "\n");
14      writer.close();
15      out.println("Done writing to " + filePath);
16    }
17  }
```

```
1
2
4
8
16
32
64
128
256
512
1024
2048
4096
8192
16384
32768
```

Example 12.6. Writing to a file.

```
Done writing to /Users/marwan/powers_of_2.txt
```

The output of the program is shown above, and the contents of the new file, that is, the powers of 2, are shown in the margin. The "\n" notation denotes a newline character which causes the output to advance to a new line. The following sections discuss the above example in further detail.

File Paths

After running the code in example 12.6, you should be able to find the file that was written by the program in your home directory. Your home directory is retrieved by the Java program using the syntax `System.getProperty("user.home")`, and then stored in the `directory` string. The file path consists of the directory name followed by a slash, followed by the file name. The file extension in our case is ".txt", but you can specify any extension that you want, or no extension at all.

If you're on Windows, your home directory is under "c:\users". If you're on a Mac, it's under "/Users".

Relative paths are allowed as well, and if used, will be relative to your project's root directory in Eclipse. To see this in action, you can just use the file name as the file path, without the directory name or slash. After the program runs, right-click on the project's root in Package Explorer and choose "Refresh", after which you'll see the "powers_of_2.txt" file in the project's file tree alongside the "src" directory. You can even double click on it in Package Explorer to open the file in Eclipse.

Exceptions

Since creating a `FileWriter` object may throw an exception, either the `FileWriter` creation has to be placed in a `try` block, or the method declaration has to include a "throws" clause. In example 12.6 we've added the `throws` clause to the `main` method, but you can choose to wrap file I/O in try-catch blocks if that's your preference.

Appending to a File

To append to an existing file instead of creating a new file, add another parameter to the `FileWriter`'s constructor with the value `true`. This tells the `FileWriter` to keep the existing file if it's already there, and append to the file's existing contents.

Exercises

12.1   Write a program that prompts the user for a recipe's name, its ingredient list and preparation instructions, then creates a text file containing the information that was entered by the user.

12.2   Use exercise 8.2 as a starting point. After creating the NewsStory class, create a NewsStory object using data entered by the user, then save the story record to a file.

12.3 Reading from a File

Reading from a file in Java is very similar to writing to a file. You would create a `File` object, passing its constructor the path to the file that you want to read. Then you'd create a `FileReader` object, passing its constructor the `File` object. We'll go a step further and create a `BufferedReader` object, passing its constructor the `FileReader` object, and this allows us to use the `readLine` method of the `BufferedReader` class to easily read each line of the file. Example 12.7 shows how to read the file that was written in example 12.6,

```
1   import static java.lang.System.out;
2   import java.io.BufferedReader;
3   import java.io.File;
4   import java.io.FileReader;
5   import java.io.IOException;
6
7   public class Test {
8     public static void main(String[] args) throws IOException {
9
10      String filePath = System.getProperty("user.home") + "/powers_of_2.txt";
11      File file = new File(filePath);
12      FileReader reader = new FileReader(file);
13      BufferedReader bufferedReader = new BufferedReader(reader);
14      do {
15        String line = bufferedReader.readLine();
16        if (line == null)
17          break;
18        out.println(line);
19      } while (true);
20      bufferedReader.close();
21    }
22  }
```

Example 12.7. Reading from a file.

```
1
2
4
8
16
32
64
128
256
512
1024
2048
4096
8192
16384
32768
```

note that the program doesn't make any assumption with regard to the length of the file. It keeps looping until the `readLine` method returns null, at which point it exits from the "do-while" loop. It's also possible to use `Scanner` to read from a text file, which allows us to use the convenient methods `nextInt`, `nextDouble`, and so on. Example 12.8 shows how to use the `Scanner` class to read numbers from the "powers_of_2.txt" file, add them up and display the total,

```
1   import static java.lang.System.out;
2   import java.io.File;
3   import java.io.IOException;
4   import java.util.Scanner;
5
6   public class Test {
7     public static void main(String[] args) throws IOException {
8
9       String filePath = System.getProperty("user.home") + "/powers_of_2.txt";
10      File file = new File(filePath);
```

Example 12.8. Reading from a file using `Scanner`.

```
11    Scanner reader = new Scanner(file);
12    int sum = 0;
13    while (reader.hasNext())
14      sum += reader.nextInt();
15    reader.close();
16    out.println("The sum of the first fifteen powers of 2 is " + sum);
17  }
18 }
```

```
The sum of the first fifteen powers of 2 is 65535
```

Note the use of `hasNext` in example 12.8, which allows the concise loop syntax as opposed to the loop in example 12.7.

`BufferedReader` and `Scanner` are higher level classes which use the lower level `FileReader` class under the hood. They're both good examples of abstraction. Reading with `FileReader` in our program would entail more code because it doesn't have `nextLine`, `hasNext`, `nextInt` and other convenient methods. Abstractions usually allow more concise syntax, but with that benefit comes hidden danger. You should always think about runtime performance when using abstractions because you usually don't know exactly how they're implemented.

Tip 9. Be cautious when using abstractions. Although using abstractions is encouraged, you should investigate the runtime performance characteristics of classes or methods that you utilize. Unless you wrote it yourself, you aren't usually aware of what the code is doing under the hood.

Exercises

12.3 Download a text file that contains a list of English words, for example search for "Google 10000 words" to find `google-10000-english.txt`. Write a program that reads this file and prints out the word containing the most vowels.

12.4 Repeat exercise 12.3 and find the word that ends with the most vowels.

12.4 Binary I/O

Binary input and output are similar to text-based I/O, but the data you're reading or writing is stored within the file in its native format. For example, a signed integer would be stored in the standard two's compliment format and occupies four bytes in the file. Binary format is useful in some situations to reduce the file size and also speed up input and output, since numeric data doesn't need to be converted to and from a text format. Example 12.9 shows how to write the first fifteen powers of 2 to a binary file, while example 12.10 shows how to read the same numbers from a binary file,

```java
import static java.lang.System.out;
import java.io.DataOutputStream;
import java.io.FileOutputStream;
import java.io.IOException;

public class Test {

  public static void main(String[] args) throws IOException {
    String filePath = "powers_of_2.bin";
    DataOutputStream stream = new DataOutputStream (new FileOutputStream(
      filePath));
    for (int i = 0; i <= 15; i++)
      stream.writeInt((int) Math.pow(2, i));
    stream.close();
    out.println("Done writing to " + filePath);
  }
}
```

Example 12.9. Writing to a binary file.

```
Done writing to powers_of_2.bin
```

```java
import static java.lang.System.out;
import java.io.DataInputStream;
import java.io.FileInputStream;
import java.io.IOException;

public class Test {

  public static void main(String[] args) throws IOException {
    String filePath = "powers_of_2.bin";
    DataInputStream stream = new DataInputStream(new FileInputStream(filePath))
      ;
    int sum = 0;
    while (stream.available() > 0)
      sum += stream.readInt();
    stream.close();
    out.println("The sum is " + sum);
  }
}
```

Example 12.10. Reading from a binary file.

```
The sum is 65535
```

The code is similar to the text-based examples, but writing binary data uses the DataOutputStream class with its writeInt method, while reading binary data uses the DataInputStream class with its readInt and available methods. The binary file is 64 bytes in size, with each of the sixteen integers using four bytes.

Exercises

12.5   Write a program that saves the numbers 1 to 10 to a binary file. Download a free hex editor and view the file. Identify the bytes that represent each of the ten integers. Look up hexadecimal format online if you're not familiar with it.

12.6   Repeat exercise 12.5 with a short string.

12.7   Repeat exercise 12.5 with the integers -1 through -10. Look up two's compliment format online to learn more about it.

12.8   Repeat exercise 12.5 with the floating point numbers 1, 1000 and 0.001. Look up the IEEE 754 format online to learn more about it.

12.5 Object Serialization

To *serialize* an object is to write it to a file. To *deserialize* an object is to read it from a file. Serialization is sometimes called *persistence*.

When writing objects to a file, or reading them from a file, you can use the techniques shown in the previous section to write and read each of the object's fields separately. But, there's a more convenient way to write objects to files and read them from files. It involves the object's class implementing the `Serializable` interface. Once this is done, the `ObjectOutputStream` and `ObjectInputStream` classes can be used to write an object to a file in one step, and read it from a file in one step. Example 12.11 shows a class named `Language`, which implements the `Serializable` interface. This interface doesn't include any methods, but lets the serialization methods know that the class can be serialized.

Example 12.11. Implementing a serializable class.

```
1   import java.io.Serializable;
2
3   class Language implements Serializable {
4
5       private String name;
6       private char[] firstFewLetters;
7       private int speakers;
8
9       public Language (String name, char[] firstFewLetters, int speakers) {
10          this.name = name;
11          this.firstFewLetters = new char[firstFewLetters.length];
```

```
12    for (int i = 0; i < firstFewLetters.length; i++)
13      this.firstFewLetters[i] = firstFewLetters[i];
14    this.speakers = speakers;
15  }
16
17  @Override
18  public String toString() {
19    String result = name + ", " + speakers + " speakers: [";
20    for (char ch : firstFewLetters)
21      result += ch + ",";
22    result += "...]";
23    return result;
24  }
25 }
```

Note that the `firstFewLetters` character array in example 12.11 is copied from an array that's passed in, as opposed to copying the array reference. This means the `Language` object has its own copy that won't be affected in case the array that was passed into its constructor is later modified by the caller.

The `main` method in the next example (12.12) creates several `Language` objects, writes them to a file, then reads the language data from the file and prints it out.

```
1  import static java.lang.System.out;
2  import java.io.FileInputStream;
3  import java.io.FileOutputStream;
4  import java.io.IOException;
5  import java.io.ObjectInputStream;
6  import java.io.ObjectOutputStream;
7
8  public class Test {
9
10   public static void main(String[] args) throws IOException,
11       ClassNotFoundException {
12
12     Language english = new Language ("English", new char[] { 'a', 'b', 'c', 'd'
         , 'e' }, 510_000_000);
13     Language japanese = new Language ("Japanese", new char[] { '\u3041', '\
         u3042', '\u3043', '\u3044', '\u3045' }, 127_000_000);
14     Language urdu = new Language ("Urdu", new char[] { '\u0627', '\u0628', '\
         u067e', '\u062a', '\u0679' }, 104_000_000);
15
16     ObjectOutputStream outputStream = new ObjectOutputStream(new
         FileOutputStream("languages.bin"));
17     outputStream.writeInt(3); // write number of objects being saved
18     outputStream.writeObject(english);
19     outputStream.writeObject(japanese);
20     outputStream.writeObject(urdu);
21     outputStream.close();
22
23     ObjectInputStream inputStream = new ObjectInputStream(new FileInputStream("
         languages.bin"));
24     int count = inputStream.readInt();  // read number of objects to load
25     for (int i = 0; i < count; i++) {
26       Language language = (Language) inputStream.readObject();
27       out.println(language);
```

Example 12.12. Serializing objects.

If foreign language characters don't appear properly in the output, go into the Run Configurations dialog, choose the current run configuration, then go to the Common tab, and change the encoding to UTF-8 in the Encoding section.

```
28      }
29      inputStream.close();
30    }
31 }
```

```
English, 510000000 speakers: [a,b,c,d,e,...]
Japanese, 127000000 speakers: [あ,ぁ,い,ぃ,う,...]
Urdu, 104000000 speakers: [ث,ٹ,پ,ب,ا,...]
```

Syntactic sugar is alternate syntax that doesn't change the meaning of code, but makes it easier to read.

Java allows you to add underlines to in an integer constant to make it easier to read, thus `127_000_000` is the same as `127000000`.

In Java, characters hold data in the Unicode format, which represent letters in any language. Non-English characters typically occupy two bytes or more, and may be represented as a hexadecimal constant such as `\u3041`. Each byte is represented by two hex digits.

It's important for you to be familiar with the binary and hexadecimal number systems, and to be able to convert numbers between binary, hexadecimal and decimal. There are many good online tutorials on number systems.

In example 12.12, three `Language` objects are created. An `ObjectOutputStream` object is created, the number of languages (three) is written to the output stream, then each of the languages is written and the stream is closed. The code then creates an `ObjectInputStream` object and reads the number of languages from the file. Finally, each language is read and printed to the console.

Exercises

12.9   Start with example 8.8. Save a few `Car` objects to a file, then write another program that reads the `Car` objects from the file and prints them to the console.

12.6 Example: Flight Database

Now that we know how to write to, and read from files, we'll update the flight database example from chapter 10. When the program starts up, it reads flights from a data file. If the file doesn't exist, it creates the sample flights. When the program exits, it writes the flights to the data file, so the data is preserved until the next run.

Example 12.13. Adding serialization to the flight management application.

```java
1   ...
2   import java.io.FileInputStream;
3   import java.io.FileOutputStream;
4   import java.io.IOException;
5   import java.io.ObjectInputStream;
6   import java.io.ObjectOutputStream;
7   import java.io.Serializable;
8   ...
9     public static void main(String[] args) {
10  ...
11      ArrayList<Flight> flights = new ArrayList<>();
12      readFlights(flights);
13
14      boolean done = false;
15      while (!done) {
16  ...
17      }
18
19      writeFlights(flights);
20      input.close();
21    }
22  ...
23    private static void readFlights(ArrayList<Flight> flights) {
24      try {
25        ObjectInputStream inputStream = new ObjectInputStream(new FileInputStream
          ("flights.dat"));
26        int count = inputStream.readInt();  // read number of objects to load
27        for (int i = 0; i < count; i++) {
28          Flight flight = (Flight) inputStream.readObject();
29          flights.add(flight);
30        }
31        inputStream.close();
32      }
33      catch (IOException ex) {
34        out.println("An error occurred reading flight data: " + ex.getMessage());
35
36        // add default sample data
37        flights.add(new Flight("JFK", "MCO", "Delta", 1100, 13, 30, 16, 11));
38        flights.add(new Flight("LGA", "LAX", "United", 29, 6, 0, 9, 21));
39        flights.add(new Flight("CLE", "PDX", "Delta", 412, 9, 59, 11, 15));
40        flights.add(new Flight("SAT", "BWI", "American", 11, 20, 42, 1, 2));
41        flights.add(new Flight("LFT", "ATL", "Delta", 90, 12, 0, 15, 57));
42        flights.add(new Flight("SNA", "CVG", "Southwest", 170, 10, 30, 12, 28));
43      }
44      catch (ClassNotFoundException ex) {
45        out.println("An error occurred reading flight data: " + ex.getMessage());
46      }
47    }
48
49    private static void writeFlights(ArrayList<Flight> flights) {
50      try {
51        ObjectOutputStream outputStream = new ObjectOutputStream(new
          FileOutputStream("flights.dat"));
52        outputStream.writeInt(flights.size()); // write number of flights being
          saved
53        for (Flight flight : flights)
54          outputStream.writeObject(flight);
55        outputStream.close();
56      }
57      catch (IOException ex) {
58        out.println("An error occurred writing flight data: " + ex.getMessage());
59      }
```

```
60   }
61   ...
62   class Flight implements Serializable {
63   ...
64   }
```

```
l
Delta 1100 (JFK 13:30 -> MCO 16:11)
United 29 (LGA 06:00 -> LAX 09:21)
Delta 412 (CLE 09:59 -> PDX 11:15)
American 11 (SAT 20:42 -> BWI 01:02)
Delta 90 (LFT 12:00 -> ATL 15:57)
Southwest 170 (SNA 10:30 -> CVG 12:28)

(A)dd flight
(D)elete flight
(C)hange a flight
(L)ist all flights
(1)Search by airline and flight number
(2)Search by destination
(E)xit
d
Airline: delta
Flight number: 1100
Deleted

(A)dd flight
(D)elete flight
(C)hange a flight
(L)ist all flights
(1)Search by airline and flight number
(2)Search by destination
(E)xit
e
```

```
(A)dd flight
(D)elete flight
(C)hange a flight
(L)ist all flights
(1)Search by airline and flight number
(2)Search by destination
(E)xit
l
United 29 (LGA 06:00 -> LAX 09:21)
Delta 412 (CLE 09:59 -> PDX 11:15)
American 11 (SAT 20:42 -> BWI 01:02)
Delta 90 (LFT 12:00 -> ATL 15:57)
Southwest 170 (SNA 10:30 -> CVG 12:28)
```

The code in example 12.13 to write and read flights mirrors the serialization of language objects in example 12.12. The flight database is read upon startup, and written when the program exits. The sample output shows deleting one flight, exiting, restarting, and listing the flights again to verify the change was saved.

Chapter Summary

- An exception occurs in case of an exceptional error. Code can catch such an exception and handle it appropriately.
- A Java program can write text to, and read text from a text file.
- A program can read and write data in its native format to a binary data file.
- Objects of a Java class can be written to a binary data file if the class implements the `Serializable` interface.

Creating `File` object

`throws` **block**

Creating `FileReader` **object**

Creating `BufferedReader` **object**

Reading a line

Closing reader

```java
 1  public static void main(String[] args) throws IOException {
 2
 3      File file = new File("datafile.txt");
 4      FileReader reader = new FileReader(file);
 5      BufferedReader bufferedReader = new BufferedReader(reader)
 6      List<String> lines = new ArrayList<>();
 7      do {
 8          String line = bufferedReader.readLine();
 9          if (line == null)
10              break;
11          lines.add(line);
12      } while (true);
13      bufferedReader.close();
14  }
```

Exercise Solutions

12.1
```java
 1  import static java.lang.System.out;
 2  import java.io.File;
 3  import java.io.FileWriter;
 4  import java.io.IOException;
 5  import java.util.Scanner;
 6
 7  public class Test {
 8
 9      public static void main(String[] args) throws IOException {
10
11          Scanner input = new Scanner(System.in);
12          out.print("Enter recipe name: ");
13          String name = input.nextLine();
14          out.print("Enter ingredient list: ");
15          String ingredients = input.nextLine();
16          out.print("Enter preparation instructions: ");
```

```
17      String instructions = input.nextLine();
18      input.close();
19
20      FileWriter writer = new FileWriter(new File("recipe.txt"));
21      writer.write(name + "\n");
22      writer.write(ingredients + "\n");
23      writer.write(instructions + "\n");
24      writer.close();
25      out.println("Done");
26    }
27  }
```

```
Enter recipe name: Easy Tuna Casserole
Enter ingredient list: 3 cups cooked macaroni, 1 can tuna, 1 can cream of chicken soup, 1 cup
Enter preparation instructions: Preheat oven to 350 degrees, combine the macaroni, tuna and so
Done
```

12.2

```
1   import static java.lang.System.out;
2   import java.io.File;
3   import java.io.FileWriter;
4   import java.io.IOException;
5   import java.io.Serializable;
6   import java.util.Scanner;
7
8
9   public class Test {
10
11    public static void main(String[] args) throws IOException {
12
13      Scanner input = new Scanner(System.in);
14
15      NewsStory story = new NewsStory();
16      out.print("Enter title: ");
17      story.title = input.nextLine();
18      out.print("Enter summary: ");
19      story.summary = input.nextLine();
20      out.print("Enter author: ");
21      story.author = input.nextLine();
22      out.print("Enter publication year: ");
23      story.publicationYear = input.nextInt();
24      input.nextLine();
25
26      input.close();
27
28      FileWriter writer = new FileWriter(new File("story.txt"));
29      writer.write(story.title + "\n");
30      writer.write(story.summary + "\n");
31      writer.write(story.author + "\n");
32      writer.write(story.publicationYear + "\n");
33      writer.close();
34      out.println("Done");
35    }
36  }
37
38  class NewsStory {
39    String title;
40    String summary;
41    String author;
42    int publicationYear;
43  }
```

```
Enter title: How fast is the universe expanding? Galaxies provide one answer
Enter summary: Determining how rapidly the universe is expanding is key to un
Enter author: Robert Sanders
Enter publication year: 2021
Done
```

12.3

```java
1  import static java.lang.System.out;
2  import java.io.File;
3  import java.io.IOException;
4  import java.util.Scanner;
5
6  public class Test {
7
8    public static void main(String[] args) throws IOException {
9
10     Scanner dictionary = new Scanner(new File("google-10000-english.
         txt"));
11
12     String result = "";
13     int resultVowels = 0;
14     while (dictionary.hasNext()) {
15       String word = dictionary.nextLine();
16       int vowels = wordVowels(word);
17       if (vowels > resultVowels) {
18         result = word;
19         resultVowels = vowels;
20       }
21     }
22
23     dictionary.close();
24     out.println("The word with the most vowels is " + result);
25   }
26
27   private static int wordVowels (String word) {
28     int count = 0;
29     for (int i = 0; i < word.length(); i++) {
30       char ch = word.charAt(i);
31       if (ch == 'i' || ch == 'o' || ch == 'e' || ch == 'u' || ch ==
         'a')
32         count++;
33     }
34     return count;
35   }
36 }
```

```
The word with the most vowels is telecommunications
```

12.4

```java
1  import static java.lang.System.out;
2  import java.io.File;
3  import java.io.IOException;
4  import java.util.Scanner;
5
6  public class Test {
7
8    public static void main(String[] args) throws IOException {
9
10     Scanner dictionary = new Scanner(new File("google-10000-english.
         txt"));
11
12     String result = "";
```

```
13    int resultVowels = 0;
14    while (dictionary.hasNext()) {
15      String word = dictionary.nextLine();
16      int vowels = trailingVowels(word);
17      if (vowels > resultVowels) {
18        result = word;
19        resultVowels = vowels;
20      }
21    }
22
23    dictionary.close();
24    out.println("The word that ends with the most vowels is " +
        result);
25  }
26
27  private static int trailingVowels (String word) {
28    int count = 0;
29    for (int i = word.length() - 1; i >= 0; i--) {
30      char ch = word.charAt(i);
31      if (ch != 'i' && ch != 'o' && ch != 'e' && ch != 'u' && ch !=
        'a')
32        break;
33      count++;
34    }
35    return count;
36  }
37 }
```

```
The word that ends with the most vowels is ieee
```

12.5
```
1  import static java.lang.System.out;
2  import java.io.DataOutputStream;
3  import java.io.FileOutputStream;
4  import java.io.IOException;
5
6  public class Test {
7
8    public static void main(String[] args) throws IOException {
9      String filePath = "data.bin";
10     DataOutputStream stream = new DataOutputStream (new
         FileOutputStream(filePath));
11     for (int i = 1; i <= 10; i++)
12       stream.writeInt(i);
13     stream.close();
14     out.println("Done writing to " + filePath);
15   }
16 }
```

```
00000000  00 00 00 01 00 00 00 02  00 00 00 03 00 00 00 04  |................|
00000010  00 00 00 05 00 00 00 06  00 00 00 07 00 00 00 08  |................|
00000020  00 00 00 09 00 00 00 0a ~10                        |........|
00000028       1
```

12.6
```
1  import static java.lang.System.out;
2  import java.io.DataOutputStream;
3  import java.io.FileOutputStream;
4  import java.io.IOException;
5
6  public class Test {
7
```

```
8    public static void main(String[] args) throws IOException {
9      String filePath = "data.bin";
10     DataOutputStream stream = new DataOutputStream (new
         FileOutputStream(filePath));
11     stream.writeBytes("Make a long story short.");
12     stream.close();
13     out.println("Done writing to " + filePath);
14   }
15 }
```

```
00000000   4d 61 6b 65 20 61 20 6c  6f 6e 67 20 73 74 6f 72   |Make a long stor|
00000010   79 20 73 68 6f 72 74 2e                            |y short.|
00000018
```

12.7
```
1  import static java.lang.System.out;
2  import java.io.DataOutputStream;
3  import java.io.FileOutputStream;
4  import java.io.IOException;
5
6  public class Test {
7
8    public static void main(String[] args) throws IOException {
9      String filePath = "data.bin";
10     DataOutputStream stream = new DataOutputStream (new
         FileOutputStream(filePath));
11     for (int i = -1; i >= -10; i--)
12       stream.writeInt(i);
13     stream.close();
14     out.println("Done writing to " + filePath);
15   }
16 }
```

```
00000000   ff ff ff ff  ff ff ff fe  ff ff ff fd ff ff ff fc   |................|
00000010   ff ff ff fb  ff ff ff fa  ff ff ff f9 ff ff ff f8   |................|
00000020   ff ff ff f7  ff ff ff f6                            |........|
00000028      -1                     -10      -2
```

12.8
```
1  import static java.lang.System.out;
2  import java.io.DataOutputStream;
3  import java.io.FileOutputStream;
4  import java.io.IOException;
5
6  public class Test {
7
8    public static void main(String[] args) throws IOException {
9      String filePath = "data.bin";
10     DataOutputStream stream = new DataOutputStream (new
         FileOutputStream(filePath));
11     stream.writeFloat(1);
12     stream.writeFloat(1000);
13     stream.writeFloat(0.001f);
14     stream.close();
15     out.println("Done writing to " + filePath);
16   }
17 }
```

```
00000000   3f 80 00 00  44 7a 00 00  3a 83 12 6f               |?...Dz..:..o|
0000000c       1           1000        0.001
```

12.9
```
1  import static java.lang.System.out;
2  import java.io.FileInputStream;
```

```
3  import java.io.FileOutputStream;
4  import java.io.IOException;
5  import java.io.ObjectInputStream;
6  import java.io.ObjectOutputStream;
7  import java.io.Serializable;
8
9  public class Test {
10
11    public static void main(String[] args) throws IOException,
          ClassNotFoundException {
12      Car car1 = new Car(34, "Honda", "Civic", 21);
13      Car car2 = new Car("Ford", "Fiesta");
14      Car car3 = new Car(19, "Toyota", "Corola", 22);
15
16      ObjectOutputStream outputStream = new ObjectOutputStream(new
          FileOutputStream("cars.bin"));
17      outputStream.writeInt(3); // write number of objects being saved
18      outputStream.writeObject(car1);
19      outputStream.writeObject(car2);
20      outputStream.writeObject(car3);
21      outputStream.close();
22
23      ObjectInputStream inputStream = new ObjectInputStream(new
          FileInputStream("cars.bin"));
24      int count = inputStream.readInt();  // read number of objects to
          load
25      for (int i = 0; i < count; i++) {
26        Car car = (Car) inputStream.readObject();
27        out.println(car);
28      }
29      inputStream.close();
30    }
31  }
32
33  class Car implements Serializable {
34    double mpg;
35    String make;
36    String model;
37    double tankCapacity;
38
39    static final double DEFAULT_MPG = 20;
40    static final double DEFAULT_TANK_CAPACITY = 15;
41
42    public Car(double mpg, String make, String model, double
          tankCapacity) {
43      this.mpg = mpg;
44      this.make = make;
45      this.model = model;
46      this.tankCapacity = tankCapacity;
47    }
48
49    public Car(String make, String model) {
50      this(DEFAULT_MPG, make, model, DEFAULT_TANK_CAPACITY);
51    }
52
53    double getRange() {
54      return tankCapacity * mpg;
55    }
56
57    @Override
58    public String toString() {
59      return make + " " + model + " [MPG " + mpg + "]";
```

```
60      }
61  }
```

```
Honda Civic [MPG 34.0]
Ford Fiesta [MPG 20.0]
Toyota Corola [MPG 19.0]
```

Program Performance | 13

13.1 Implementing ArrayList

In this chapter, we'll learn how to analyze program performance. We'll begin our discussion by implementing our own versions of ArrayList and LinkedList, then we'll analyze their performance characteristics.

The MyList Interface

Our own versions of ArrayList and LinkedList will omit some of the functionality offered by Java's built-in versions, while keeping the implementations realistic and comparable to Java's versions. We begin by defining the generic MyList interface which both will implement,

```
interface MyList<E> {
  public void insert (int index, E object) throws Exception;
  public void add (E object);
  public E get (int index) throws Exception;
  public int indexOf (E object);
  public int lastIndexOf (E object);
  public E remove(int index) throws Exception;
  public E set (int index, E object) throws Exception;
  public int size();
}
```

Example 13.1. The MyList interface

The Test Program

We also need a program to test our versions of MyArrayList and MyLinkedList. It tests each method of the MyList interface,

Example 13.2. Test program for
`MyArrayList` and `MyLinkedList`.

```java
public class Test {

  public static void main(String[] args) throws Exception {

    MyList<String> names = new MyArrayList<>();
    names.add("Peter");
    names.add("Mary");
    names.add("Heather");
    names.add("Henry");
    names.add("Elizabeth");
    names.add("Mary");

    out.println("Initially, list contents are: " + names);

    names.insert(2, "George");
    out.println("After inserting George at index 2, list contents are: " +
      names);

    names.insert(0, "Betty");
    out.println("After inserting Betty at index 0, list contents are: " + names
      );

    out.println("List size is: " + names.size());
    out.println("Element at index 3 is: " + names.get(3));
    out.println("Index of Mary is: " + names.indexOf("Mary"));
    out.println("lastIndexOf Mary is: " + names.lastIndexOf("Mary"));

    String removedName = names.remove(2);
    out.println("After removing index 2 (" + removedName + "), list contents
      are: " + names);

    names.set(1, "John");
    out.println("After putting John at index 1, list contents are: " + names);
  }
}
```

MyArrayList Constructor and Data Members

We'll begin with an empty version of `MyArrayList`, shown in example 13.3. This just contains a constructor and three private data
members,

- `array` is a native array containing the list's data, each element
  being of the generic type `E`.
- `size` keeps track of the number of array elements in use.
- `capacity` holds the size of `array`, which is always equal to or
  greater than `size`.

An `ArrayList` is a wrapper around a native array. It lets the caller
add elements to the internal array, remove elements from the internal
array, and so on. When the array grows past the size of the internal

native array, it creates a new, larger, internal array to hold the data, and copies the existing array's contents to the new array.

```
1  class MyArrayList<E> implements MyList<E> {
2
3    private E[] array = null;
4    private int size = 0;
5    private int capacity = 0;
6
7    public MyArrayList() {
8      capacity = 10;
9      array = (E[]) new Object[capacity];
10   }
11 }
```

Example 13.3. Empty version of MyArrayList.

The initial capacity in our implementation is 10. The constructor creates the internal array as an array of `Object` references, and each of the array's elements is able to hold a reference to an object of the generic type `E`, since Object is a superclass of `E`. This roundabout way of creating an array of `E` object references is due to one of the limitations of generics in Java, which is that a generic class can't create an array of the generic type.

MyArrayList.add()

In our implementation, each time the internal array grows, the capacity doubles. Java's version doesn't guarantee a specific increase in capacity beyond stipulating that adding an element has a fixed amortized runtime cost. Growing the internal array too frequently would cause a program using the `ArrayList` to be too slow, since each time the internal array grows, its contents must be copied to the new array. Example 13.4 shows the `toString` method, the `add` method, and the utility method `expandIfNeeded`, which is called from `add`,

```
1  class MyArrayList<E> implements MyList<E> {
2  ...
3    private void expandIfNeeded () {
4      if (size == capacity) {
5        int oldCapacity = capacity;
6        capacity *= 2;
7
8        // allocate new array
9        E[] newArray = (E[]) new Object[capacity];
10
11       // copy everything from the old array to the new array
12       for (int i = 0; i < oldCapacity; i++)
13         newArray[i] = array[i];
14
15       array = newArray;
```

Example 13.4. MyArrayList.add().

```
16      }
17    }
18
19    public void add (E object) {
20      expandIfNeeded();
21      array[size++] = object;
22    }
23
24    @Override
25    public String toString() {
26      String result = "[";
27      for (int i = 0; i < size; i++) {
28        result += array[i];
29        if (i < size-1)
30          result += ", ";
31      }
32      return result + "]";
33    }
34  ...
35 }
```

The `expandIfNeeded` method compares the size with the capacity. If there is no more free space, a new internal array is allocated with twice the capacity of the old one, then the contents of the old internal array are copied to the new internal array. Finally, the array reference is set to the newly-allocated array.

The "plus plus" operator is called the post-increment operator when it's used after a variable. When used before a variable, it increments the variable's value before using the value in the enclosing expression, and is called the pre-increment operator.

The `add` method expands the array if needed, then adds the object passed in to the end of the internal array. Note that the "plus plus" operator increments the `size` variable *after* the expression "array[size++]" is evaluated. That is, "size" is taken as the index into `array`, then "size" is incremented.

Finally, `toString` prints the elements of the array as comma-separated values within square brackets.

We have enough to start testing. We'll just need to add placeholders for the rest of the methods, so we can run a test,

Example 13.5. Placeholders for remaining `MyArrayList` methods.

```
1   public void insert (int index, E object) throws Exception {
2   }
3
4   public E get (int index) throws Exception {
5     return null;
6   }
7
8   public int indexOf (E object) {
9     return -1;
10  }
11
12  public int lastIndexOf (E object) {
13    return -1;
14  }
15
16  public E remove(int index) throws Exception {
```

```
17       return null;
18     }
19
20     public E set (int index, E object) throws Exception {
21       return null;
22     }
23
24     public int size() {
25       return size;
26     }
```

```
Initially, list contents are: [Peter, Mary, Heather, Henry, Elizabeth, Mary]
After inserting George at index 2, list contents are: [Peter, Mary, Heather, He
After inserting Betty at index 0, list contents are: [Peter, Mary, Heather, Her
List size is: 6
Element at index 3 is: null
Index of Mary is: -1
lastIndexOf Mary is: -1
After removing index 2 (null), list contents are: [Peter, Mary, Heather, Henry
After putting John at index 1, list contents are: [Peter, Mary, Heather, Henry
```

The above screen shot shows that the add, toString and size methods work, while the rest are yet to be implemented. We've started testing as soon as possible in keeping with technique 16 on page 192.

We'll proceed next to implement the remaining six methods. Normally we'd test after adding each method, but here we'll test after all six are added, to save some space.

MyArrayList.insert()

The insert method receives an object of type E to be inserted, and the index at which to insert it into the list. It performs the following steps,

1. Check that the index is valid. The index must refer to an existing list element. If it's not, an exception is thrown.
2. Expand the internal array if needed.
3. Move each element of the internal array over to the right, starting with the index at which the new data element will be inserted.
4. Set the contents of the array at the specified index to its new data value.
5. Increment the array size.

Example **13.6.**
MyArrayList.insert().

```
1   public void insert (int index, E object) throws Exception {
2     if (index < 0 || index > size - 1)
3       throw new Exception ("Invalid index");
4
5     expandIfNeeded();
6     for (int i = size - 1; i >= index; i--)
7       array[i+1] = array[i];
8     array[index] = object;
9     size++;
10  }
```

Inserting an element into an array list.

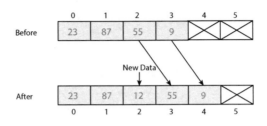

MyArrayList.get()

The **get** method takes one parameter, the index of the list element to be retrieved. It returns the list element of type E that's stored in the array at the specified index. It simply checks that the index is valid (if not, it throws an exception), then returns the element at the specified index.

Example 13.7. MyArrayList.get().

```
1   public E get (int index) throws Exception {
2     if (index < 0 || index > size - 1)
3       throw new Exception ("Invalid index");
4     return array[index];
5   }
```

MyArrayList.indexOf()

The **indexOf** method takes one parameter, an object of type **E**, and returns the first index at which that object occurs. If the object isn't found, it returns -1. The implementation simply loops from the beginning to the end of the array and returns immediately when the object being searched for is found. If the array terminates, -1 is returned since the object wasn't found. Note that the **equals** method is used to compare the parameter to each element of the array. Had we used the equality operator (==) instead, it would be testing whether the two refer to the *same object instance*.

```
1   public int indexOf (E object) {
2     for (int i = 0; i < size; i++)
3       if (object.equals(array[i]))
4         return i;
5     return -1;
6   }
```

Example 13.8.
MyArrayList.indexOf().

MyArrayList.lastIndexOf()

The lastIndexOf method works the same way as indexOf, except that it goes through the array backwards from the end. As with indexOf, it returns immediately if the object being searched for is found.

```
1   public int lastIndexOf (E object) {
2     for (int i = size - 1; i >= 0; i--)
3       if (object.equals(array[i]))
4         return i;
5     return -1;
6   }
```

Example 13.9.
MyArrayList.lastIndexOf().

MyArrayList.remove()

The remove method is similar to insert because it has to shift the array's contents starting at a particular index. This time though, it's shifting each element to the left and decrementing the list's size instead of incrementing it. The steps taken by remove are,

The remove method's implementation is a good example of the kind of iteration that you should be comfortable writing.

1. Check that the index is valid. The index must refer to an existing list element. If it's not, an exception is thrown.
2. Save the element that is to be removed in a temporary variable called result.
3. Move each element of the internal array over to the left, starting at the index after that of the list element to be removed, up to the end of the array.
4. Decrement the array size.
5. Return the element of type E that was removed.

```
1   public E remove(int index) throws Exception {
2     if (index < 0 || index > size - 1)
3       throw new Exception ("Invalid index");
4
5     E result = array[index];
6     for (int i = index; i < size - 1; i++)
7       array[i] = array[i+1];
8     size --;
```

Example 13.10.
MyArrayList.remove().

```
 9
10      return result;
11    }
```

MyArrayList.set()

The set method takes an index and an element to insert within the list at that index. It follows this procedure,

1. Check that the index is valid. The index must refer to an existing list element. If it's not, an exception is thrown.
2. Save the element that's currently at the specified index of the array in a temporary variable called result.
3. Save the new data within the array at the specified index.
4. Return the element of type E that was overwritten by the new data.

Example 13.11. MyArrayList.set().

```java
public E set (int index, E object) throws Exception {
  if (index < 0 || index > size - 1)
    throw new Exception ("Invalid index");

  E result = array[index];
  array[index] = object;
  return result;
}
```

Having implemented all the class's methods, we can run the test code again and we get the correct output as shown below,

```
Initially, list contents are: [Peter, Mary, Heather, Henry, Elizabeth, Mary]
After inserting George at index 2, list contents are: [Peter, Mary, George, Heather, Henry, Elizabeth, Mary]
After inserting Betty at index 0, list contents are: [Betty, Peter, Mary, George, Heather, Henry, Elizabeth, Mary]
List size is: 8
Element at index 3 is: George
Index of Mary is: 2
lastIndexOf Mary is: 7
After removing index 2 (Mary), list contents are: [Betty, Peter, George, Heather, Henry, Elizabeth, Mary]
After putting John at index 1, list contents are: [Betty, John, George, Heather, Henry, Elizabeth, Mary]
```

We shouldn't move on without testing the dynamic growth capability of MyArrayList. We'll test that next by adding 100 numbers to a MyArrayList, then printing them out. If all goes well, the internal array will grow as needed from its default capacity of 10 as more elements are added to the array,

Example 13.12. Testing the automatic growth of the MyArrayList's internal array.

```java
MyList<Integer> countdown = new MyArrayList<>();
for (int i = 99; i >= 0; i--)
  countdown.add(i);
for (int i = 0; i < countdown.size(); i++) {
  if (i % 20 == 0)
    out.println();
  out.printf("%4d", countdown.get(i));
}
```

```
99  98  97  96  95  94  93  92  91  90  89  88  87  86  85  84  83  82  81  80
79  78  77  76  75  74  73  72  71  70  69  68  67  66  65  64  63  62  61  60
59  58  57  56  55  54  53  52  51  50  49  48  47  46  45  44  43  42  41  40
39  38  37  36  35  34  33  32  31  30  29  28  27  26  25  24  23  22  21  20
19  18  17  16  15  14  13  12  11  10   9   8   7   6   5   4   3   2   1   0
```

While our implementation of `ArrayList` lacks the `iterator` method, and a few other details, it's a realistic example of how Java's `ArrayList` is implemented, and has similar performance characteristics. We'll start discussing performance in the next section.

Exercises

13.1 Add the following methods from the `List` interface to the `MyList` interface, then implement them in `MyArrayList`.

  a. void clear(): clears all elements of the list.
  b. boolean isEmpty(): returns `true` if the list is empty, and `false` otherwise.
  c. boolean remove(Object o): removes the first occurrence of the specified object from the list. Returns `true` if an element was removed, and `false` otherwise.

13.2 Program Performance

When we analyze program performance, we aim to find the relative performance of different algorithms on the same computer, not the relative performance of the same algorithm running on different computers. We compare different algorithms that accomplish the same task in order to determine which is the better algorithm. For example, we can compare different sorting algorithms to see which one is faster.

Comparing algorithms, not computers.

Comparing different algorithms that perform the same task, not algorithms that perform different tasks.

In addition, when we analyze program performance, we don't measure performance in seconds. Rather, we measure performance as it relates to the size of the program's input. As the size of the input grows, we observe how the algorithm's runtime grows. For example, an algorithm that has linear runtime is one whose runtime grows proportionally to the size of the input. An algorithm that has constant runtime is one whose runtime doesn't change no matter what the size of its input is.

We compare an algorithm's runtime to the size of its input.

We look at the worst-case performance of an algorithm, based on the possible input values, not the best-case scenario.

Another thing to keep in mind when analyzing program performance is that we're considering the worst case runtime. An algorithm can have different performance characteristics depending on the input, so it may be fast for some inputs and slow for others. Typically, we're only concerned with the *worst case* performance of the algorithm.

In most cases, we're only interested in the time performance of an algorithm, not how much space it requires to hold its data structures. In some cases though, the space requirements play a role in our decision making when choosing an algorithm.

Keeping in mind what was just said, let's look at an example. The `MyArrayList.indexOf` method in example 13.8 receives a parameter, which is the element we want to find in the list. But the algorithm implemented by this method actually has two inputs:

- The element that we want to find, the `object` parameter.
- The `array` class variable, which holds the internal array of list elements.

We have to think about the time it takes this algorithm to run, as it relates to the size of the input. In our case, the size of the input is the size of the internal array. Recall that the algorithm loops from the start of the array to its end looking for the object that was passed in as a parameter. Once it finds the object in question, the loop terminates even if it hasn't gone all the way to the end of the array.

In the best-case scenario, the object being searched for is at the very start of the internal array. The loop only executes once. Since the object is at the start of the array, it's found right away and the algorithm is done. But we can't consider this case. We have to assume the worst-case scenario. For this algorithm, the worst-case scenario is that the object being searched for isn't in the list, in which case the loop examines every element of the array and then -1 is returned indicating the object wasn't found.

O(n) runtime performance means the runtime is *linear* in the size of the input.

Since the actions taken in each iteration of the loop run in constant time, we now know that the algorithm's runtime is proportional to the size of the input. As the array's size grows, the runtime grows proportionally to it. It's traditional to denote the size of the input with the variable n. When the runtime is proportional to the input's size, we say that it is *on the order of n*, and we denote it as $O(n)$. This notation expresses the runtime as a function of the input size.

Suppose two algorithms perform the same task in O(n) runtime because they both have a loop that iterates once for each element of the input. They may perform the task in different ways, with different operations within the loop for each algorithm. One of the two algorithms may execute a loop iteration faster than the other when running on the same computer. Nevertheless, we consider them equivalent because we're only interested in the *approximate* runtime (hence the expression *on the order of*).

Sequences

Suppose an algorithm has two parts that are run in sequence, and each part runs in O(n) time. The overall runtime is 2*O(n). We discard the constant 2 because we're only interested in the *rough* measure of performance as related to the size of the input. Thus, after discarding the constant, we say that the overall runtime is actually O(n).

When analyzing runtime, we discard constant coefficients (multipliers).

If an algorithm has two parts that run in sequence, one having O(n) runtime and the other having $O(n^2)$ runtime, we discard the part with the smaller runtime and keep the one with the larger runtime. Again, this is because we're only interested in a *rough* measure of the runtime performance as related to the input size. Thus in this case, the overall runtime would be $O(n^2)$.

When analyzing runtime, we discard parts with lower runtime and keep the part with the higher runtime.

For example, suppose a method takes as input a two-dimensional array of grades, one row for each student's grades. Let's suppose this method computes the average grade for each student, then goes through the student list and prints each student's grade average. This method is shown in example 13.13,

```
1   public static void main(String[] args) throws Exception {
2
3       int[][] grades = new int[][] {
4           { 100,  90,  95,  98, 100,  90,  85 },
5           {  77,  94,  95,  95,  81,  93, 100 },
6           { 100,  91, 100,  98,  99,  85, 100 },
7           {  99,  75, 100,  50,  92,  99,  95 },
8       };
9
10      printGradeAverages(grades);
11  }
12
13  private static void printGradeAverages (int[][] grades) {
14
15      double[] averages = new double[grades.length];
16      for (int student = 0; student < grades.length; student++) {
17          int sum = 0;
```

Example 13.13. Printing student grade averages.

```
Student 1: 94.00
Student 2: 90.71
Student 3: 96.14
Student 4: 87.14
```

```
18      for (int grade = 0; grade < grades[student].length; grade++)
19        sum += grades[student][grade];
20      averages[student] = (double) sum / grades[student].length;
21    }
22
23    for (int student = 0; student < averages.length; student++)
24      out.printf("Student %d: %.2f\n", student + 1, averages[student]);
25  }
```

The `printGradeAverages` method contains two sections. The top section runs in O(nm) time where n is the number of students, and m is the number of grades per student. That's because it has a nested loop, the outer loop processing each student, and the inner processing each grade for the student. The bottom section runs in O(n) time because it loops once per student. So the overall runtime is O(nm) since that is larger than O(n).

Selections

When analyzing runtime of a selection, we add the runtime cost of evaluating the condition to that of the slower of the two alternative sections of code.

When an algorithm contains a selection, such as an if statement with an else clause, one of two sections of code will run, but not both. In this case, as with the cases we discussed above, we have to assume the worst and use the slower section's runtime as the overall runtime. But we should also take into account the time it takes to compute the if statement's *condition*. For example, suppose we have the following section of code,

```
1   if (names.contains(userName)) {
2     out.println("The user " + userName + " is in the list.");
3   }
4   else {
5     out.println("The user " + userName + " is not in the list.");
6   }
```

The notation we've been using is known as *Big-O notation*. An algorithm's runtime expressed in big-O notation is often referred to as its *runtime complexity*, or just its *complexity*. You can use these terms interchangeably.

The `if` clause contains one print statement which runs in constant time (that is, its runtime doesn't vary with the size of the input, which is the length of the name list). Likewise, the else clause also contains a single print statement, also having a constant runtime. But, the `if` condition evaluation takes O(n) time to run because the `contains` method loops over the list. So the overall runtime is O(n) because the slower of the `if` and `else` clauses runs in constant time and evaluating the `if` condition has O(n) runtime.

The runtime of a section of code that runs in constant time is denoted O(1). Note that n doesn't appear in the expression since the runtime is independent of it.

Figure 13.1 shows a visual comparison of the growth rates of some common runtimes, and figure 13.2 shows the same chart in a wider view (note the Y axis values in both figures). These figures illustrate what you already knew intuitively—a runtime that is quadratic grows very fast as the size of the input grows. Most algorithms that you will use frequently have a logarithmic, linear, or O(n log n) complexity. We'll discuss logarithmic complexity and provide an example later on in section 14.1. Table 13.1 lists these common runtimes with an example of each one.

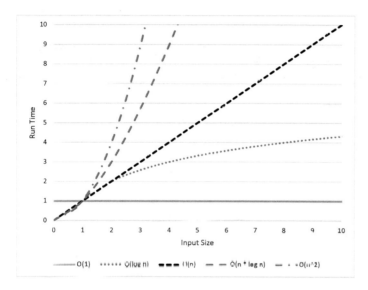

Figure 13.1: Comparing common runtimes.

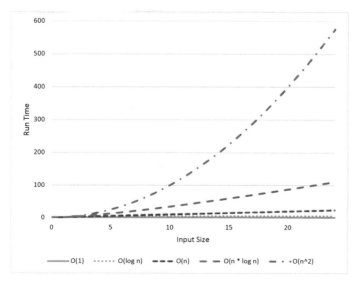

Figure 13.2: Comparing common runtimes (wide view).

Table 13.1: Common runtimes.

Logarithmic complexity, O(log n) is often written as O(lg n) when the logarithm has base 2. In this book, I will use O(log n) to refer to a base 2 logarithm, so you should consider O(log n) and O(lg n) as equivalent.

Runtime	Name	Example
O(1)	Constant	`MyArrayList.get()`
O(log n)	Logarithmic	Binary search (chapter 14)
O(n)	Linear	`MyArrayList.insert()`
O(n log n)	Log-linear	Merge sort (chapter 16)
$O(n^2)$	Quadratic	Bubble sort (chapter 16)

Referring back to the previous section, we can now analyze the complexity of each method of the `MyArrayList` class,

- `add`: This method expands the array if needed, then sets the value at a particular array index to the new data value, a constant-time operation, since using an index to access a particular element of a native Java array takes constant time. The expansion of the array takes place at infrequent intervals, doubling the array's size each time it's expanded. This effectively amortizes the runtime cost of expanding the array and the overall complexity of the `add` operation is constant, or O(1).
- `insert`: This expands the array if needed, and shifts all elements from a certain point to the end of the array over to the right by one. In the worst case, it loops through the whole array, so the complexity is linear, or O(n).
- `get`: This returns the value at a particular array index, a constant time operation, so its complexity is constant, or O(1).
- `indexOf`: This loops through the array in search of a particular value. At worst, it has to go through the whole array, so its complexity is linear, or O(n).
- `lastIndexOf`: This loops through the array in search of a particular value. At worst, it has to go through the whole array, so its complexity is linear, or O(n).
- `remove`: This contains a loop that shifts all elements after a certain point by one space to the left. In the worst case, this goes through most of the array, so the complexity is linear, or O(n).
- `set`: This sets a particular array element to a new value, a constant time operation, so its complexity is O(1).
- `size`: This returns the current size, which is stored in the private `size` data member, a constant time operation, so its complexity is O(1).

Operation	Complexity	Reason
add	O(1)	It just writes to the end of the array.
insert	O(n)	It shifts elements to the right starting at the index inserted into.
get	O(1)	It just gets the array element at a certain index.
indexOf	O(n)	It loops through the array looking for a particular value.
lastIndexOf	O(n)	It loops through the array looking for a particular value.
remove	O(n)	It shifts elements to the left starting after the index removed from.
set	O(1)	It just writes to a particular index in the array.
size	O(1)	It just returns the internal size variable.

Table 13.2: Complexity of each MyArrayList operation.

Exercises

13.2 What is the time complexity of this code?

```
1  int addAges(int[] ageArray) {
2    int sum = 0;
3    for (int i = 0; i < ageArray.length; i++)
4      sum += ageArray[i];
5    return sum;
6  }
```

13.3 What is the time complexity of this code?

```
1  ArrayList<Integer> doSomething(int[] array) {
2    ArrayList<Integer> results = new ArrayList<>();
3    for (int i = 0; i < array.length; i++) {
4      for (int j = i + 1; j < array.length; j++) {
5        results.add(array[i] + array[j]);
6      }
7    }
8    return results;
9  }
```

13.4 The following method computes a*b. What is its runtime?

```
1  int product(int a, int b) {
2    int sum = 0;
3    for (int i = 0; i < b; i++)
4      sum += a;
5    return sum;
6  }
```

13.5   The following method computes a%b, where "a" and "b" are positive integers. What is its runtime?

```
1   int mod(int a, int b) {
2     if (b <= 0)
3       return -1;
4     int div = a / b;
5     return a - div * b;
6   }
```

13.3 Implementing LinkedList

As we did with `ArrayList`, we'll implement our own version of Java's `LinkedList` and analyze its performance. A linked list implements the `List` interface just as the array list does, but the internal structure is completely different, and it has its own pros and cons in terms of performance when compared to an array list. For example, deleting the first element is a constant time operation in a linked list, whereas its complexity is linear in an array list.

The `Node` class

Each data element in a linked list is wrapped in a separate container object, which we'll call a *node*. In addition to the data element, each node has a pointer to the next node in the list. While `MyArrayList` contains an internal native array, `MyLinkedList` doesn't contain an array but a series of nodes, with each node pointing to the next one in the list. The `MyLinkedList` object keeps references to the first and last nodes. Example 13.14 shows the `Node` class and the beginnings of the `MyLinkedList` class.

Example 13.14. Node and MyLinkedList.

```
1   class Node<E> {
2     E element;
3     Node<E> next;
4
5     public Node (E element) {
6       this.element = element;
7     }
8   }
9
10  class MyLinkedList<E> implements MyList<E> {
11
12    Node<E> head = null;
13    Node<E> tail = null;
14    int size = 0;
15
16    public void add (E object) {
17    }
```

```
18
19    public void insert (int index, E object) throws Exception {
20    }
21
22    public E get (int index) throws Exception {
23      return null;
24    }
25
26    public int indexOf (E object) {
27      return -1;
28    }
29
30    public int lastIndexOf (E object) {
31      return -1;
32    }
33
34    public E remove(int index) throws Exception {
35      return null;
36    }
37
38    public E set (int index, E object) throws Exception {
39      return null;
40    }
41
42    public int size() {
43      return size;
44    }
45 }
```

Note that `Node` is generic, and its internal data is of the generic type `E`. `MyLinkedList` keeps track of the list's size in its `size` variable, and holds references to the first and last node in the `head` and `tail` member variables.

We'll use the same test code for `LinkedList` as we did for `ArrayList`. We just need to change the name `list` to a linked list,

```
1    MyList<String> names = new MyLinkedList<>();
```

Other than the above simple change, the rest of the test program can be used as shown in example 13.2. This illustrates the power of polymorphism, defined on page 208.

MyLinkedList.add()

Now that we have the outline of the `MyLinkedList` class and its testing code, our goal should be to get something minimal working so that we can start testing, in keeping with technique 16 on page 192. To do this, we'll just need to override `toString` and implement either `add` or `insert`. We'll choose `add` since it's simpler.

The `MyLinkedList.add` method adds a new list element to the end of the list by following these steps,

- Create a new `Node` object, initializing it with the data of type `E` being added to the list.
- Increment the internal `size` variable, which keeps track of the size of the list.
- Add the new `Node` object to the end of the linked list. There are two cases to consider:
  - If the list is empty when `add` is called, both `head` and `tail` are null. In this case, both `head` and `tail` will be set to the new node.
  - If the list is not empty, the existing last node will have a `null` value in its `next` reference. Its `next` reference will be changed to point to the new node, and the `tail` reference will also be set to the new node. Note that `tail` will be set to the new node in both of these cases.

The code implementing the above steps is shown in example 13.15,

Example 13.15. `MyLinkedList.add`.

```
1   public void add (E object) {
2
3       // create new node to hold the new data value
4       Node<E> newNode = new Node<E>(object);
5
6       // increment list size
7       size++;
8
9       // insert the new node at the end of the linked list
10      if (head == null)
11          head = newNode;
12      else
13          tail.next = newNode;
14      tail = newNode;
15  }
```

MyLinkedList.toString()

We're almost able to start testing. The only thing we need to do before running the first test is to write the `toString` method. The `toString` method follows the chain of nodes from the head to the tail, adding the data (i.e., the list element) contained in each node to the string that it returns. Following the linked list in this way is sometimes called *walking* the linked list.

The terms *pointer* and *reference* are often used interchangeably, especially by developers who work in both C and Java. A reference in C is called a pointer.

To walk the linked list, we create a new node pointer called `current`, and set its value to the `head`. Then we repeatedly process the current node and increment `current` to point to the next node, terminating once `current` is null at which point we've processed the last node in the chain. This process is illustrated in example 13.16,

```
1   Node<E> current = head;
2   while (current != null) {
3
4     // process the current node. The current node's data is accessed with the
        syntax 'current.element'
5     ...
6
7     // advance to the next node
8     current = current.next;
9   }
```

Example 13.16. Walking a linked list.

It is critical that you understand examples 13.16 and 13.17, especially the way that the `current` reference is dereferenced to access the current node's `element` (its data) and its `next` reference (the pointer to the next node). This kind of code is at the heart of linked lists, and many other data structures.

Loops are the way arrays are often processed. Loops are the algorithmic counterpart of the array data structure. In the same way, the pattern in example 13.16 is the algorithmic counterpart of the linked list data structure. It's a very common way of traversing a linked list to perform some operation on each node, and you'll see examples of this repeatedly throughout the rest of this section starting with example 13.17 that implements the `MyLinkedList.toString` method.

`MyLinkedList.toString` iterates through the linked list, adding each node's data to the string that is ultimately returned. The rest of the methods will be implemented next.

```
1    @Override
2    public String toString() {
3
4      String result = "[";
5      Node<E> current = head;
6      while (current != null) {
7
8        // add this node's data to the resulting string
9        result += current.element;
10       if (current.next != null)
11         result += ", ";
12
13       // advance to the next node
14       current = current.next;
15     }
16     return result + "]";
17   }
```

Example 13.17. `MyLinkedList.toString`.

At first glance, `MyLinkedList.toString` has linear runtime, but the repeated string concatenations are problematic, since each time a data element is concatenated to the result, a new string is created, and the list's contents 'so far' are copied to it. This technically makes it $O(n^2)$, and the same applies to `MyArrayList.toString`. Section 15.7 reveals the way to fix this.

```
Initially, list contents are: [Peter, Mary, Heather, Henry, Elizabeth, Mary]
After inserting George at index 2, list contents are: [Peter, Mary, Heather, Henry, Elizabeth, Mary]
After inserting Betty at index 0, list contents are: [Peter, Mary, Heather, Henry, Elizabeth, Mary]
List size is: 6
Element at index 3 is: null
Index of Mary is: -1
lastIndexOf Mary is: -1
After removing index 2 (null), list contents are: [Peter, Mary, Heather, Henry, Elizabeth, Mary]
After putting John at index 1, list contents are: [Peter, Mary, Heather, Henry, Elizabeth, Mary]
```

MyLinkedList.get()

The **get** method takes an integer index and returns the data element at that index within the list. It walks the linked list to get to the node at the specified index, then returns the node's data.

Example
MyLinkedList.get().

13.18.

```
1  public E get (int index) throws Exception {
2    if (index < 0 || index > size - 1)
3      throw new Exception ("Invalid index");
4
5    Node<E> current = head;
6    int counter = 0;
7    while (counter < index) {
8      current = current.next;
9      counter ++;
10   }
11
12   return current.element;
13 }
```

MyLinkedList.indexOf()

The **indexOf** method takes an object to look for in the list, and returns the index of the first occurrence of the object. It walks the linked list from the beginning until it finds the data it's looking for, or reaches the end of the list, in which case it returns -1.

Example
MyLinkedList.indexOf().

13.19.

```
1  public int indexOf (E object) {
2
3    Node<E> current = head;
4    int index = 0;
5    while (current != null) {
6      if (object.equals(current.element))
7        return index;
8      current = current.next;
9      index ++;
10   }
11
12   return -1;
13 }
```

MyLinkedList.lastIndexOf()

The **lastIndexOf** method takes an object to look for in the list, and returns the last index at which the object occurs within the list. It walks the linked list from the beginning to the end, keeping the last index at which it finds the data it's looking for. If the data isn't found, it returns -1.

```
1   public int lastIndexOf (E object) {
2
3       int result = -1;
4       Node<E> current = head;
5       int index = 0;
6       while (current != null) {
7         if (object.equals(current.element))
8           result = index;
9         current = current.next;
10        index ++;
11      }
12
13      return result;
14  }
```

Example   13.20.
MyLinkedList.lastIndexOf().

MyLinkedList.set()

The set method takes an index and a data item of type E, and writes the data item to the node at the specified index. It also returns the data that was previously at that index.

```
1   public E set (int index, E object) throws Exception {
2       if (index < 0 || index > size - 1)
3         throw new Exception ("Invalid index");
4
5       Node<E> current = head;
6       int counter = 0;
7       while (counter < index) {
8         current = current.next;
9         counter ++;
10      }
11
12      E result = current.element;
13      current.element = object;
14      return result;
15  }
```

Example   13.21.
MyLinkedList.set().

MyLinkedList.insert()

The insert method takes an index and an object to insert at that index within the list. It walks the list from the beginning until the node prior to the desired index (previous), then inserts the new data element into the chain after previous. This is done by setting the new node's next pointer to previous.next, then setting previous.next to the new node. Special handling is performed when the new node is inserted at the start or the end of the linked list.

Example   **13.22.**
`MyLinkedList.insert()`.

```java
 1  public void insert (int index, E object) throws Exception {
 2    if (index < 0 || index > size)
 3      throw new Exception ("Invalid index");
 4
 5    Node<E> newNode = new Node<>(object);
 6
 7    Node<E> current = head;
 8    int counter = 0;
 9    Node<E> previous = null;
10    while (counter < index) {
11      previous = current;
12      current = current.next;
13      counter++;
14    }
15
16    if (previous != null)
17      previous.next = newNode;
18    newNode.next = current;
19
20    size ++;
21
22    if (index == 0)
23      head = newNode;
24    if (index == size - 1)
25      tail = newNode;
26  }
```

Inserting an element into a linked list.

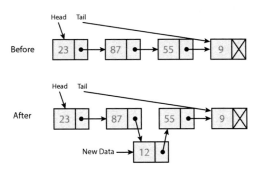

MyLinkedList.remove()

The `remove` method takes an index and removes the object at that index within the list. It walks the list from the beginning, finding the node to be deleted and the one prior to it (`previous`), then deletes the proper node by setting `previous.next` to `current.next`. Special handling is performed when the node to delete is at the start or the end of the linked list. In addition, the deleted data is returned by the `remove` method.

```
1   public E remove(int index) throws Exception {
2     if (index < 0 || index > size - 1)
3       throw new Exception ("Invalid index");
4
5     Node<E> current = head;
6     int counter = 0;
7     Node<E> previous = null;
8     while (counter < index) {
9       previous = current;
10      current = current.next;
11      counter++;
12    }
13
14    if (previous != null)
15      previous.next = current.next;
16    E result = current.element;
17
18    size --;
19
20    if (index == 0)
21      head = current.next;
22    if (index == size - 1)
23      tail = previous;
24
25    return result;
26  }
```

Example **13.23**.
`MyLinkedList.remove()`.

```
Initially, list contents are: [Peter, Mary, Heather, Henry, Elizabeth, Mary]
After inserting George at index 2, list contents are: [Peter, Mary, George, Heather, Henry, Elizabeth, Mary]
After inserting Betty at index 0, list contents are: [Betty, Peter, Mary, George, Heather, Henry, Elizabeth, Ma
List size is: 8
Element at index 3 is: George
Index of Mary is: 2
lastIndexOf Mary is: 7
After removing index 2 (Mary), list contents are: [Betty, Peter, George, Heather, Henry, Elizabeth, Mary]
After putting John at index 1, list contents are: [Betty, John, George, Heather, Henry, Elizabeth, Mary]
```

Each method's complexity can be analyzed as was done with `MyArrayList`,

- `add`: This creates a new node and points the existing last node to it, which requires constant time, so it runs in O(1) time.
- `insert`: This method needs to walk the linked list from the beginning to the desired index, which takes O(n) time.
- `get`: This walks the linked list from the start to the desired index, so it takes O(n) time.
- `indexOf`: Walks the linked list looking for a particular data item. In the worst case, it takes O(n) time.
- `lastIndexOf`: Walks the entire linked list and finds the last occurrence of a particular data item, so its complexity is O(n).
- `remove`: Walks the linked list to a specified index, so its complexity is O(n).
- `set`: Walks the linked list to a specified index, so its complexity is O(n).

Table 13.3: Complexity of each operation for both list implementations.

Operation	MyArrayList	MyLinkedList
add	O(1)	O(1)
insert	O(n)	O(n)
get	O(1)	O(n)
indexOf	O(n)	O(n)
lastIndexOf	O(n)	O(n)
remove	O(n)	O(n)
set	O(1)	O(n)
size	O(1)	O(1)
Removing first element	O(n)	O(1)
Inserting at beginning	O(n)	O(1)

- size: Returns the internal size data member, requiring constant time, so its complexity is O(1).

Table 13.3 shows the complexity of each operation for each of MyArrayList and MyLinkedList. A couple more rows have been added to show the relative performance of removing the first list element, and adding a new list element at the start of the list. The table highlights the pros and cons of ArrayList and LinkedList. ArrayList is a good choice in most cases, but LinkedList is very handy in certain cases. For example, the queue implementation shown in example 11.2 uses a list to hold the queue's elements. It uses add to add a new item to the queue, and remove(0) to remove an item from the queue. Both of those operations run in constant time when using a linked list, while an array list adds an item in constant time but requires O(n) time when removing the first element of the list.

Exercises

13.6 Repeat exercise 13.1 for MyLinkedList. Write the remove method's loop manually to get more coding practice (i.e., don't use the indexOf or remove(int) methods in the implementation of remove(Object)).

13.4 Timing Tests

To corroborate the above performance analysis, example 13.24 adds numbers to a `MyLinkedList`, then repeatedly deletes the first element until the list is empty. This is repeated with different list sizes and the time it takes to delete the numbers from the list is reported. Then, the process is repeated with a `MyLinkedList`. The results are charted in figure 13.3, and show that deleting the first element from a linked list has constant runtime, while deleting the first element from an array list runs in time linear in the array size.

```
1   public static void main(String[] args) throws Exception {
2
3     for (int size = 0; size <= 100000; size += 10000)
4       doTest(size, false);
5     for (int size = 0; size <= 100000; size += 10000)
6       doTest(size, true);
7   }
8
9   public static void doTest(int size, boolean useArrayList) throws Exception {
10
11    MyList<Integer> list = useArrayList ? new MyArrayList<>() : new
      MyLinkedList<>();
12
13    for (int i = 0; i < size; i++)
14      list.add((int) (Math.random() * 100));
15
16    long startTime = System.nanoTime();
17    while (list.size() != 0)
18      list.remove(0);
19    long endTime = System.nanoTime();
20
21    out.printf("Removing elements from %s of size %d took %d microseconds\n",
        useArrayList ? "array list" : "linked list", size, (endTime - startTime)
        /1000);
22  }
```

Example 13.24. Testing runtime of `remove(0)`.

```
Removing elements from linked list of size 0 took 2 microseconds
Removing elements from linked list of size 10000 took 906 microseconds
Removing elements from linked list of size 20000 took 1220 microseconds
Removing elements from linked list of size 30000 took 368 microseconds
Removing elements from linked list of size 40000 took 383 microseconds
Removing elements from linked list of size 50000 took 483 microseconds
Removing elements from linked list of size 60000 took 595 microseconds
Removing elements from linked list of size 70000 took 758 microseconds
Removing elements from linked list of size 80000 took 401 microseconds
Removing elements from linked list of size 90000 took 449 microseconds
Removing elements from linked list of size 100000 took 454 microseconds
Removing elements from array list of size 0 took 1 microseconds
Removing elements from array list of size 10000 took 169067 microseconds
Removing elements from array list of size 20000 took 714610 microseconds
Removing elements from array list of size 30000 took 1566097 microseconds
Removing elements from array list of size 40000 took 2772301 microseconds
Removing elements from array list of size 50000 took 4265944 microseconds
Removing elements from array list of size 60000 took 6151599 microseconds
Removing elements from array list of size 70000 took 8379022 microseconds
Removing elements from array list of size 80000 took 10922787 microseconds
Removing elements from array list of size 90000 took 13825244 microseconds
Removing elements from array list of size 100000 took 17107247 microseconds
```

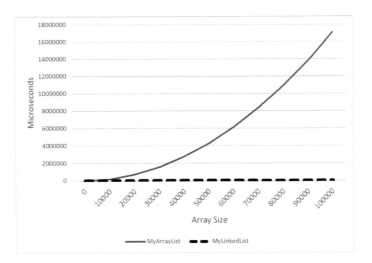

Figure 13.3: Runtime comparison of `ArrayList` and `LinkedList` when deleting first list element.

Finally, we'll run a similar timing test comparing `MyArrayList` and `MyLinkedList`, but this time the test will retrieve array elements by index. The results are charted in figure 13.4, and show that getting an element by index from an array list has constant runtime, while doing so with a linked list runs in time linear in the array size.

Example 13.25. Testing runtime of `get`.

```java
public static void main(String[] args) throws Exception {

  for (int size = 0; size <= 100000; size += 10000)
    doTest(size, false);
  for (int size = 0; size <= 100000; size += 10000)
    doTest(size, true);
}

public static void doTest(int size, boolean useArrayList) throws Exception {

  MyList<Integer> list = useArrayList ? new MyArrayList<>() : new
    MyLinkedList<>();

  for (int i = 0; i < size; i++)
    list.add((int) (Math.random() * 100));

  long startTime = System.nanoTime();
  for (int i = 0; i < size; i++)
    list.get(i);
  long endTime = System.nanoTime();

  out.printf("Getting elements from %s of size %d took %d microseconds\n",
    useArrayList ? "array list" : "linked list", size, (endTime - startTime)
    /1000);
}
```

```
Getting elements from linked list of size 0 took 0 microseconds
Getting elements from linked list of size 10000 took 93462 microseconds
Getting elements from linked list of size 20000 took 361789 microseconds
Getting elements from linked list of size 30000 took 881576 microseconds
Getting elements from linked list of size 40000 took 1499290 microseconds
Getting elements from linked list of size 50000 took 2310426 microseconds
Getting elements from linked list of size 60000 took 3498410 microseconds
Getting elements from linked list of size 70000 took 4723476 microseconds
Getting elements from linked list of size 80000 took 6150266 microseconds
Getting elements from linked list of size 90000 took 7646067 microseconds
Getting elements from linked list of size 100000 took 9688306 microseconds
Getting elements from array list of size 0 took 0 microseconds
Getting elements from array list of size 10000 took 839 microseconds
Getting elements from array list of size 20000 took 153 microseconds
Getting elements from array list of size 30000 took 246 microseconds
Getting elements from array list of size 40000 took 299 microseconds
Getting elements from array list of size 50000 took 375 microseconds
Getting elements from array list of size 60000 took 449 microseconds
Getting elements from array list of size 70000 took 523 microseconds
Getting elements from array list of size 80000 took 607 microseconds
Getting elements from array list of size 90000 took 719 microseconds
Getting elements from array list of size 100000 took 840 microseconds
```

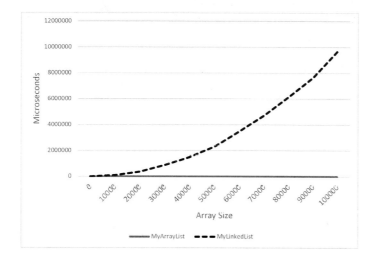

Figure 13.4: Runtime comparison of `ArrayList` and `LinkedList` when getting an element by index.

Chapter Summary

- `ArrayList` and `LinkedList` each implement the `List` interface, but have different performance characteristics, and each is appropriate to use in certain situations.
- When analyzing program performance, we focus on comparing different algorithms with respect to the size of the input.
- When analyzing program performance, we're concerned mainly with worst-case running time.

- Big-O notation summarizes runtime performance by expressing the runtime as a rough function of the input size.
- Timing tests can be used to verify performance analysis by measuring the runtime as the size of the input increases.

```
1  class MyLinkedList<E> implements MyList<E> {
2
3    Node<E> head = null;
4    Node<E> tail = null;
5    int size = 0;
6
7    public int indexOf (E object) {
8
9      Node<E> current = head;                       Start at the head
10     int index = 0;
11     while (current != null) {                     Loop until end of list
12       if (object.equals(current.element))
13         return index;                             Process each node
14       current = current.next;
15       index ++;                                   Advance current reference
16     }
17
18     return -1;
19   }
20 }
```

Exercise Solutions

13.1
```
1  interface MyList<E> {
2    ...
3
4    public void clear();
5    public boolean isEmpty();
6    public boolean remove(Object o) throws Exception;
7  }
8
9  class MyArrayList<E> implements MyList<E> {
10   ...
11
12   public void clear() {
13     size = 0;
14   }
15
16   public boolean isEmpty() {
17     return size == 0;
18   }
19
20   public boolean remove(Object o) throws Exception {
21     int index = indexOf((E) o);
22     if (index == -1)
23       return false;
24     remove(index);
25     return true;
```

```
26 |   }
27 | }
28 |
29 | public class Test {
30 |   public static void main(String[] args) throws Exception {
31 |
32 |     MyList<String> names = new MyArrayList<>();
33 |     names.add("Peter");
34 |     names.add("Mary");
35 |     names.add("Heather");
36 |     names.add("Mary");
37 |     out.println("names = " + names);
38 |     out.println("names.isEmpty() = " + names.isEmpty());
39 |     names.remove("Mary");
40 |     out.println("After removing Mary, names = " + names);
41 |     names.clear();
42 |     out.println("After clearing, names = " + names);
43 |   }
44 | }
```

```
names = [Peter, Mary, Heather, Mary]
names.isEmpty() = false
After removing Mary, names = [Peter, Heather, Mary]
After clearing, names = []
```

13.2 It loops once for each element of the array, so the complexity is O(n).

13.3 The outer loop iterates once for each element of the array. The inner loop iterates from i to the end of the array. The first time through the outer loop, the inner loop iterates n times. The last time through the outer loop, the inner loop iterates one time. On average, the inner loop iterates $n/2$ times. So the overall complexity is $O(n^2/2)$, or $1/2\ O(n^2)$. Discarding the constant (1/2), the complexity is O(n).

13.4 It loops from 0 to b, so the complexity is O(n) where n is the *value* of b.

13.5 Each operation in the method runs in constant time, so the complexity is O(1).

13.6
```
 1 | interface MyList<E> {
 2 |   ...
 3 |
 4 |   public void clear();
 5 |   public boolean isEmpty();
 6 |   public boolean remove(Object o) throws Exception;
 7 | }
 8 |
 9 | class MyLinkedList<E> implements MyList<E> {
10 |   ...
11 |
12 |   public void clear() {
13 |     head = tail = null;
14 |     size = 0;
```

```
15    }
16
17    public boolean isEmpty() {
18      return size == 0;
19    }
20
21    public boolean remove(Object o) throws Exception {
22
23      Node<E> current = head;
24      Node<E> previous = null;
25      while (current != null) {
26
27        // if object is found, remove it
28        if (current.element.equals(o)) {
29
30          size --;
31
32          // take the current node out of the chain
33          if (previous != null)
34            previous.next = current.next;
35
36          // if this is the first node, special handling is needed
37          if (current == head)
38            head = current.next;
39
40          // if this is the last node, special handling is needed
41          if (current == tail)
42            tail = previous;
43
44          return true;
45        }
46
47        previous = current;
48        current = current.next;
49      }
50
51      // object not found
52      return false;
53    }
54  }
55
56  public class Test {
57    public static void main(String[] args) throws Exception {
58
59      MyList<String> names = new MyLinkedList<>();
60      names.add("Peter");
61      names.add("Mary");
62      names.add("Heather");
63      names.add("Mary");
64      out.println("names = " + names);
65      out.println("names.isEmpty() = " + names.isEmpty());
66      names.remove("Mary");
67      out.println("After removing Mary, names = " + names);
68      names.clear();
69      out.println("After clearing, names = " + names);
70    }
71  }
```

```
names = [Peter, Mary, Heather, Mary]
names.isEmpty() = false
After removing Mary, names = [Peter, Heather, Mary]
After clearing, names = []
```

Maps and Hashing | 14

14.1 Binary Search

Maps are efficient collection classes that allow us to store key/value pairs, where the key and value are both generic types. We begin our discussion of maps with an example of looking up a record using its name. For this, we'll use a publicly available database of asteroids, and get an asteroid's information by name. Any other data set can be used for this example, as long as it's in text format and has enough rows. We'll begin by downloading the data set from `http://www.minorplanet.info/lightcurvedatabase.html` (LCDB; Warner et al., 2009). On that web page, we locate the link to LCLIST_-PUB_CURRENT.zip and download it. After unzipping the file, we copy the data file "LC_SUM_PUB.TXT" to the root of our Eclipse project (this can be done by dragging it onto the project root in Eclipse's Package Explorer view). After doing this, it will appear alongside the "src" folder in the Package Explorer, as shown in figure 14.1.

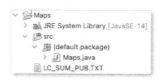

Figure 14.1: Data file under the project root in the Package Explorer window.

The data file has about 34,000 records, one row for each record, with columns for the various data fields. It can be opened in Eclipse as shown in figure 14.2.

```
ASTEROID LIGHTCURVE DATABASE (LCDB) SUMMARY (Complete)
GENERATED: Oct 22, 2020

NUMBER    NAME                  DESIG           FAM     S CLASS S F DIA.
---------------------------------------------------------------------------
     1    Ceres                                 MB-O    S C       L   973.89
     2    Pallas                                MB-O    S B       C   512.59
     3 *  Juno                                  MB-M    S S       L   252.
     4    Vesta                                 V       S V       D   464.64
     5    Astraea                               MB-I    S S       L   115.
     6 *  Hebe                                  MB-I    S S       D   182.31
     7 *  Iris                                  MB-I    S S       D   198.97
     8    Flora                                 FLOR    T S       L   138.81
```

Figure 14.2: Asteroids data file opened in Eclipse.

We'll write a program that reads the data from this file, line by line, using the techniques we learned in chapter 12. We'll use the

Scanning goes through a string, separating its components. *Parsing* is similar, but can handle nested structures that are arbitrarily deep. Colloquially, the term *parsing* is often used in place of the term *scanning*.

string manipulation techniques we learned in chapter 2 to scan each line, extracting the relevant data fields (we'll only read some of the data fields that are of interest to us). And, we'll use the techniques we learned in chapter 8 to create an `Asteroid` class that holds each asteroid's data. We'll also use the techniques we learned in chapter 10 to hold the asteroid objects in an `ArrayList`. The `Asteroid` class implements `Comparable` as discussed in chapter 11 to facilitate sorting the list of asteroids. Our first version is shown in example 14.1,

Example 14.1. `Asteroid` class and its test program.

```java
import static java.lang.System.out;
import java.io.File;
import java.io.FileNotFoundException;
import java.util.ArrayList;
import java.util.Collections;
import java.util.List;
import java.util.Scanner;

public class Maps {

  public static void main(String[] args) throws FileNotFoundException {

    List<Asteroid> asteroids = new ArrayList<>();

    File file = new File("LC_SUM_PUB.TXT");
    Scanner input = new Scanner(file);

    // ignore first 5 lines (the header)
    for (int i = 0; i < 5; i++)
      input.nextLine();

    // process each asteroid (one line)
    while (input.hasNext()) {
      String line = input.nextLine();

      int number = Integer.parseInt(line.substring(0, 8).trim());
      String name = line.substring(10, 40).trim();
      float diameter = readFloat (line, 84, 91);
      float reflectivity = readFloat(line, 109, 115);
      float period = readFloat(line, 118, 129);
      Asteroid asteroid = new Asteroid(number, name, diameter, reflectivity,
        period);
      asteroids.add(asteroid);
    }

    out.println("Read " + asteroids.size() + " asteroids...");

    // sort asteroid list
    Collections.sort(asteroids);

    // display first and last (alphabetically)
    out.println("The first asteroid is: " + asteroids.get(0));
    out.println("The last asteroid is: " + asteroids.get(asteroids.size()-1));

    input.close();
  }

  private static float readFloat(String line, int startIndex, int endIndex) {
```

```
48      float num = 0;
49      String str = line.substring(startIndex, endIndex).trim();
50      if (!str.isEmpty())
51        num = Float.parseFloat(str);
52      return num;
53    }
54  }
55
56  class Asteroid implements Comparable<Asteroid> {
57
58    int number;
59    String name;      // name or designation
60    float diameter;   // diameter in kilometers
61    float reflectivity; // Albedo ranges from 1 (perfectly reflecting) to 0 (
          perfectly absorbing)
62    float period;     // rotation period in hours
63
64    public Asteroid (int number, String name, float diameter, float reflectivity,
          float period) {
65      this.number = number;
66      this.name = name;
67      this.diameter = diameter;
68      this.reflectivity = reflectivity;
69      this.period = period;
70    }
71
72    @Override
73    public String toString() {
74      return name + " (ID " + number + "), reflectivity: " + reflectivity + ",
          diameter: " + diameter + " km, period: " + period + " hours";
75    }
76
77    @Override
78    public int compareTo(Asteroid other) {
79      return name.compareToIgnoreCase(other.name);
80    }
81  }
```

```
Read 34190 asteroids...
The first asteroid is: 05s07 (ID 0), reflectivity: 0.1, diameter: 122.3 km, period: 6.54 hours
The last asteroid is: Zyskin (ID 2098), reflectivity: 0.2, diameter: 8.91 km, period: 3.92 hours
```

Next, we'll search for a particular asteroid in two different ways, while comparing the speed of this search in a way similar to the timing tests you saw in the last chapter. The first method will look for an asteroid by examining each element of the asteroid list. This is referred to as a linear search. The second method is more efficient, and is called a binary search. Let's look at the code first, then we'll discuss how binary search works,

```
1   public static void main(String[] args) throws FileNotFoundException {
2   ...
3       // display first and last (alphabetically)
4       //out.println("The first asteroid is: " + asteroids.get(0));
5       //out.println("The last asteroid is: " + asteroids.get(asteroids.size()-1))
          ;
6
7       input.close();
```

Example 14.2. Comparing linear search and binary search.

```
 8
 9    // linear search
10    Asteroid asteroid = null;
11    long start = System.currentTimeMillis();
12    for (int i = 0; i < 50000; i++) {
13      asteroid = linearSearch(asteroids, "Pluto");
14    }
15    long end = System.currentTimeMillis();
16    out.println("Linear search: Pluto's record is " + asteroid);
17    out.println("Linear search: Time to find Pluto: " + (end-start) + "
      milliseconds");
18
19    // binary search
20    Collections.sort(asteroids);
21    start = System.currentTimeMillis();
22    int index = -1;
23    for (int i = 0; i < 50000; i++) {
24      index = Collections.binarySearch(asteroids, new Asteroid(0, "Pluto", 0,
        0, 0));
25    }
26    end = System.currentTimeMillis();
27    out.println("Binary search: Pluto's record is " + asteroids.get(index));
28    out.println("Binary search: Time to find Pluto: " + (end-start) + "
      milliseconds");
29  }
30
31  private static Asteroid linearSearch (List<Asteroid> asteroids, String
      asteroidName) {
32    for (int i = 0; i < asteroids.size(); i++)
33      if (asteroids.get(i).name.equals(asteroidName))
34        return asteroids.get(i);
35    return null;
36  }
```

```
Read 34190 asteroids...
Linear search: Pluto's record is Pluto (ID 134340), reflectivity: 0.65, diameter: 339.0 km,
Linear search: Time to find Pluto: 13751 milliseconds
Binary search: Pluto's record is Pluto (ID 134340), reflectivity: 0.65, diameter: 339.0 km,
Binary search: Time to find Pluto: 21 milliseconds
```

The timing results reveal that finding Pluto 50,000 times in the list of asteroids using binary search takes about 21 milliseconds, while finding it using the brute force method (linear search) takes about 13,000 milliseconds, so binary search is about 500 times faster in this case.

A binary search is like the children's game where you guess an unknown number between 1 and 100. After each guess, you are told whether the unknown number is higher or lower than the number you guessed. Your first guess is likely to be the number 50. If you are told the unknown number is higher, your next guess is likely to be 75, and so on.

Binary search only works when searching for an item in a sorted list. It works by keeping track of the range of items within the list where the desired record might be, then looking at the middle of that range. Since the list is sorted, comparing the middle item of the range to the desired item will tell whether the desired item is in the upper or lower half of the range. Then the new range is set accordingly and the process is repeated. When starting the binary search process, the range is initially set to the entire list. If we were to write this algorithm as pseudocode, it could look something like this,

1. *Let the list be T, and the desired item be I*
2. *Set the upper index U to the topmost index of T, and the lower index L to 0*
3. *Repeat until I is found, or the upper index U and lower index L are the same,*
   a) *If U = L, and the list item at index U isn't the desired item I, we're done (I is not found)*
   b) *Get the index at the middle of the current range: let M = (U + L) / 2*
   c) *Get the item at index M. If it's the desired item I, we're done*
   d) *If the item at index M is larger than the desired item I, set the lower index L to M*
   e) *Otherwise, the item at index M is smaller than the desired item I, so set the upper index U to M*

Suppose we're looking for the number 58 in the list (-22, 0, 3, 3, 4, 4, 11, 12, 58, 99, 101). The binary search process for these inputs, following the above pseudocode, is illustrated in figure 14.3. The search terminates by finding the number 58 after 3 steps, cutting the range to search by half in each step. Note that the algorithm still works if the list contains duplicate elements.

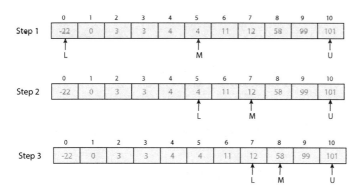

Figure 14.3: Binary search.

The observant reader may wonder how much overhead sorting the list causes, and whether it's worthwhile. Sorting a list runs in O(n log n) time, which makes it worthwhile to sort the list if binary search is used many times. If only one search operation is needed, linear search is faster than having to sort and then do a binary search.

Binary search cuts the current search range by half in each step. At most, the number of steps required is the base 2 logarithm of n, where n is the size of the list. This represents the number of times a list can be cut in half before narrowing down to one element. For example, a list of size 8 can be cut in half three times before reaching size 1. The base 2 log of n is the power of 2 that yields n. In the example just mentioned, raising 2 to the power 3 is 8. Table 14.1 shows the base 2 log for various values of n. As the list's size grows larger and larger, the value of binary search becomes more and more apparent. To find an item in a sorted list with a million numbers using binary search, it only takes 20 steps. To put it in big-O terms, linear search runs in O(n) time, while binary search runs in O(log n) time (refer to table 13.1 on page 256).

Table 14.1: Base 2 logarithms.

n	$log_2(n)$	n	$log_2(n)$
1	0	1,024	10
2	1	2,048	11
4	2	4,096	12
8	3	8,192	13
16	4	16,384	14
32	5	32,768	15
64	6	65,536	16
128	7	131,072	17
256	8	262,144	18
512	9	524,288	19
		1,048,576	20

Exercises

14.1 Download stellar data and put it in a collection. Look up stars by name using binary search. For example, try the file "hygfull.csv" at this address: `https://github.com/astronexus/HYG-Database`.

14.2 Maps

A map is a collection that stores key/value pairs where both the key and value are generic types. The map can only hold one value for each unique key, and looking up a value by its key is very fast. In Java, the Map interface defines methods such as put and get, and is analogous to the List interface for lists because multiple map classes implement Map just as multiple list classes implement List. The HashMap class implements the Map interface, and is used frequently. The TreeMap class also implements Map but is specialized and less often used (it holds the keys in sorted order, but is slower when looking up a value by its key). Just like ArrayList is your go-to list class, HashMap is your go-to class for storing key/value pairs and looking up values by their keys.

We'll illustrate maps by updating example 14.2, adding a new way of looking up astroids by name. In example 14.3, we add a new collection, asteroidMap of type HashMap<String, Asteroid>. This maps string values to Asteroid objects.

Example 14.3. Using HashMap.

```
1  ...
2  import java.util.HashMap;
3  import java.util.Map;
4
5    public static void main(String[] args) throws FileNotFoundException {
6
7      List<Asteroid> asteroids = new ArrayList<>();
8      Map<String, Asteroid> asteroidMap = new HashMap<>();
9  ...
10     // process each asteroid (one line)
11     while (input.hasNext()) {
12 ...
13       asteroids.add(asteroid);
14       asteroidMap.put(asteroid.name, asteroid);
15     }
16
17 ...
18     // map search
19     start = System.currentTimeMillis();
20     for (int i = 0; i < 50000; i++) {
21       asteroid = asteroidMap.get("Pluto");
22     }
23     end = System.currentTimeMillis();
24     out.println("Map search: Pluto's record is " + asteroid);
25     out.println("Map search: Time to find Pluto: " + (end-start) + "
         milliseconds");
26   }
27 ...
```

```
Read 34190 asteroids...
Linear search: Pluto's record is Pluto (ID 134340), reflectivity: 0.65, diameter: 339.0 km,
Linear search: Time to find Pluto: 13266 milliseconds
Binary search: Pluto's record is Pluto (ID 134340), reflectivity: 0.65, diameter: 339.0 km,
Binary search: Time to find Pluto: 21 milliseconds
Map search: Pluto's record is Pluto (ID 134340), reflectivity: 0.65, diameter: 339.0 km, per
Map search: Time to find Pluto: 2 milliseconds
```

Note the following details about the code in example 14.3,

- The map is created on line 8, as a `HashMap<String, Asteroid>`. The key type is `String` and the value type is `Asteroid`.
- Each time an asteroid is added to the list (line 13), it's also added to the asteroid map (line 14), mapping the asteroid's name to the asteroid object using the `put` method of the `HashMap` class.
- The `get` method of the `HashMap` class is used on line 21 to retrieve an `Asteroid` object from the map using its key, the asteroid's name.

The output shows that looking up an asteroid using the map is about ten times faster than the binary search method, in this case. Each time the code in example 14.3 adds an asteroid to the list of asteroids, it also adds it to the asteroid map, mapping the asteroid's name to the asteroid object. In this way, the asteroid map functions as an index into the asteroid list. We create `Asteroid` objects and add them to two separate collections, each holding separate references to the same objects.

The speed of looking up a value in `HashMap` is one of two things in programming that feel like magic (the other is recursion, discussed in chapter 15), and it's thanks to hashing, which we discuss in the next section.

Looking up a value using its key in a `HashMap` is so fast that it approaches constant runtime, O(1), as opposed to logarithmic runtime for binary search and linear runtime for linear search.

Technique 21. Use a `HashMap` as an index to speed up lookups

You can use a separate `HashMap` collection as an index to speed up looking up objects by a specific key, such as an ID or a name. This separate index has to be updated when a new object is added or removed from the main collection, so there is overhead, but it's often much faster in the end to add this separate index.

Occasionally, you'll need to iterate through a map's entries. The `Map` interface provides a way for you to do this,

Example 14.4. Iterating through a Map's entries.

```
1  import java.util.Map.Entry;
2  ...
3    // iterate through the map's entries
4    for (Entry<String, Asteroid> entry : asteroidMap.entrySet())
5      out.println("key = " + entry.getKey() + ", value = " + entry.getValue());
```

```
key = Amelia, value = Amelia (ID 986), reflectivity: 0.1183, diameter
key = 2000 RW50, value = 2000 RW50 (ID 92967), reflectivity: 0.21, di
key = Cosicosi, value = Cosicosi (ID 2129), reflectivity: 0.24, diame
key = 2013 GU92, value = 2013 GU92 (ID 368116), reflectivity: 0.1, di
```

The `Map.entrySet` method returns a collection of `Map.Entry` objects, each of which allows retrieval of the key and value of a single entry using the `getKey` and `getValue` methods. Note that `HashMap`'s implementation of `entrySet` doesn't provide the entries in a particular order.

Exercises

14.2   Use the dictionary file that you downloaded for exercise 12.3. Read each word and add it to a map, mapping the word to *true* (the `HashMap` will map `String` to `Boolean`). This will allow fast lookup of dictionary words. Use this dictionary to spell check a file of the user's choosing and output words that aren't capitalized and don't appear in the dictionary.

14.3 Hashing

Hashing is a technique that boils down the data in an object to a number. The hash code of any object is returned by the `hashCode` method, which takes no parameters. Every class has this method since every class is ultimately derived from Object, and `Object` provides a default implementation. Classes that might be used as keys in a `HashMap` need to override `hashCode`. The number returned by `hashCode` should be different for each instance of an object containing different data. Example 14.5 shows some objects with their hash codes,

```
1    Integer number = 123;
2    out.println("hashCode of " + number + " is " + number.hashCode());
3
4    String str = "To be or not to be";
5    out.println("hashCode of '" + str + "' is " + str.hashCode());
6    str = "To be or not to bee";
7    out.println("hashCode of '" + str + "' is " + str.hashCode());
8
9    Boolean bool = true;
10   out.println("hashCode of " + bool + " is " + bool.hashCode());
11
12   Float decimalNumber = 3.141f;
13   out.println("hashCode of " + decimalNumber + " is " + decimalNumber.hashCode
        ());
14   decimalNumber = 3.142f;
15   out.println("hashCode of " + decimalNumber + " is " + decimalNumber.hashCode
        ());
```

Example 14.5. Hash code examples.

```
hashCode of 123 is 123
hashCode of `To be or not to be' is 557539254
hashCode of `To be or not to bee' is 103847791
hashCode of true is 1231
hashCode of 3.141 is 1078527525
hashCode of 3.142 is 1078531719
```

The `hashCode` implementation for each class essentially maps the class data's possible values to the set of integers. Obviously, this can't be a one-to-one mapping, since a class has an arbitrary number of data elements. But, it should perform this mapping in such a way that ensures good distribution of its set of possible data values to the set of integers. When two instances of a class that have different data result in the same number returned by `hashCode`, it's called a hash value collision. Since collisions are inevitable (because it's not a one-to-one mapping), the goal of `hashCode` is simply to minimize collisions and get an even distribution of internal data values to integer hash codes. It's also desirable for objects with similar data values to produce hash codes that aren't close together, as this produces less clustering of hash codes. Note in example 14.5's output that adding a letter to the end of a string produced a very different hash code.

Without overriding `hashCode`, a custom class inherits the default implementation provided by `Object`. This returns the memory address at which the object resides. In this case, two instances that have the same data will produce different hash codes, which is usually not the desired behavior. Example 14.6 shows this,

Example 14.6. Default `hashCode` implementation.

```
1  import static java.lang.System.out;
2
3  public class TestFilm {
4
5    public static void main(String[] args) {
6
7      Film film1 = new Film("Gone with the Wind", "Victor Fleming", 1939);
8      Film film2 = new Film("Gone with the Wind", "Victor Fleming", 1939);
9      out.println("Film1's hash code is " + film1.hashCode());
10     out.println("Film2's hash code is " + film2.hashCode());
11   }
12 }
13
14 class Film {
15   String title;
16   String director;
17   int year;
18
19   public Film(String title, String director, int year) {
20     super();
21     this.title = title;
22     this.director = director;
23     this.year = year;
24   }
```

```
25
26   @Override
27   public String toString() {
28     return "Film [title=" + title + ", director=" + director + ", year=" + year
           + "]";
29   }
30 }
```

```
Film1's hash code is 225534817
Film2's hash code is 1878246837
```

As mentioned earlier, if you intend for your class to be used as a key in a `HashMap`, you should override `hashCode` and ensure it has a good distribution of hash codes, as well as producing the same hash code for two instances with the same data. The standard technique for doing this is shown in example 14.7,

```
1  import java.util.HashMap;
2  import java.util.Map;
3  import java.util.Map.Entry;
4  ...
5    public static void main(String[] args) {
6
7      Film film1 = new Film("Gone with the Wind", "Victor Fleming", 1939);
8      Film film2 = new Film("Gone with the Wind", "Victor Fleming", 1939);
9      out.println("Film1's hash code is " + film1.hashCode());
10     out.println("Film2's hash code is " + film2.hashCode());
11
12     Map<Film, Float> ratings = new HashMap<>();
13     ratings.put(film1, 5f);
14     ratings.put(film2, 4.5f);
15
16     for (Entry<Film, Float> entry : ratings.entrySet())
17       out.println(entry.getKey() + " (" + entry.getValue() + " stars)");
18   }
19 ...
20   @Override
21   public int hashCode() {
22     final int prime = 31;
23     int result = 1;
24     result = prime * result + ((director == null) ? 0 : director.hashCode());
25     result = prime * result + ((title == null) ? 0 : title.hashCode());
26     result = prime * result + year;
27     return result;
28   }
29
30   @Override
31   public boolean equals(Object object2) {
32
33     // if second film is null or not a film object, return false
34     if (object2 == null || object2.getClass() != getClass())
35       return false;
36
37     Film film2 = (Film) object2;
38
39     // if titles aren't equal, return false
40     if ((title == null && film2.title != null) ||
```

Example 14.7. Overriding `hashCode`.

As noted on page 64, shortcut operators can be used to avoid errors. We're using that technique in `equals`.

```
41        (title != null && film2.title == null) ||
42        !title.equals(film2.title))
43        return false;
44
45    // if directors aren't equal, return false
46    if ((director == null && film2.director != null) ||
47        (director != null && film2.director == null) ||
48        !director.equals(film2.director))
49        return false;
50
51    // if years aren't equal, return false
52    if (year != film2.year)
53        return false;
54
55    return true;
56 }
```

```
Film1's hash code is 830722461
Film2's hash code is 830722461
Film [title=Gone with the Wind, director=Victor Fleming, year=1939] (4.5 stars)
```

We're assuming that `String.hashCode` runs in constant time. The observant reader may ask how it does this. The answer is that the hash code is computed once with linear time complexity and saved so that `String.hashCode` just needs to return the saved value. Strings are immutable, which guarantees that the hash code only needs to be computed once.

The standard `hashCode` implementation shown in example 14.7 starts with a result of 1, then factors in the hash code of each data element of the class. When factoring in the hash code of each data element, the existing result is multiplied by a prime number, and added to the hash code of the data element. This method was developed over time and generally produces a good distribution with minimal collisions. Note that this implementation of `hashCode` runs in constant time.

We also override the `Object.equals` method, which receives a `Film` parameter and returns true or false depending on whether the data in this instance matches the data in the `Film` instance passed in. Without overriding *both* `hashCode` and `equals`, a class can't be used properly as a key within a `HashMap`. Removing the `equals` override from `Film` results in the hash map not recognizing `film1` and `film2` as the same film, causing two entries to be output as shown below,

```
Film1's hash code is 830722461
Film2's hash code is 830722461
Film [title=Gone with the Wind, director=Victor Fleming, year=1939] (5.0 stars)
Film [title=Gone with the Wind, director=Victor Fleming, year=1939] (4.5 stars)
```

Now that we understand how hashing works, we can discuss how `HashMap` stores key/value pairs and performs `get` operations in constant time. The `HashMap` contains an array of linked lists called chained buckets, with each linked list node containing a pair (a key and a value), as shown in figure 14.4. Each key's hash code is mapped to an index of this array by computing its modulus with respect to the array's length. For example, if the array's length is 9, the hash

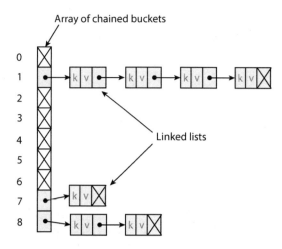

Array of chained buckets

Linked lists

Figure 14.4: Internal structure of HashMap.

code 830722461 maps to the index 6 because 830722461 mod 9 is 6. When adding a key/value pair with that key, the HashMap creates a new linked list node containing that key/value pair and adds it to the linked list at index 6 of the array. The array is expanded periodically as more key/value pairs are added to the map, similar to the way that ArrayList grows. This periodic growth ensures that the chains are short (assuming that the hash codes aren't clustered). When the array grows, each existing key/value pair is re-mapped so that it's in the right chain. Too many hash code collisions result in some of the array indexes having much longer chains than other indexes.

The HashMap.get method performs the following steps to find a key's value in this internal structure,

- Call the key's hashCode method to get its hash code. This is a constant-time operation.
- Compute the modulus of hash code with respect to the array length, to find the array index. This is a constant-time operation.
- Traverse the linked list at that array index to find the key, and if it exists, return its value. This is a constant-time operation as long as the chains are short.

When the key's hashCode method produces an even distribution of hash codes, the internal structure is well balanced, the chains are short, and the get method runs in constant time, O(1). Finally, note that adding new pairs to a `HashMap` (using `put`) is also a constant-time operation, since it uses the same steps as the `get` operation, except that the linked list is changed by adding new key/value pair or updating an existing key's value.

Chapter Summary

- Maps are collections that store key/value pairs, where the key and value are generic types.
- A `HashMap` allow fast lookup of a value using its key.
- The `hashCode` method returns an integer, where different internal data map to different hash integers.
- To use a custom class as a key within a `HashMap` requires overriding `equals` and `hashCode`.

Create `HashMap` collection

```
1   Map<String, Asteroid> asteroidMap = new HashMap<>();
2
3   // read data
4   while (input.hasNext()) {
5       ...
6       asteroidMap.put(asteroid.name, asteroid);
7   }
8
9   asteroid = asteroidMap.get("Pluto");
```

Add key/value pair to the map

Get a value using its key

Recursion | 15

15.1 Recursion

Recursion is when a method calls itself. Let's consider for example the mathematical definition of a factorial. The factorial of a positive integer n is the product of integers from 1 to n,

$$f(n) = \prod_{i=1}^{n} i$$

Computing factorial is simple using a loop,

```java
public static void main(String[] args) {

    int n = 6;
    int factorial = 1;
    for (int i = 1; i <= n; i++)
        factorial *= i;

    out.println("The factorial of " + n + " is " + factorial);
}
```

Example 15.1. Computing factorial with a loop.

```
The factorial of 6 is 720
```

Another mathematical definition of factorial is the following,

$$f(n) = \begin{cases} 1, & n = 1 \\ n * f(n-1), & n > 1 \end{cases}$$

In this recursive definition, the factorial of an integer n is computed by multiplying n by the factorial of $n - 1$. Every recursive definition has at least one *recursive case*, where the function is used within its own definition with a different parameter value, and at least one *base* case. Here, the base case is when $n = 1$, and the recursive case is when $n > 1$.

Recursive case: The set of inputs causing a function to refer to itself.

Base case: The set of inputs that don't cause a function to refer to itself.

With the recursive definition of factorial, we can compute the factorial of 6 as follows,

$$f(6) = 6 \times f(5)$$
$$f(6) = 6 \times 5 \times f(4)$$
$$f(6) = 6 \times 5 \times 4 \times f(3)$$
$$f(6) = 6 \times 5 \times 4 \times 3 \times f(2)$$
$$f(6) = 6 \times 5 \times 4 \times 3 \times 2 \times f(1)$$
$$f(6) = 6 \times 5 \times 4 \times 3 \times 2 \times 1$$
$$f(6) = 720$$

Note that this computation required the factorial function to be evaluated six times. The recursive definition of factorial is implemented as a recursive method in example 15.2,

Example 15.2. Computing factorial recursively.

```
1   public static void main(String[] args) {
2
3       int n = 6;
4       out.println("The factorial of " + n + " is " + factorial(n));
5   }
6
7   public static int factorial(int n) {
8
9       // base case
10      if (n == 1)
11          return 1;
12
13      // recursive case
14      return n * factorial (n - 1);
15  }
```

```
The factorial of 6 is 720
```

By the time execution reaches line 11, the `return` statement belonging to the base case, several nested calls from `factorial` to itself have occurred. The invocation of `factorial` with parameter value 6 waits for the invocation with parameter value 5 to return, which in turn waits for the invocation with parameter 4 to return, and so on. Each of these method calls has a corresponding stack frame. To see this in action, we place a breakpoint on line 11 and run the program in debug mode. When the program stops at the breakpoint (figure 15.1), the Debug view shows the call stack with the most recent stack frame at the top. Each frame on the call stack corresponds to one method call—the `main` method is seen at the bottom of the stack, followed

When a recursive method calls itself, the method invocation that made the call waits for the nested call to return, and its local data is saved in its stack frame on the call stack.

by the six calls to `factorial`, with parameter values ranging from 6 to 1. You can click on each stack frame in the Debug view to select it, showing the local variables for that frame in the Variables view on the right of the Eclipse window. Figure 15.2 shows the same program with the second-to-last frame selected, where `factorial` has been called with the parameter value 2.

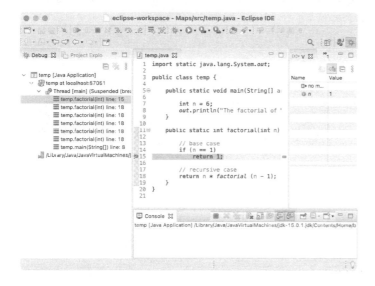

Figure 15.1: Debug view with call stack.

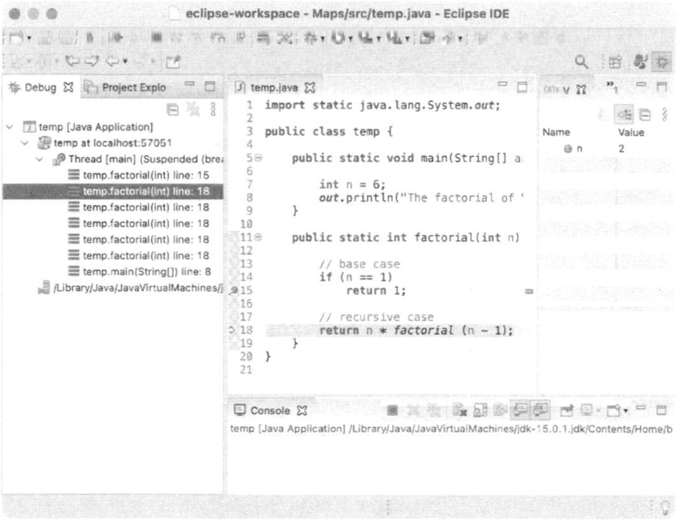

Figure 15.2: Selecting a different stack frame in the debugger.

Examples 15.1 and 15.2 implement factorial in different ways, one using a loop and the other using recursion. Iteration and recursion accomplish the same thing, just in different ways, and they each

Iteration and recursion are equivalent in the sense that each recursive implementation can be made iterative, and vice versa. But each is more natural and preferable to the other in certain situations.

have different pros and cons. In some cases, iteration is easier to implement and in other cases recursion is.

The call stack's memory is large enough that you don't need to worry about the number of nested calls. But the call stack's memory is finite, so if a bug in the recursive method keeps it from terminating, the recursion doesn't terminate and continues until the call stack overflows, resulting in an exception. Example 15.3 shows this scenario, where the base case tests for "n == 10" instead of "n == 1",

Example 15.3. The stack overflow exception.

```
1   public static void main(String[] args) {
2
3       int n = 6;
4       out.println("The factorial of " + n + " is " + factorial(n));
5   }
6
7   public static int factorial(int n) {
8
9       // base case
10      if (n == 10)
11          return 1;
12
13      // recursive case
14      return n * factorial (n - 1);
15  }
```

```
Exception in thread "main" java.lang.StackOverflowError
        at temp.factorial(temp.java:18)
        at temp.factorial(temp.java:18)
        at temp.factorial(temp.java:18)
        at temp.factorial(temp.java:18)
        at temp.factorial(temp.java:18)
        at temp.factorial(temp.java:18)
        at temp.factorial(temp.java:18)
        at temp factorial(temp java:18)
```

Using recursion to implement the factorial function isn't a good example of recursion in the real world, since factorial is better implemented using iteration. In the next section we'll introduce trees, and we'll see examples where recursion is preferable to iteration.

Exercises

15.1 Write a recursive method that computes the sum of numbers in an integer array.

15.2 Write a recursive method that concatenates the strings in a list of strings.

15.2 Trees

A tree is a data structure where each node can have multiple child nodes. The tree data structure can model many real-world hierarchical structures. In this section we'll model the organizational structure of the Department of Energy, using information from the DOE's website as seen in figure 15.3.

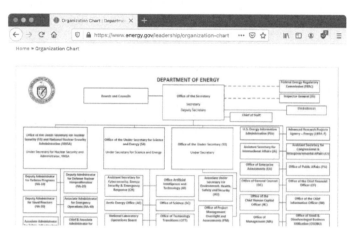

Figure 15.3: Organizational structure of the Department of Energy.

The Java class that will represent a department is `DepartmentNode`, and is shown in example 15.4. It has fields for the department's name, the number of employees, the department budget and a list of child departments. The `DepartmentNode` class resembles the `Node` class in example 13.14, except that a `DepartmentNode` can have multiple children, while `Node` can only have one child.

Example 15.4. The `DepartmentNode` class and test code.

```
1  import static java.lang.System.out;
2  import java.util.ArrayList;
3  import java.util.List;
4
5  public class Trees {
6
7    public static void main(String[] args) {
8
9      DepartmentNode node1 = new DepartmentNode("Bonneville Power Administration"
           , 21, 150000);
10     DepartmentNode node2 = new DepartmentNode("Southeastern Power
           Administration", 11, 190000);
11     DepartmentNode node3 = new DepartmentNode("Southwestern Power
           Administration", 15, 110000);
12     DepartmentNode node4 = new DepartmentNode("Western Area Power
           Administration", 14, 120000);
13
14     DepartmentNode node5 = new DepartmentNode("Assistant Secretary for
           Electricity", 12, 191000, node1, node2, node3, node4);
15     DepartmentNode node6 = new DepartmentNode("Assistant Secretary for Fossil
           Energy", 10, 100000);
```

```
16    DepartmentNode node7 = new DepartmentNode("Assistant Secretary for Nuclear
         Energy", 10, 100000);
17    DepartmentNode node8 = new DepartmentNode("Assistant Secretary for Energy
         Efficiency and Renewable Energy", 10, 100000);
18
19    DepartmentNode node9 = new DepartmentNode("Office of the Undersecretary of
         Energy", 10, 100000, node5, node6, node7, node8);
20
21    DepartmentNode node10 = new DepartmentNode("Office of Science", 15, 110000)
         ;
22    DepartmentNode node11 = new DepartmentNode("Office of Artificial
         Intelligence and Technology", 14, 120000);
23    DepartmentNode node12 = new DepartmentNode("Office of the Undersecretary
         for Science", 12, 191000, node10, node11);
24
25    DepartmentNode node13 = new DepartmentNode("Chief of Staff", 1, 50000);
26    DepartmentNode node14 = new DepartmentNode("Ombudsman", 1, 50000);
27
28    DepartmentNode root = new DepartmentNode("Office of the Secretary", 12,
         191000, node12, node9, node13, node14);
29    }
30  }
31
32  class DepartmentNode {
33
34    String name;
35    int employees;
36    int budget;
37    List<DepartmentNode> children = new ArrayList<>();
38
39    public DepartmentNode (String name, int employees, int budget, DepartmentNode
         ... departmentNodes) {
40      this.name = name;
41      this.employees = employees;
42      this.budget = budget;
43      for (DepartmentNode child : departmentNodes)
44        this.children.add(child);
45    }
46  }
```

In addition to the department name, employee count and budget,
the `DepartmentNode`'s constructor receives a varargs parameter
containing a list of child department nodes. The test code adds
several nodes to the tree, with fictitious numbers for the employee
count and budget of each department. The lower nodes are created
first so that each can be passed into its parent node's constructor.
Once the root node is created, it represents the entire tree.

15.3 Traversing Trees with Iteration

To traverse a tree is to process each of its nodes, applying some
action to each node such as printing it out. We can use a loop to do
this using the following algorithm,

- Create an empty stack of nodes.
- Push the tree's root onto the stack.
- Repeat the following steps until the stack is empty:
  - Pop a node *n* from the stack.
  - Process the node *n*, e.g., print it out.
  - Push each of *n*'s children onto the stack.

Example 15.5 applies the above algorithm to print the tree,

```java
public static void main(String[] args) {
...
    DepartmentNode root = new DepartmentNode("Office of the Secretary", 12,
      191000, node12, node9, node13, node14);
    printTreeIterative(root);
}

private static void printTreeIterative(DepartmentNode root) {
    Map<DepartmentNode, Integer> nodeLevelMap = new HashMap<>();
    List<DepartmentNode> stack = new ArrayList<>();

    stack.add(root);
    nodeLevelMap.put(root, 0);

    while (!stack.isEmpty()) {

        // pop a node from the stack
        DepartmentNode currentNode = stack.remove(stack.size() - 1);

        // process the node
        int currentNodeLevel = nodeLevelMap.get(currentNode);
        for (int i = 0; i < currentNodeLevel; i++)
            out.print("  ");
        out.println(currentNode.name);

        // push each of the current node's children onto the stack
        for (DepartmentNode child : currentNode.children) {
            stack.add(child);
            nodeLevelMap.put(child, currentNodeLevel + 1);
        }
    }
}
```

Example 15.5. Printing a tree using iteration.

```
Office of the Secretary
  Ombudsman
  Chief of Staff
  Office of the Undersecretary of Energy
    Assistant Secretary for Energy Efficiency and Renewable Energy
    Assistant Secretary for Nuclear Energy
    Assistant Secretary for Fossil Energy
    Assistant Secretary for Electricity
      Western Area Power Administration
      Southwestern Power Administration
      Southeastern Power Administration
      Bonneville Power Administration
  Office of the Undersecretary for Science
    Office of Artificial Intelligence and Technology
    Office of Science
```

In example 15.5, the tree traversal algorithm is used to print the tree:

- Create an empty stack of nodes (line 9).
- Push the tree's root onto the stack (line 11).
- Repeat the following steps until the stack is empty (lines 14-30):
  - Pop a node *n* from the stack (line 17).
  - Process the node *n* by printing it out (lines 20-23).
  - Push each of *n*'s children onto the stack (lines 26-29).

We've added a map to store the level of each node. The first node pushed onto the stack has level 0, and each further node pushed onto the stack is one level deeper than its parent. The level is used when processing each node to indent it properly. The output shows the tree structure of the department hierarchy.

We'll show one more example of traversing the tree iteratively, this time adding up the departmental budgets for all departments in the tree, and printing out the total budget,

Example 15.6. Summation over a tree using iteration.

```
1   public static void main(String[] args) {
2   ...
3       DepartmentNode root = new DepartmentNode("Office of the Secretary", 12,
            191000, node12, node9, node13, node14);
4       out.println("Total budget is " + totalBudget(root));
5   }
6
7   private static int totalBudget(DepartmentNode root) {
8
9       List<DepartmentNode> stack = new ArrayList<>();
10      stack.add(root);
11      int totalBudget = 0;
12
13      while (!stack.isEmpty()) {
14
15          // pop a node from the stack
16          DepartmentNode currentNode = stack.remove(stack.size() - 1);
17
18          // process the node
19          totalBudget += currentNode.budget;
20
21          // push each of the current node's children onto the stack
22          for (DepartmentNode child : currentNode.children)
23              stack.add(child);
24      }
25
26      return totalBudget;
27  }
```

```
Total budget is 1873000
```

The same pattern is used in example 15.6—the stack is created, the root is pushed onto the stack, then a loop repeatedly pops a node from the stack and processes it, then pushes its own children onto the stack. This time, the act of processing a node is simply adding its budget to the total budget.

Exercises

15.3   Modify example 15.6 to print the number of departments in the tree.

15.4 Traversing Trees with Recursion

Traversing a tree is simpler and more natural using recursion than it is using iteration. There's no need for a queue of nodes. Processing a node consists of performing an operation, e.g., printing the node, then recursively processing each of its subtrees. Example 15.7 prints the department tree and sums the department budgets using recursion,

```
1   public static void main(String[] args) {
2   ...
3       DepartmentNode root = new DepartmentNode("Office of the Secretary", 12,
            191000, node12, node9, node13, node14);
4       root.PrintSubtree(0);
5       out.println("Total budget is " + root.totalBudget());
6   }
7   ...
8   public void PrintSubtree(int level) {
9       for (int i = 0; i < level; i++)
10          out.print("  ");
11      out.println(name);
12
13      for (DepartmentNode child : children)
14          child.PrintSubtree(level+1);
15  }
16
17  public int totalBudget () {
18      int answer = budget;
19      for (DepartmentNode child : children)
20          answer += child.totalBudget();
21      return answer;
22  }
```

Example 15.7. Traversing a tree with recursion.

```
Office of the Secretary
  Office of the Undersecretary for Science
    Office of Science
    Office of Artificial Intelligence and Technology
  Office of the Undersecretary of Energy
    Assistant Secretary for Electricity
      Bonneville Power Administration
      Southeastern Power Administration
      Southwestern Power Administration
      Western Area Power Administration
    Assistant Secretary for Fossil Energy
    Assistant Secretary for Nuclear Energy
    Assistant Secretary for Energy Efficiency and Renewable Energy
  Chief of Staff
  Ombudsman
Total budget is 1873000
```

The recursive versions are simpler, more intuitive and easier to maintain. The `printSubtree` method receives the node's level as a parameter, prints out the node (lines 9-11), then recursively processes each of the node's children while incrementing the level (lines 13-14). The `totalBudget` method adds the node's budget (line 18) to the total budgets of each of its children (lines 19-20), and returns the sum (line 21).

Exercises

15.4   Modify example 15.7 to print the number of departments in the tree.

15.5   Extend exercise 15.4 to print the average budget of a department.

15.5 Graphs

Graph: A tree that can have cycles.

As you have seen, trees are represented by nodes that have references from parent to child. A graph is a tree that can have cycles. To see that in action, we'll look at a program that navigates a maze. Figure 15.4 shows a maze with one entrance and one exit.

To represent this as a graph, we'll number the squares, as shown in figure 15.5,

Each square is connected to an adjacent square if there is no wall between them. Thus, square 2 is connected to squares 1 and 3, but

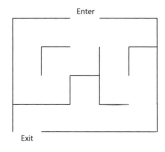

Figure 15.4: Maze example.

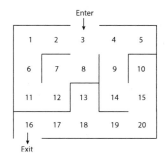

Figure 15.5: Maze example with numbered squares.

not square 7. Each square can be represented in Java as a node, just as we did with trees. The connections between adjacent squares are bidirectional, so two adjacent nodes will each have a reference to the other. Note that the graph representing this maze has a cycle because the player can move from square 3 to 8, then to 7, 12, 11, 6, 1, 2 and back to 3. Square 3 is special because it's the starting point, and square 16 is special because it's the only exit. Example 15.8 shows the Node class and a test program that constructs the graph shown in figure 15.5,

```java
import static java.lang.System.out;
import java.util.ArrayList;
import java.util.List;

public class Test {

  public static void main(String[] args) {

    // make 20 nodes
    List<Node> nodes = new ArrayList<>();
    for (int i = 0; i < 20; i++)
      nodes.add(new Node(i+1));

    // node 16 (with index 15) is an exit
    nodes.get(15).isExit = true;

    // connect the nodes to represent the maze
    connect(nodes, 1, 2);
    connect(nodes, 2, 3);
```

Example 15.8. Representing a maze as a graph in Java.

```
20      connect(nodes, 3, 4);
21      connect(nodes, 4, 5);
22      connect(nodes, 1, 6);
23      connect(nodes, 3, 8);
24      connect(nodes, 4, 9);
25      connect(nodes, 7, 8);
26      connect(nodes, 6, 11);
27      connect(nodes, 7, 12);
28      connect(nodes, 9, 14);
29      connect(nodes, 10, 15);
30      connect(nodes, 11, 12);
31      connect(nodes, 14, 15);
32      connect(nodes, 13, 18);
33      connect(nodes, 15, 20);
34      connect(nodes, 16, 17);
35      connect(nodes, 17, 18);
36      connect(nodes, 18, 19);
37      connect(nodes, 19, 20);
38    }
39
40   private static void connect(List<Node> nodes, int nodeId1, int nodeId2) {
41      // point the first node to the second node, and the second to the first
42      nodes.get(nodeId1 - 1).children.add(nodes.get(nodeId2 - 1));
43      nodes.get(nodeId2 - 1).children.add(nodes.get(nodeId1 - 1));
44    }
45  }
46
47  class Node {
48    int id;
49    List<Node> children = new ArrayList<>();
50    boolean isExit = false;
51
52    public Node(int id) {
53      this.id = id;
54    }
55
56    @Override
57    public String toString() {
58      return ((Integer) id).toString();
59    }
60  }
```

The code to find a path through the maze will perform a traversal, similar to the code that traverses trees, but we need to add logic that prevents getting stuck in a loop when a cycle is encountered in the graph. This is done by keeping a list of nodes that have already been visited, which is checked when processing each child of the current node. If a child node has already been visited, it isn't processed again. In addition, the code checks whether the current node is an exit, and if so, prints a message saying that the exit has been found. This is shown in example 15.9,

Example 15.9. Traversing a graph.

```
1   public static void main(String[] args) {
2 ...
3
4      List<Node> visited = new ArrayList<>();
5      solve(nodes.get(2), visited);
```

```
 6   }
 7
 8   private static boolean solve(Node node, List<Node> visited) {
 9
10       System.out.print(node.id + " ");
11       visited.add(node);
12
13       if (node.isExit) {
14         System.out.print("Found exit!");
15         return true;
16       }
17
18       for (Node child : node.children)
19         if (!visited.contains(child))
20           if (solve(child, visited))
21             return true;
22
23       return false;
24   }
```

```
3 2 1 6 11 12 7 8 4 5 9 14 15 10 20 19 18 13 17 16 Found exit!
```

The solve method processes one node at a time, and passes the visited list to itself when it recurses. The visited list contains the list of nodes that have already been seen. solve returns true when the exit has been found, in which case the traversal is cut short. Otherwise it returns false. The output shows the order in which nodes are visited. It starts at node 3, and shows the traversal to nodes 2, 1, 6, 11, 12, 7, then 8. While processing node 8, no unvisited child nodes are found, so backtracking occurs until the current node is 3 again, at which point node 4 is the only unvisited child, so the traversal resumes with node 4, and so on.

It is instructive to walk through this traversal in your head, on paper or using the debugger, and you should do this until you're comfortable with the way the traversal works.

Note that traversal is cut short once the exit is found, even if not all nodes have been visited. You can see this if you set node 18 as an exit,

```
1   public static void main(String[] args) {
2   ...
3       nodes.get(17).isExit = true;
4
5       List<Node> visited = new ArrayList<>();
6       solve(nodes.get(2), visited);
7   }
```

Example 15.10. Adding a second exit.

```
3 2 1 6 11 12 7 8 4 5 9 14 15 10 20 19 18 Found exit!
```

The output above shows the list of nodes that are visited, and the order in which they're visited. What if we just want to print out the path from the entrance to the exit? We can do this by adding another list that contains the path from the first node to the last. You can think of this new 'path' list as a stack. When a node is processed, it's pushed onto the stack. When the algorithm is done processing the node, it's popped from the path, unless the exit has been found. As the traversal reaches each node, the `path` list contains the path from the entrance to that node. The code to do this is shown in example 15.11,

Example 15.11. Displaying the path from entrance to exit.

```
1   ...
2       List<Node> visited = new ArrayList<>();
3       List<Node> path = new ArrayList<>();
4       solve(nodes.get(2), visited, path);
5   ...
6
7     private static boolean solve(Node node, List<Node> visited, List<Node> path)
      {
8
9       visited.add(node);
10      path.add(node);
11
12      if (node.isExit) {
13        System.out.print("Found path: ");
14        for (Node pathNode : path)
15          System.out.print(pathNode.id + " ");
16
17        return true;
18      }
19
20      for (Node child : node.children)
21        if (!visited.contains(child))
22          if (solve(child, visited, path))
23            return true;
24
25      path.remove(path.size() - 1);
26      return false;
27    }
```

```
Found path: 3 4 9 14 15 20 19 18
```

15.6 Example: Letter Combinations

As another example of using recursion, we'll look at a program that takes a word and finds the set of words that can be formed using the original word's letters. In this example, not all letters in the original word need to be used to make a new word.

```
 1  import static java.lang.System.out;
 2  import java.io.File;
 3  import java.io.FileNotFoundException;
 4  import java.util.ArrayList;
 5  import java.util.HashMap;
 6  import java.util.List;
 7  import java.util.Map;
 8  import java.util.Scanner;
 9
10  public class Words {
11
12    public static void main(String[] args) throws FileNotFoundException {
13
14      String word = "epidemics";
15      WordFinder wordFinder = new WordFinder();
16
17      long start = System.currentTimeMillis();
18      List<String> words = wordFinder.getWords(word);
19      long end = System.currentTimeMillis();
20
21      out.println("Done in " + (end-start) + " microseconds");
22      out.println("Words contained in '" + word + "': " + words);
23    }
24  }
25
26  class WordFinder {
27
28    private Map<String, Boolean> dictionary = new HashMap<>();
29
30    public WordFinder() throws FileNotFoundException {
31
32      // read dictionary
33      File file = new File("corncob_lowercase.txt");
34      Scanner fileScanner = new Scanner(file);
35      while (fileScanner.hasNext()) {
36        String word = fileScanner.nextLine();
37        dictionary.put(word, true);
38      }
39      fileScanner.close();
40    }
41
42    // Returns words that can be composed from the letters in a word. Not all
43          letters need to be used
43    public List<String> getWords (String word) {
44      return getWordsInternal("", word);
45    }
46
47    private List<String> getWordsInternal(String word, String remainingLetters) {
48      List<String> words = new ArrayList<>();
49
50      // Base case: if there are no more letters to add, test the word
51      if (remainingLetters.isEmpty()) {
52        if (dictionary.containsKey(word) && !words.contains(word))
53          words.add(word);
54        return words;
55      }
56
57      // Recursive case: try adding each letter from the remaining letters to the
              word, and recurse
58      for (int i = 0; i < remainingLetters.length(); i++) {
59
60        char letter = remainingLetters.charAt(i);
```

Example 15.12. Letter Combinations.

```
61
62        // Remove this letter from remaining letters
63        String remainder = remainingLetters.substring(0, i) + remainingLetters.
          substring(i+1);
64
65        List<String> newWords = getWordsInternal(word + letter, remainder);
66        for (String newWord : newWords) // merge results
67          if (!words.contains(newWord))
68            words.add(newWord);
69
70        // Also try without the letter
71        newWords = getWordsInternal(word, remainder);
72        for (String newWord : newWords) // merge results
73          if (!words.contains(newWord))
74            words.add(newWord);
75      }
76
77    return words;
78  }
79 }
```

```
Done in 19876 milliseconds
Words contained in 'epidemics': [epidemics, epidemic, epics, epic, ems, em
```

The `main` method (line 12) creates an instance of the `WordFinder` class and calls its `getWords` method, which returns a list of words found. The `main` method then prints the resulting words as well as the time it took to perform the computation.

The `WordFinder` class contains a dictionary, which is a map of strings to boolean values. The dictionary is loaded by the `WordFinder` constructor. Each word from the dictionary file is loaded into the map as a key, with `true` as the boolean value. The dictionary we use here contains about $50,000$ English words, and can be downloaded by searching for 'corncob dictionary file' and downloading 'corncob_-lowercase.txt'. Alternatively, the 'google-10000-english.txt' file from chapter 12 can be used.

The HashSet class, which we haven't mentioned yet, can be used to store the dictionary. A `HashSet` is similar to a `HashMap` but only stores the keys without mapping them to values.

The `WordFinder.getWords` method (line 43) calls an internal version, `getWordsInternal`, that accepts two parameters. The helper method `getWordsInternal` is recursive.

It's common for a recursive method to be be called from another method that passes a default initial value for one of its parameters, like we've done in example 15.12 with `getWords` and `getWordsInternal`.

The `getWordsInternal` method (line 47) implements the following algorithm,

- `getWordsInternal` takes two parameters, a string containing part of a word being constructed, and a second string containing letters that haven't been used yet, and can potentially be used in building the word.

- Base case (lines 51-55): If the list of remaining letters is empty, test the first parameter (the word). If it's a proper word, add the word to the result list and return the result list.
- Recursive case (lines 58-77): Create empty list for the result word list. For each letter L in the list of remaining letters, perform the following steps,

  - Remove the letter L from the list of remaining letters (lines 60-63).
  - Add the letter L to the end of the word, and recursively get a list of results from the new word and new list of remaining letters. Add the results to the result list. (lines 65-68).
  - Recursively get a list of results from the original word and the new list of remaining letters. Add the results to the result list (lines 71-74).

The essence of the algorithm is to construct the possible candidate words by repeatedly taking each possible letter from the input and adding it to the candidate word. Each recursive call uses one more letter from the input, so the depth of recursion will equal the length of the input. The looping performed in each recursive invocation ensures each possible letter is used to construct the next part of the candidate word. Figure 15.6 shows the recursive control flow for the input 'put'.

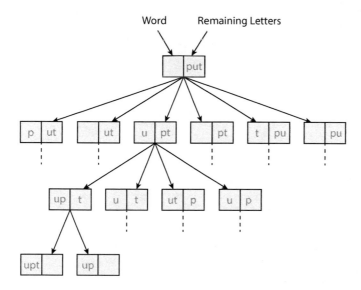

Figure 15.6: Recursive control flow for `getWordsInternal`.

Cache: A set of key/value pairs that's used to remember the results of a computation for particular input values. When the computation needs to be done later with the same set of input values, the result can be retrieved quickly from the cache.

To speed up the algorithm, a cache can be added to remember previous computations performed by the `getWordsInternal` method. The `Map` collection is perfect for such a cache. The key would be the inputs into the method, and the values are the corresponding outputs. This will speed up the program by eliminating all the duplicate calls with the same input values,

Example 15.13. Letter Combinations with cache.

```
1  class WordFinder {
2
3    private Map<String, Boolean> dictionary = new HashMap<>();
4    private Map<String, List<String>> cache = new HashMap<>();
5    ...
6
7    private List<String> getWordsInternal(String word, String remainingLetters) {
8
9      // check cache
10     if (cache.containsKey(word + "_" + remainingLetters))
11       return cache.get(word + "_" + remainingLetters);
12
13     List<String> words = new ArrayList<>();
14
15     // Base case: if there are no more letters to add, test the word
16     if (remainingLetters.isEmpty()) {
17       if (dictionary.containsKey(word) && !words.contains(word))
18         words.add(word);
19
20       // cache the result
21       cache.put(word + "_" + remainingLetters, words);
22
23       return words;
24     }
25
26     // Recursive case: try adding each letter from the remaining letters to the
         word, and recurse
27     ...
28     // cache the result
29     cache.put(word + "_" + remainingLetters, words);
30
31     return words;
32   }
33  }
```

The cache is created as a static variable on line 4 of example 15.13. Technique 15 on page 184 cautions against using global variables, but the use of a static variable for this purpose is fine, since the cache is *meant* to be shared by multiple invocations of `getWordsInternal`. If your program is multithreaded, be aware that `Map` isn't thread safe. Instead, use `ConcurrentHashMap`.

```
Done in 1117 milliseconds
Words contained in 'epidemics': [epidemics, epidemic, epics, epic, ems, em
```

The cache is created on line 4 of example 15.13. Before returning a result, the `getWordsInternal` method caches the results on lines 21 and 29. At the top of `getWordsInternal`, the cache is checked and used if the input exists in the cache. Caching is a very common optimization technique, used in many places in hardware and software layers of all computer systems. In the above example, the runtime was reduced to about 6% of the runtime without using the cache. The difference gets much more pronounced as the size of the input grows. The runtime for the input 'electronic' with the use of caching is about 3% of the runtime without it.

```
Done in 10452 milliseconds
Words contained in 'electronic': [electronic, electron, electro, electric, el
```

```
Done in 380505 milliseconds
Words contained in 'electronic': [electronic, electron, electro, electric, el
```

> **Technique 22. Use caching to speed up your program**
>
> Caching can be used to speed up runtime performance dramatically. The `HashMap` class is a good choice for cache implementation.

Since we're discussing runtime performance, we'll present one more important performance enhancement technique in the next section.

15.7 StringBuilder

Strings in Java are immutable. This means they can't be directly modified. When we add two strings together, a new string is made to hold the result. This can cause performance issues if there is a lot of string manipulation in your program. Java offers a special class for this, called `StringBuilder`. The `StringBuilder` class allows you to modify a string without having to allocate a new string to hold the result. Once you're done with your changes to the string, you can copy the final string from the `StringBuilder` object to a `string` object.

The next example (15.14) eliminates punctuation and numbers from a string, with two implementations, one using `String` and the other using `StringBuilder`,

```
1  import static java.lang.System.out;
2
3  public class TestStrings {
4
5    public static void main(String[] args) {
6
7      String result = "";
```

Example 15.14. Using StringBuilder.

```
 8    String input = "The Olympic Games are on the way with Japan set to host the
         29th edition of the modern games. Over 11,000 competitors from 206
         nations will descend on Tokyo in 2021 to aim for glory in their
         respective fields. A total of 33 sports will be shown at the Olympics
         including five new sports for fans to sink their teeth into.";
 9
10    long start = System.currentTimeMillis();
11    for (int i = 0; i < 1000000; i++)
12      result = eliminatePunctuation(input);
13    long end = System.currentTimeMillis();
14
15    out.println("String - Done in " + (end-start) + " milliseconds");
16    out.println("String - Result: " + result);
17
18    start = System.currentTimeMillis();
19    for (int i = 0; i < 1000000; i++)
20      result = eliminatePunctuation2(input);
21    end = System.currentTimeMillis();
22
23    out.println("StringBuilder - Done in " + (end-start) + " milliseconds");
24    out.println("StringBuilder - Result: " + result);
25  }
26
27  private static String eliminatePunctuation(String input) {
28    String result = "";
29    for (int i = 0; i < input.length(); i++) {
30      char ch = input.charAt(i);
31      if ((ch >= 'a' && ch <= 'z') ||
32        (ch >= 'A' && ch <= 'Z') ||
33        ch == ' ')
34        result += ch;
35    }
36    return result;
37  }
38
39  private static String eliminatePunctuation2(String input) {
40    StringBuilder result = new StringBuilder();
41    for (int i = 0; i < input.length(); i++) {
42      char ch = input.charAt(i);
43      if ((ch >= 'a' && ch <= 'z') ||
44        (ch >= 'A' && ch <= 'Z') ||
45        ch == ' ')
46        result.append(ch);
47    }
48    return result.toString();
49  }
50 }
```

```
String - Done in 16682 milliseconds
String - Result: The Olympic Games are on the way with Japan set to host the th edition o
StringBuilder - Done in 1566 milliseconds
StringBuilder - Result: The Olympic Games are on the way with Japan set to host the th ed
```

The `String` implementation of `eliminatePunctuation` builds a string one character at a time. Punctuation characters and digits are filtered out using the `if` condition on lines 31-33. Each time a character is added to the string result on line 34, a new string object has to be allocated, copying the old string to the new one. This slows down processing and also puts pressure on the memory system since strings are allocated on the heap.

In contrast, the `eliminatePunctuation2` implementation allocates a `StringBuilder` object that doesn't cause this repeated allocation of new strings. Text can be appended to a `StringBuilder` without allocating a new object or copying the previous contents of the `StringBuilder`. The timing test with this particular test data show that the `StringBuilder` implementation uses about 10% of the time that the `String` implementation does.

> **Technique 23. Use `StringBuilder` to speed up string processing**
>
> `StringBuilder` can be used to speed up string operations that require the string to be modified, such as adding to the string, or deleting part of it.

Chapter Summary

- Recursion is when a method calls itself. Problems that require iteration can also be solved using recursion. In some situations, recursive code is much simpler and more maintainable than its iterative counterpart.
- Every recursive method has a base case, which tests for a termination condition, and a recursive case, where the recursive method calls itself.
- Caching is a common technique for increasing the runtime performance of a program.
- The `StringBuilder` class allows manipulation of string data that's faster than using the `String` class.

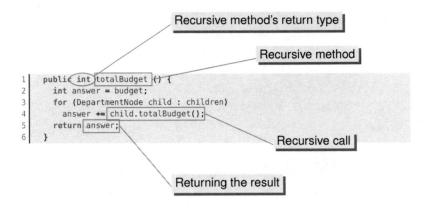

```
1    public int totalBudget () {
2      int answer = budget;
3      for (DepartmentNode child : children)
4        answer += child.totalBudget();
5      return answer;
6    }
```

Recursive method's return type

Recursive method

Recursive call

Returning the result

Exercise Solutions

15.1

The sum is 24

```
1    public static void main(String[] args) {
2
3      int[] array = { 10, 12, -3, 5 };
4      out.print("The sum is " + sumArray(array));
5    }
6
7    public static int sumArray(int[] array) {
8      return sumArray(array, 0);
9    }
10
11   public static int sumArray(int[] array, int index) {
12
13     // base case
14     if (array.length == index)
15       return 0;
16
17     // recursive case
18     return array[index] + sumArray(array, index + 1);
19   }
```

15.2

The merged string is MondayTuesdayFriday

```
1    public static void main(String[] args) {
2
3      List<String> days = new ArrayList<>();
4      days.add("Monday");
5      days.add("Tuesday");
6      days.add("Friday");
7      out.print("The merged string is " + concatenateStrings(days));
8    }
9
```

```
10    public static String concatenateStrings(List<String> strings) {
11      return concatenateStrings(strings, 0);
12    }
13
14    public static String concatenateStrings(List<String> strings, int
        index) {
15
16      // base case
17      if (index == strings.size())
18        return "";
19
20      // recursive case
21      return strings.get(index) + concatenateStrings(strings, index +
        1);
22    }
```

15.3

```
1     public static void main(String[] args) {
2     ...
3       DepartmentNode root = new DepartmentNode("Office of the
          Secretary", 12, 191000, node12, node9, node13, node14);
4       out.println("Number of departments in the tree is: " +
          countDepartments(root));
5     }
6
7     private static int countDepartments(DepartmentNode root) {
8
9       List<DepartmentNode> stack = new ArrayList<>();
10      stack.add(root);
11      int totalDepartments = 0;
12
13      while (!stack.isEmpty()) {
14
15        // pop a node from the stack
16        DepartmentNode currentNode = stack.remove(stack.size() - 1);
17
18        // process the node
19        totalDepartments ++;
20
21        // push each of the current node's children onto the stack
22        for (DepartmentNode child : currentNode.children)
23          stack.add(child);
24      }
25
26      return totalDepartments;
27    }
```

`Number of departments in the tree is: 15`

15.4

```
1     public static void main(String[] args) {
2     ...
3       DepartmentNode root = new DepartmentNode("Office of the
          Secretary", 12, 191000, node12, node9, node13, node14);
4       out.println("Number of departments is: " + root.countNodes());
5     }
6
7     class DepartmentNode {
8     ...
9       public int countNodes () {
10        int answer = 1;
```

`Number of departments is: 15`

```
11      for (DepartmentNode child : children)
12        answer += child.countNodes();
13      return answer;
14    }
15  }
```

15.5

```
Average budget is: 124866
```

```
1   public static void main(String[] args) {
2   ...
3      DepartmentNode root = new DepartmentNode("Office of the
         Secretary", 12, 191000, node12, node9, node13, node14);
4      out.println("Average budget is: " + root.totalBudget() / root.
         countNodes());
5    }
6
7  class DepartmentNode {
8  ...
9    public int totalBudget () {
10     int answer = budget;
11     for (DepartmentNode child : children)
12       answer += child.totalBudget();
13     return answer;
14   }
15 }
```

Sorting | 16

16.1 Bubble Sort

As you saw in section 11.4, a list can be sorted using `Collec-tions.sort` as long as the list holds elements of a type that implements `Comparable`. We'll repeat example 11.6 here as example 16.1,

```java
import static java.lang.System.out;
import java.util.ArrayList;
import java.util.Collections;
import java.util.List;

public class SortTest {

  public static void main(String[] args) {

    // Generate 10 random numbers between 1 and 20
    List<Integer> list = new ArrayList<Integer>();
    for (int i = 0; i < 10; i++)
      list.add((int) (Math.random() * 20) + 1);

    out.println("Before sorting: " + list);
    Collections.sort(list);
    out.println("After sorting: " + list);
  }
}
```

Example 16.1. Sorting a list of numbers.

```
Before sorting: [10, 9, 7, 19, 8, 4, 7, 14, 9, 16]
After sorting: [4, 7, 7, 8, 9, 9, 10, 14, 16, 19]
```

What if we wanted to sort the list ourselves without using Java's built-in `sort` method? A simple sort algorithm called bubble sort can be used instead of the sort operation on line 16 of example 16.1. The bubble sort algorithm works by repeatedly swapping two numbers that are in the wrong order, until the list is sorted. This is shown in example 16.2,

```java
  public static void main(String[] args) {
    ...
    out.println("Before sorting: " + list);
    bubbleSort(list);
    out.println("After sorting: " + list);
  }
```

Example 16.2. Bubble sort.

```
7
8     public static void bubbleSort(List<Integer> list) {
9
10        // loop 'n' times, where n is the size of the list
11        for (int counter1 = 0; counter1 < list.size(); counter1++) {
12
13            // loop 'n' times, where n is the size of the list
14            for (int counter2 = 0; counter2 < list.size() - 1; counter2++) {
15
16                // if we see two elements out of order, swap them
17                if (list.get(counter2) > list.get(counter2 + 1)) {
18                    int temp = list.get(counter2);
19                    list.set(counter2, list.get(counter2 + 1));
20                    list.set(counter2 + 1, temp);
21                }
22            }
23        }
24    }
```

```
Before sorting: [19, 3, 18, 14, 3, 20, 18, 4, 7, 2]
After sorting:  [2, 3, 3, 4, 7, 14, 18, 18, 19, 20]
```

The sort method makes multiple passes, and during each pass examines successive pairs of numbers in the list. When a pair is in the wrong order, i.e., the first number is bigger than the second, the two numbers are swapped before the next pair is examined. After each pair is examined, the larger one is part of the next pair that is examined. Figure 16.1 shows the first three steps of the inner loop, within the first pass of the outer loop:

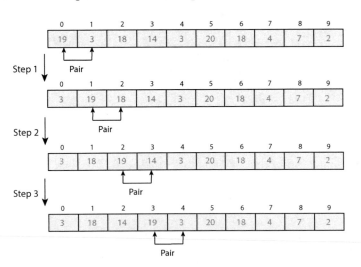

Figure 16.1: The first few steps of the inner loop of the Bubble sort algorithm.

- In step 1, the first pair is examined, with indexes 0 and 1. They're swapped since they're in the wrong order.

- In step 2, the second pair is examined, with indexes 1 and 2. They're swapped.
- In step 3, the third pair is examined, with indexes 2 and 3. They're swapped.

Once the inner loop goes through all pairs, the first pass of the outer loop is over. Note that after the first pass of the outer loop, the largest number, 20, will have been moved to the end of the array. After the second pass of the outer loop, the second-largest number, 19, will be in the right place, and so on. The numbers bubble over to their correct positions, hence the algorithm's name. Figure 16.2 shows the array's contents after the first three passes of the outer loop.

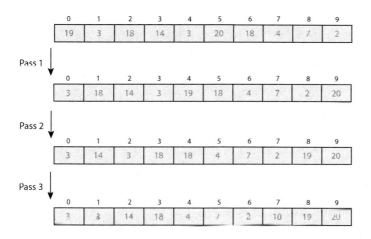

Figure 16.2: The first few steps of the outer loop of the Bubble sort algorithm.

Applying the techniques we learned in chapter 13, it's clear since the outer and inner loop both loop from 1 to n, where n is the list's size, that the algorithm's time complexity is $O(n^2)$.

We're not quite done, because the bubble sort in example 16.2 takes a list of integers as a parameter, so it's not capable of sorting a list of strings or other `Comparable` types. It can be converted to accept a generic type, stipulating that the type implements the `Comparable` interface, as shown in example 16.3,

```
1   public static void main(String[] args) {
2
3     List<Integer> numbers = new ArrayList<>();
4     for (int i = 0; i < 10; i++)
5       numbers.add((int) (Math.random() * 20) + 1);
6     out.println("Numbers before sorting: " + numbers);
7     bubbleSort(numbers);
8     out.println("Numbers after sorting : " + numbers);
9
```

Example 16.3. Generic bubble sort.

```
10      List<String> names = new ArrayList<>();
11      names.add("Samantha");
12      names.add("Jon");
13      names.add("Pierre");
14      names.add("Chris");
15      out.println("Names before sorting: " + names);
16      bubbleSort(names);
17      out.println("Names after sorting : " + names);
18  }
19
20  public static <E extends Comparable<E>> void bubbleSort(List<E> list) {
21
22      // loop 'n' times, where n is the size of the list
23      for (int counter1 = 0; counter1 < list.size(); counter1++) {
24
25          // loop 'n' times, where n is the size of the list
26          for (int counter2 = 0; counter2 < list.size() - 1; counter2++) {
27
28              // if we see two elements out of order, swap them
29              if (list.get(counter2).compareTo(list.get(counter2 + 1)) > 0) {
30                  E temp = list.get(counter2);
31                  list.set(counter2, list.get(counter2 + 1));
32                  list.set(counter2 + 1, temp);
33              }
34          }
35      }
36  }
```

```
Numbers before sorting: [7, 6, 9, 19, 17, 2, 13, 16, 19, 18]
Numbers after sorting : [2, 6, 7, 9, 13, 16, 17, 18, 19, 19]
Names before sorting: [Samantha, Jon, Pierre, Chris]
Names after sorting : [Chris, Jon, Pierre, Samantha]
```

Example 16.3 shows bubble sort as a generic method. Generic methods, which we haven't discussed yet, are similar to generic types in that they accept a type as a parameter. The generic type is shown in angle brackets after the `static` keyword on line 20 of example 16.3, and stipulates that the generic type `E` implements the `Comparable<E>` interface (the `extends` keyword is used here instead of `implements`). The other changes we had to make were to change the `temp` variable on line 30 from `int` to `E`, and to use `compareTo` instead of an arithmetic comparison operator to compare two instances of `E` on line 29.

A common optimization of bubble sort is to end the inner loop at `list.size()` - `counter1`, which allows it to avoid looking at numbers that have already reached their proper position in the list. Another common optimization is to terminate the outer loop if the previous iteration didn't result in any pairs being swapped, which helps if the list was nearly sorted to begin with. Neither of these optimizations change the algorithm's time complexity.

Sort algorithms generally fall in two categories, slow ones that perform in quadratic time, $O(n^2)$, and fast ones that perform in log-linear time, O(n log n). In the next section, we'll look at one of the faster ones.

Exercises

16.1 Update example 16.3 to implement the following optimization. Have the outer loop terminate if the previous iteration didn't result in any pairs being swapped.

16.2 Merge Sort

One of the faster sorting algorithms is merge sort. It's a recursive algorithm that can be summarized as follows,

- Take the input list L, of size n, and break it into two halves, *H1* and *H2*, each of size $n/2$.
- Recursively sort each of the two halves, *H1* and *H2*.
- Merge the sorted halves, *H1* and *H2*, by looping through both halves in parallel and repeatedly moving the smaller number from either half to a new list, which will contain the sorted contents of the original list *L*.

The first part is just to break the list into two halves, and there's no re-arranging of list items in that part. The real work of sorting happens during the second phase which merges the two sorted halves. Figure 16.3 illustrates the merge sort algorithm sorting a list of four numbers.

As seen in figure 16.3, the input list has four numbers, which is split into two lists of size 2. Each of the two smaller lists is further split into lists of size 1. The lists of size 1 are sorted by definition, and therein lies the base case of the recursive algorithm. Each two sorted lists of size 1 are merged into a list of size 2, and the two lists of size 2 are merged into the result which has a size of 4. Note that each point where a list is split into two lists represents one invocation of the recursive merge sort algorithm, and there are three such invocations in this example. Each of those three invocations performs a merge,

Note that the recursion depth is the log of the input size.

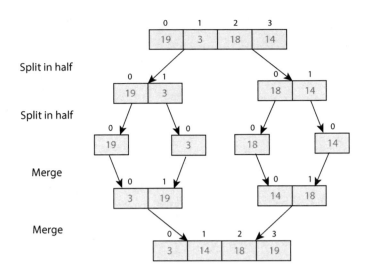

Figure 16.3: Sorting a list using the Merge sort algorithm.

seen in figure 16.3 where two lists are merged into one. The merge sort implementation is shown in example 16.4,

Example 16.4. Merge sort.

```java
public static void main(String[] args) {
...
  out.println("Before sorting: " + list);
  list = mergeSort(list);
  out.println("After sorting: " + list);
}

public static List<Integer> mergeSort(List<Integer> list) {

  // base case - nothing to do if the list is empty or has just one element
  if (list.size() < 2)
    return list;

  // partition the list into two halves, and recurse

  // copy first half of the input list into 'half1', and sort 'half1'
  List<Integer> half1 = new ArrayList<>();
  for (int i = 0; i < list.size() / 2; i++)
    half1.add(list.get(i));
  half1 = mergeSort(half1);

  // copy second half of the input list into 'half2', and sort 'half2'
  List<Integer> half2 = new ArrayList<>();
  for (int i = list.size() / 2; i < list.size(); i++)
    half2.add(list.get(i));
  half2 = mergeSort(half2);

  // merge the two sorted halves
  return merge(half1, half2);
}

public static List<Integer> merge(List<Integer> half1, List<Integer> half2) {

  List<Integer> result = new ArrayList<>();
```

```
35    int index1 = 0;
36    int index2 = 0;
37
38    // loop until both halves are depleted
39    while (index1 < half1.size() || index2 < half2.size()) {
40
41      // if half1 is depleted, take from half2
42      if (index1 == half1.size())
43        result.add(half2.get(index2++));
44
45      // if half2 is depleted, take from half1
46      else if (index2 == half2.size())
47        result.add(half1.get(index1++));
48
49      // if neither half is depleted, take the smaller list element from half1
      or half2
50      else {
51        if (half1.get(index1) > half2.get(index2))
52          result.add(half2.get(index2++));
53        else
54          result.add(half1.get(index1++));
55      }
56    }
57
58    return result;
59  }
```

```
Before sorting: [11, 4, 16, 7, 10, 12, 13, 18, 5, 6]
After sorting:  [4, 5, 6, 7, 10, 11, 12, 13, 16, 18]
```

Example 16.4 contains two methods, `mergeSort` which splits the input into two halves and calls itself recursively, and `merge` which merges two sorted lists into one. These two methods implement the algorithm summarized in the beginning of this section. Note that the algorithm still works when the input's size is odd, in which case one of the two halves is larger than the other by one element. The merge method walks through both input lists in parallel which requires two indexes, one for each list. In each iteration of the main merge loop, the smaller number at the index point of each input list is moved to the output list.

To illustrate the speed difference between the two sorting algorithms, we'll modify the main method to repeatedly test both with different input sizes. Figure 16.4 shows the relative speed as the input grows.

```
1  public static void main(String[] args) {
2
3    for (int i = 8000; i <= 64000; i += 8000)
4      runTest(i);
5  }
6
7  private static void runTest (int size) {
8
```

Example 16.5. Comparing bubble sort and merge sort.

```
9      // Generate random numbers between 1 and 1000000
10     List<Integer> list1 = new ArrayList<Integer>();
11     List<Integer> list2 = new ArrayList<>();
12     for (int i = 0; i < size; i++) {
13       int number = (int) (Math.random() * 1000000) + 1;
14       list1.add(number);
15       list2.add(number);
16     }
17
18     long start = System.currentTimeMillis();
19     bubbleSort(list1);
20     long end = System.currentTimeMillis();
21     out.println("List size " + size + ", Bubble sort took " + (end-start) + "
         milliseconds");
22
23     start = System.currentTimeMillis();
24     list2 = mergeSort(list2);
25     end = System.currentTimeMillis();
26     out.println("List size " + size + ", Merge sort took " + (end-start) + "
         milliseconds");
27   }
```

```
List size 8000, Bubble sort took 453 milliseconds
List size 8000, Merge sort took 16 milliseconds
List size 16000, Bubble sort took 1839 milliseconds
List size 16000, Merge sort took 11 milliseconds
List size 24000, Bubble sort took 4332 milliseconds
List size 24000, Merge sort took 19 milliseconds
List size 32000, Bubble sort took 8050 milliseconds
List size 32000, Merge sort took 19 milliseconds
List size 40000, Bubble sort took 13543 milliseconds
List size 40000, Merge sort took 33 milliseconds
List size 48000, Bubble sort took 19495 milliseconds
List size 48000, Merge sort took 42 milliseconds
List size 56000, Bubble sort took 26959 milliseconds
List size 56000, Merge sort took 48 milliseconds
List size 64000, Bubble sort took 40264 milliseconds
List size 64000, Merge sort took 48 milliseconds
```

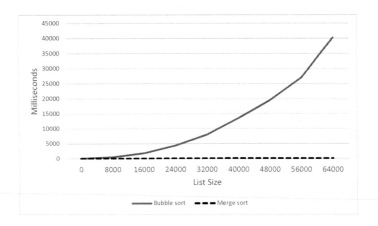

Figure 16.4: Comparing bubble sort and merge sort.

Exercises

16.2 Change the merge sort method in example 16.4 so that it's generic, as was done with bubble sort in the last section.

16.3 Recurrence Relations

Let's discuss the runtime performance of merge sort. There are three parts to the merge sort algorithm,

- Splitting the input list into two lists. This is O(n) since it loops once through the input.
- Recursively calling merge sort on each of the two lists, each containing half of the original input.
- Merging the two sorted lists, each of size $n/2$. This is O(n) since it's done with one pass through both of them simultaneously.

In the second step above, the algorithm calls itself twice, each time with an input size that's half the original input size n. The rest (steps 1 and 3 above) is done in O(n) time. The following recurrence relation describes the runtime:

$$T(n) = 2T(n/2) + O(n) \quad \Rightarrow \quad O(n \ log \ n)$$

A recurrence relation describes the runtime of an algorithm with an input size of n using its own runtime with a smaller input, and in this case the smaller input size is $n/2$. The equation shown above tells us that the runtime of a method that does O(n) work in addition to calling itself twice, each time with half the original input size, is equal to O(n log n). Recall from table 13.1 that O(n log n) is known as log-linear time, and from figure 13.2 that log-linear algorithms are far faster than those that are quadratic. This explains the results seen in figure 16.4 illustrating the difference in runtime between merge sort and bubble sort.

Recurrence relations are useful in analyzing the time complexity of recursive algorithms. Table 16.1 shows some common recurrence

[2] explains recurrence relations in detail and describes three different ways of solving recurrence relations.

Recurrence	Complexity	Example
$T(n) = T(n/2) + O(1)$	$O(log\ n)$	Binary Search
$T(n) = T(n-1) + O(1)$	$O(n)$	Traversing a list
$T(n) = 2T(n/2) + O(1)$	$O(n)$	Traversing a tree
$T(n) = T(n-1) + O(n)$	$O(n^2)$	Bubble sort
$T(n) = 2T(n/2) + O(n)$	$O(n\ log\ n)$	Merge sort

relations with an example algorithm for each. Let's think about each one,

- Imagine binary search, first explained in section 14.1 implemented recursively. The middle of the list is found and compared to the item in question. That's the fixed cost which is O(1). Then the recursive call occurs, with search bounds narrowed down to half of the original range. So we've got $T(n) = T(n/2) + O(1)$, and the binary search terminates in a logarithmic number of iterations since the input size is cut in half in each iteration.

- Imagine the list traversal in example 13.17 implemented in a recursive way. Instead of a `while` loop to construct the string result of `toString`, the string is constructed by concatenating the current node in the linked list to the result of a recursive call with the next node as input. That's $O(1)$ fixed cost (using a `StringBuilder`) plus a recursive call to process the rest of the list. Thus we have $T(n) = T(n-1) + O(1)$. Traversing a list visits each node and has overall time cost of $O(n)$.

- Tree traversal is done by processing the current node, then recursively processing each of the node's children. Processing the current node takes $O(1)$ time, and processing each child takes $T(n/m)$ time where n is the size of the node's subtree and m is the branching factor. Thus we have $T(n) = 2T(n/2) + O(1)$ in the case of a binary tree, or $T(n) = m\ T(n/m) + O(1)$ in the case of a tree with a branching factor of m. Traversing a tree visits each node and has $O(n)$ overall time cost.

- Imagine bubble sort implemented recursively. The inner loop is performed once, with cost $O(n)$, resulting in one number bubbling to its proper location, then a recursive call is made to perform another iteration of the outer loop. That's still effectively a nested loop, with both the outer and inner loops repeating n times, performing bubble sort in $O(n^2)$ time where the recurrence relation is $T(n) = T(n-1) + O(n)$.

- The final item in table 16.1 is $T(n) = 2T(n/2) + O(n)$, exemplified by merge sort with the splitting and merging both using $O(n)$ time and two recursive calls, each processing half the input size. Merge sort runs in $O(n \, log \, n)$ time.

Sometimes memory requirements (space complexity) play a big role in deciding which algorithm to use. The merge sort algorithm allocates a new list to store the merge operation's result, and this is done in each nested call. To take pressure off the Java memory management system, for several years the internal sort algorithm used by `Arrays.sort` wasn't one of the $O(n \, log \, n)$ algorithms, but rather quick sort, which is $O(n^2)$ in the worst case, but is $O(n \, log \, n)$ in the *average* case. The big advantage of quick sort is that it sorts a list *in place* without needing to allocate space to copy the list.

Exercises

16.3   Update example 13.17 to implement `MyLinkedList.toString` using recursion instead of iteration. See the above description of list traversal with recursion.

16.4 Where To From Here?

Did you follow my advice in the introduction's "How to use this book" section? If you've internalized what this book covers, and can write the code for the book's examples on your own, I believe the hard part is over for you. Everything else that you'll encounter in the world of software development will either be easier than what you learned here, or will be a variation on the concepts you learned here. Either way, you should be able to pick it up without too much trouble, whether it's "process stuff" such as source control, tooling such as databases, infrastructure such as cloud, or platform-specific programming such as web application development. And, until you get your first full-time developer job, remember to keep practicing!

Tip 10. Until you get your first full-time developer job, remember to keep practicing!

Chapter Summary

- Sorting algorithms generally have $O(n^2)$ or $O(n \log n)$ time complexity.
- Bubble sort has $O(n^2)$ time complexity, and works by making successive passes, examining each pair of numbers in each pass, and swapping them if they're out of order.
- Merge sort has $O(n \log n)$ time complexity, and works by partitioning the list into two parts, recursively sorting each part, then merging the two sorted parts.
- Recurrence relations help to analyze the time complexity of recursive algorithms.

Outer loop

Inner loop

Check each pair

Swap two numbers

```java
1   public static void bubbleSort(List<Integer> list) {
2
3       // loop 'n' times, where n is the size of the list
4       for (int counter1 = 0; counter1 < list.size(); counter1++) {
5
6           // loop 'n' times, where n is the size of the list
7           for (int counter2 = 0; counter2 < list.size() - 1; counter2++) {
8
9               // if we see two elements out of order, swap them
10              if (list.get(counter2) > list.get(counter2 + 1)) {
11                  int temp = list.get(counter2);
12                  list.set(counter2, list.get(counter2 + 1));
13                  list.set(counter2 + 1, temp);
14              }
15          }
16      }
17  }
```

Exercise Solutions

16.1

```
1   public static void bubbleSort(List<Integer> list) {
2
3     boolean swapOccurred = true;
4     while (swapOccurred) {
5
6       swapOccurred = false;
7       for (int counter2 = 0; counter2 < list.size() - 1; counter2++)
        {
8
9         // if we see two elements out of order, swap them
10        if (list.get(counter2) > list.get(counter2 + 1)) {
11          int temp = list.get(counter2);
12          list.set(counter2, list.get(counter2 + 1));
13          list.set(counter2 + 1, temp);
14          swapOccurred = true;
15        }
16      }
17    }
18  }
```

```
Before sorting: [19, 17, 3, 6, 16, 5, 19, 14, 19, 9]
After sorting:  [3, 5, 6, 9, 14, 16, 17, 19, 19, 19]
```

16.2

```
1   public static void main(String[] args) {
2
3     List<Integer> numbers = new ArrayList<>();
4     for (int i = 0; i < 10; i++)
5       numbers.add((int) (Math.random() * 20) + 1);
6     out.println("Numbers before sorting: " + numbers);
7     numbers = mergeSort(numbers);
8     out.println("Numbers after sorting : " + numbers);
9
10    List<String> names = new ArrayList<>();
11    names.add("Samantha");
12    names.add("Jon");
13    names.add("Pierre");
14    names.add("Chris");
15    out.println("Names before sorting: " + names);
16    names = mergeSort(names);
17    out.println("Names after sorting : " + names);
18  }
19
20  public static <E extends Comparable<E>> List<E> mergeSort(List<E>
      list) {
21
22    // base case - nothing to do if the list is empty or has just
      one element
23    if (list.size() < 2)
24      return list;
25
26    // partition the list into two halves, and recurse
27
28    // copy first half of the input list into 'half1', and sort '
      half1'
29    List<E> half1 = new ArrayList<>();
```

```
30      for (int i = 0; i < list.size() / 2; i++)
31        half1.add(list.get(i));
32      half1 = mergeSort(half1);
33
34      // copy second half of the input list into 'half2', and sort '
           half2'
35      List<E> half2 = new ArrayList<>();
36      for (int i = list.size() / 2; i < list.size(); i++)
37        half2.add(list.get(i));
38      half2 = mergeSort(half2);
39
40      // merge the two sorted halves
41      return merge(half1, half2);
42    }
43
44   public static <E extends Comparable<E>> List<E> merge(List<E>
           half1, List<E> half2) {
45
46      List<E> result = new ArrayList<>();
47      int index1 = 0;
48      int index2 = 0;
49
50      // loop until both halves are depleted
51      while (index1 < half1.size() || index2 < half2.size()) {
52
53        // if half1 is depleted, take from half2
54        if (index1 == half1.size())
55          result.add(half2.get(index2++));
56
57        // if half2 is depleted, take from half1
58        else if (index2 == half2.size())
59          result.add(half1.get(index1++));
60
61        // if neither half is depleted, take the smaller list element
             from half1 or half2
62        else {
63          if (half1.get(index1).compareTo(half2.get(index2)) > 0)
64            result.add(half2.get(index2++));
65          else
66            result.add(half1.get(index1++));
67        }
68      }
69
70      return result;
71    }
```

```
Numbers before sorting: [19, 20, 18, 8, 9, 15, 2, 10, 5, 19]
Numbers after sorting : [2, 5, 8, 9, 10, 15, 18, 19, 19, 20]
Names before sorting: [Samantha, Jon, Pierre, Chris]
Names after sorting : [Chris, Jon, Pierre, Samantha]
```

16.3
```
1    @Override
2    public String toString() {
3      StringBuilder sb = new StringBuilder();
4      toString(sb, head);
5      return "[" + sb + "]";
6    }
7
8    private void toString(StringBuilder sb, Node<E> node) {
9
10     // base case - node is null
```

```
11    if (node == null)
12      return;
13
14    // base case - this is the last node in the list, no comma added
15    if (node.next == null) {
16      sb.append(node.element.toString());
17      return;
18    }
19
20    // recursive case
21    sb.append(node.element);
22    sb.append(", ");
23    toString (sb, node.next);
24  }
```

```
names = [Peter, Mary, Heather, Mary]
```

Bibliography & Further Reading

[1] ABELSON, H., AND SUSSMAN, G. J. *Structure and Interpretation of Computer Programs*, 2nd ed. The MIT Press, Cambridge, MA, USA, 1996.

[2] CORMEN, T. H., LEISERSON, C. E., RIVEST, R. L., AND STEIN, C. *Introduction to Algorithms*, 2nd ed. The MIT Press, Cambridge, MA, USA, 2001.

[3] ECLIPSE FOUNDATION. Eclipse documentation. https://www.eclipse.org/documentation, 2020. Accessed: 2020-12-17.

[4] FOOTE, B., AND YODER, J. Big Ball of Mud. In *Pattern Languages of Program Design* (1999), Addison-Wesley, pp. 653–692.

[5] GAMMA, E., HELM, R., JOHNSON, R., AND VLISSIDES, J. *Design Patterns: Elements of Reusable Object-Oriented Software*. Addison-Wesley Longman Publishing Co., Inc., USA, 1995.

[6] KNUTH, D. E. *The Art of Computer Programming, Volume 1 (3rd Ed.): Fundamental Algorithms*. Addison Wesley Longman Publishing Co., Inc., USA, 1997.

[7] ORACLE. Java documentation. https://docs.oracle.com/en/java/index.html, 2020. Accessed: 2020-12-17.

[8] SEDGEWICK, R., AND WAYNE, K. *Computer Science: An Interdisciplinary Approach*, 1st ed. Addison-Wesley Professional, 2016.

Glossary

abstraction	One of the main techniques used to organize computer programs.
algorithm	A series of steps that define how a program will accomplish its task.
argument	A data value that is passed to a method's parameter.
big-o notation	A notation relating the runtime performance of an algorithm to the size of its input.
bug	A mistake in the code that results in incorrect output for certain inputs.
caching	The act of temporarily storing computed values, or storing data from slower memory within a faster memory space, for faster retrieval later.
casting	Converting a value from one type to another.
class	A type defined by Java or by the programmer.
code block	Curly braces containing lines of code.
collection	A built-in Java class that contains objects and grows as needed when you add objects to it
compiler	A program that translates source code in a high-level language into machine code.
compile-time	When the programmer is entering the source code (compared to run-time).
compiling	Translating source code in a high-level language into machine code.
complexity	A measure of the performance (time or space) of a program or an algorithm.
constant	A named data item defined in a Java program that can't be changed at runtime.
encapsulation	When data related to an object and methods that operate on the object are bundled in a class.
enumeration	A type whose instances can only have a certain set of possible values.
exception	An unexpected error condition.
expression	A Java formula that can include data and operators, producing a result of a certain type.

generic class	A class that requires another type as a parameter.
global variable	A variable that is available to all the code within a program.
graph	A tree data structure that can contain cycles.
hardcoded value	A constant value of a particular type, used in the program's source code.
hashing	The process of converting a class's data to an integer.
heap memory	The area of memory where objects and arrays reside when allocated using the `new` keyword.
high-level language	A computer language that is easily readable by humans.
IDE	The Integrated Development Environment, a program that allows the programmer to enter the program and debug it.
immutable	Immutable data is data that can't be directly changed.
infinite loop	When a loop doesn't terminate because its termination condition is never met.
inheritance	When one class extends another, inheriting its data elements and methods.
integer division	When an integer is divided by another integer.
interface	Specifies a particular set of methods that can be implemented by one or more classes.
iteration	Performing an operation repeatedly to accomplish a task or compute a result.
local variable	A variable that's defined in a local scope, such as a method.
low-level language	A computer language that is closer to the computer's native machine language.
machine language	The native language of a CPU.
map	A collection that maps keys to values, where the key and value are arbitrary classes.
method	A named block of code that can be executed as a unit.
null reference	Using an object or array reference before it's initialized, resulting in an exception.

operator precedence	The order in which operators are evaluated within an expression.
parameter	A variable defined by a method that is initialized by the code that calls it, in order to pass information into the method.
polymorphism	When a reference to a base class or interface can refer to more than one derived class at runtime.
primitive type	A native type defined by the Java language.
program	A compiled version of the source code that is executed by the computer.
project	In Eclipse, a project is a collection of classes that, when compiled, produce an executable program.
pseudocode	An English description of the steps that make up a program's algorithm.
recurrence relation	A mathematical description of an algorithm's runtime expressed in terms of its own runtime with a smaller input.
recursion	When a method calls itself.
refactoring	Reorganizing a program so that it's more maintainable.
run-time	When a software program is running (compared to compile-time).
scope	The part of the program where an identifier can be accessed.
serialization	Saving an object to a file.
shortcut evaluation	Evaluating an expression where part of the expression isn't evaluated because it doesn't need to be.
software	A sequence of instructions that tell the computer how to perform a useful task.
stack memory	The area of memory where local variables are stored.
stack overflow	When the call stack runs out of memory because of too many nested method invocations.
ternary operator	An operator that takes three arguments, such as the ?: operator.
tree	A data structure representing hierarchical data.
type casting	Converting a value from one type to another.

UML	The Unified Modeling Language, which defines many types of useful diagrams that help to specify software components and their interactions.
unary operator	An operator that takes one argument, such as the negation operator.
variable	A named data item defined in a Java program.
workspace	A collection of projects in Eclipse.
wrapper class	A class that wraps a native Java type, and provides extra functionality for convenience.

Index

About the Author

Marwan Shaban received his B.S. in computer engineering from N.C. State University in 1988, and Ph.D. in computer science from Boston University in 1996. Subsequently, he worked as a partner, software developer, software architect and in management at companies ranging from startups to large corporations, with diverse technologies such as database, cloud, mobile and web.

During his twenty-year tenure in industry, while not writing code he could be found providing technical direction and mentoring to software teams, hiring software developers, conducting secure coding reviews, managing remediation efforts, working with QA, BA and PM teams, and myriad similar activities. He has created extensive architectural documentation and always promoted code simplicity and efficiency as primary goals.

In 2008, he was profiled in the Microsoft publication "Heroes Happen Here," which highlights 115 IT professionals from 18 countries who all share a passion for adopting the latest technologies.

From 2011 to 2015, he led the enterprise architecture team at SeaWorld Parks & Entertainment, with responsibility for high-level architecture of corporate and park software systems, including the corporate division and ten parks, with 22,000 workers, and dozens of systems and databases across eight data centers, in all lines of business such as HR, finance, park operations, ticketing and customer-facing websites.

Dr. Shaban has published work in computational linguistics and virtual reality. He is currently professor of computer programming and analysis at Seminole State College in Orlando, Florida, where he encourages students to ignore fads and focus on the fundamentals.